# THE APPEAL OF INSURANCE

# The Appeal of Insurance

*Edited by Geoffrey Clark, Gregory Anderson, Christian Thomann, and J.-Matthias Graf von der Schulenburg*

UNIVERSITY OF TORONTO PRESS
Toronto Buffalo London

Toronto Buffalo London
www.utppublishing.com
Printed in Canada

ISBN 978-1-4426-4065-8

Printed on acid-free, 100% post-consumer recycled paper with vegetable-based inks.

---

**Library and Archives Canada Cataloguing in Publication**

The appeal of insurance / edited by Geoffrey Clark ... [et al.].

Includes bibliographical references.
ISBN 978-1-4426-4065-8

1. Insurance – History. 2. Insurance. I. Clark, Geoffrey Wilson, 1959–

HG8027.A66 2010 368.009 C2010-901536-3

---

University of Toronto Press acknowledges the financial assistance to its publishing program of the Canada Council for the Arts and the Ontario Arts Council.

Canada Council for the Arts Conseil des Arts du Canada ONTARIO ARTS COUNCIL CONSEIL DES ARTS DE L'ONTARIO

University of Toronto Press acknowledges the financial support for its publishing activities of the Government of Canada through the Canada Book Fund.

# Contents

# Acknowledgments

The editors are deeply grateful to the Centre for Insurance Sciences Hanover (Kompetenzzentrum Versicherungswissenschaften GmbH), the Centre for Risk and Management at Leibniz University, Hanover, and the Insurance Law Center at the University of Connecticut School of Law for making the publication of this book possible through their generous financial support. We would especially like to thank Professor Peter Kochenburger, Executive Director, Professor Kurt Strasser, former Acting Director, and Professor Patricia McCoy, Director of the Insurance Law Center, for their personal interest in this project as well as for promoting the Insurance Law Center's mission of supporting original research on insurance, law, risk, and society. Ms Patricia Carbray of the Insurance Law Center also rendered valuable administrative assistance. In addition, the editors extend their heartfelt appreciation to Diana Ericson for her kind permission to publish her late husband's work. We are indebted to Mr Virgil Duff, Executive Editor at the University of Toronto Press, for his gracious support of this book; to the anonymous reviewers of the manuscript, who offered insightful and helpful advice; to Ms Terry Teskey for her superb copy-editing; and to Ms Patricia Alexandra Simoes, Assistant Editor at the University of Toronto Press, for her logistical help. Dr Liz McFall and Mrs Julie Anne Lambert, Librarian of the John Johnson Collection at the Bodleian Library, generously aided in locating cover art.

The ideas contained in this book were first presented at a conference hosted by the Centre for Risk and Management and most appropriately held in the former house of Gottfried Wilhelm Leibniz, a founder of actuarial mathematics and an early promoter of insurance. In addition to the sponsorship provided by the Centre for Risk and Management, the conference was also supported by grants from the Office of the Dean of Arts and Sciences and from the Research and Creative Endeavors Committee, both of the State University of New York at Potsdam. Thanks are also due Dr. Ute Lohse, Managing Director of the Centre for Insurance Science Hanover, for her work on behalf of the conference.

The theme of this book owes a large measure of its inspiration to Professor Tom Baker, formerly Director of the Insurance Law Center of the University of Connecticut and now William Maul Measey Professor of Law and Health Sciences at the University of Pennsylvania School of Law, and to the other members of the Insurance and Society Workshop, some of whom contributed directly to the conference and this volume but all of whom influenced its conception.

# Contributors

**Timothy Alborn** is Professor of History and Dean of Arts and Sciences at Lehman College, City University of New York.

**Gregory Anderson** is the former Associate Head of the School of Business, University of Salford.

**Geoffrey Clark** is Professor of History at the State University of New York at Potsdam.

**Aaron Doyle** is Associate Professor in the Department of Sociology and Anthropology, Carleton University, and Adjunct Associate Professor at the Centre for Risk and Insurance Research, BI Norwegian School of Management.

**Richard Ericson** was Professor at the Centre for Criminology, University of Toronto.

**Martin Lengwiler** is Associate Professor of Modern European History at the Historical Institute, University of Basle.

**Liz McFall** is Senior Lecturer in Sociology at the Open University.

**Robin Pearson** is Professor of Economic History at the University of Hull.

**Jerònia Pons Pons** is Senior Lecturer in Economic History at the University of Seville.

**Eve Rosenhaft** is Professor of German Historical Studies at the University of Liverpool.

**J.-Matthias Graf von der Schulenburg** is Professor of Business Administration and Director of the Center for Risk and Insurance at Leibniz University, Hanover.

**Christian Thomann** is Senior Fellow at the Center for Risk and Insurance at Leibniz University, Hanover.

# THE APPEAL OF INSURANCE

# Introduction

GEOFFREY CLARK AND GREGORY ANDERSON

In October 1907, fresh out of school and having just completed his very first week at the Prague office of the Assicurazioni Generale, Franz Kafka reported to a friend, 'The insurance business as such interests me very much, but my present work is dreary.'[1] A hundred years on, dealing with insurance and insurance companies is still often seen as a dreary business. Yet recently scholars across a number of disciplines have become fascinated, like Kafka in his more expansive moments, by the profound historical role that insurance has played in shaping contemporary economic institutions, techniques of government, mechanisms of social welfare, and patterns of thought. Because insurance is what economists term a 'sold good,' the demand for (or appeal of) insurance can never, like a better mousetrap, simply be assumed. Rather, the development of the insurance industry has always depended on a considerable dose of moral exhortation and enlightened appeal. The double entendre of the word 'appeal' (attraction versus entreaty) in the title of this book captures this duality and provides the thematic thread connecting the following essays.

Perhaps more than any other business, insurance grew in concert with a clientele largely of its own making. Left to its own devices, the public has preferred to avoid confronting the certainty of fatality or the probabilities of catastrophe. It has therefore been the particular task of insurance promoters to create a demand for their products, first, by persuading the public to see the world as ruled less by divine judgments and more by statistical patterns, and second, by proclaiming a moral imperative of hedging against death and disaster by the prudential recourse to insurance. The essays presented here examine the history of insurance as a process of negotiation between the embedded social, legal, and cultural norms out of which the practice of insurance grew, and the new arrangements and sensibilities that insurance itself helped bring into being.

Over the past three centuries the insurance business has grown into a global colossus. In Europe alone, some 5,300 life and non-life companies presently transact insurance. Altogether, these companies hold assets in the neighborhood of €7 trillion and employ over one million people. Across the Atlantic, insurance companies in the United States control assets worth $6.2 trillion, employ 2.1 per cent of the U.S. workforce, and collect premiums of $1 trillion annually. In the developing world insurance coverage is much less extensive, of course, but as countries become wealthier their propensity to insure increases apace. From 2004 to 2005, for example, the People's Republic of China saw premium growth of more than 17 per cent. Meanwhile, the total life and non-life premiums paid to insurance companies worldwide is approaching $4 trillion per year, an amount equivalent to about 7 per cent of the global gross domestic product.[2] These premiums may be seen as the ransom that fortune pays to misfortune, a kind of 'seven percent solution' insurance administers as a hedge against the inevitability of accident and loss. While insurance can never truly restore a *status quo ante*, it can at least relieve suffering and regret by dulling the blow through a compensatory anaesthetic reminiscent of Sherlock Holmes's own seven percent solution.

These therapeutic benefits have helped make insurance a fixture in the economically developed countries of the world. Indeed, were Benjamin Franklin alive today he would surely count insurance with death and taxes as among life's few certainties. But neither the financial clout of the insurance industry nor its ubiquity conveys the full measure of its social and political influence. For the insurance industry has become a primary agent of discipline and control over public and private behaviours by imposing upon them the criterion of insurability. By tracing the boundaries of acceptable (and compensated) from unacceptable (and uncompensated) risk, insurers directly or indirectly govern people, products, and markets. The introduction of new medical devices is decided not just by government regulators but also by insurers, who analyse their efficacy and cost-effectiveness and, by agreeing to supply cover, practically speaking admit them into the marketplace. It is insurance companies, in writing completion bonds for Hollywood financiers, who set exhaustive terms for what film stars may or may not do during production, or what they may or may not wear on the set and off. Bond insurers (notoriously) claim to provide a cushion against the downside risk of securitized mortgages by spreading the risk of default of the underlying mortgages. The legal scholar Kenneth S. Abraham observes that the spread of liability insurance in the last century has deeply affected the tort system in the United States, with insurance and tort each taking on certain features of the other.[3] A vast array of consumer products are only marketable with the safety certification of Underwriters' Laboratories, established in 1894 at the behest of insurers in order to contain the heightened threat of fire posed by the introduction of electric power. Florida waterfront homeowners are gradually being nudged away from the coast not so much by civic planners as by insurers who have slapped hefty premiums on their hurricane-prone homes. In numerous ways, insurance companies act as guardians of safety, guarantors of investment vehicles, and gatekeepers who admit or deny entrance to markets or to risky activities.

For most of its history insurance focused on protecting against maritime loss, fire, death, and a little later illness and injury incident to travel, but more recently the range of insured contingencies has proliferated to handle exotic risks or to leverage entrepreneurial undertakings. To cite just a few examples, Rolling Stones guitarist Keith Richards insured his hands for £1 million, celebrity footballer David Beckham his legs for $70 million. Until the development of effective anti-retroviral cocktails in the 1990s, a flourishing market in 'viatical contracts' existed, enabling investors to assume the life insurance policies of AIDS victims in return for a lump-sum payment based on actuarial expectation. The $10 million purse for the Ansari X Prize, awarded for the first private space shots, was financed through a so-called 'hole-in-one' insurance policy in which the underwriters bet (wrongly) that the feat would not be accomplished by the end of the year 2004.

Although the insurance technique has been applied to marvellous effect in nearly every area of contemporary life, its omnipresence arguably has lessened rather than increased the popular and scholarly attention paid to it, much in the way that the superabundance of Coca-Cola signs has diminished their visual impact by transforming them into an unremarkable feature of the natural landscape. But neither as an institution, as a way of associating, nor as a way of thinking can insurance be regarded as anything like a natural feature of life. As the following essays clearly demonstrate, in its development over the past three hundred years the practice of insurance battled entrenched ideas about the operation of the world and the proper comportment of people within the established social, moral, or divine order. Not only was insurance controversial with respect to these prevailing norms, it played a pivotal role in redefining the contours of social solidarity, the boundaries between speculative and prudential behaviour, the bases of social and intellectual authority, the extent of property relationships, and the balance between public and private action in promoting social welfare.

Eve Rosenhaft's opening essay introduces several of these themes in her study of widows' and orphans' funds, an early form of life insurance provision, in eighteenth-century Hanover. Focusing on the financial crises experienced by the Christliche Gesellschaft zur Versorgung von Witwen und Waysen (Christian Society for the Maintenance of Widows and Orphans) in the 1720s and the Calenbergische Witwenversorgungs-Gesellschaft (Calenberg Widows' Maintenance Society) sixty years later, Rosenhaft detects a striking shift in the legitimating ideas and operational assumptions underpinning the two associations. Whereas members of the earlier society answered a religious and charitable call to support widows and orphans and trusted in their own good intentions and in God to assure the success of the venture, their later counterparts in the Calenberg adopted a less passive stance with respect to the fortunes of their society, placing their faith above all in technical expertise that empowered them to transform fatalistic uncertainties into managed risks. This 'taming of chance,' a borrowing from Ian Hacking's book of the same name, by means of mathematics was not yet the preserve of a highly trained cadre of actuaries but a more general competence and sensibility possessed by the sort of educated professionals who formed the market for these early experiments in mutual insurance, and who justified their common endeavour by reference to the sound policy of preventing poverty. This commitment to actuarialism testifies to a change from the hopeful fatalism evident in the earlier period to a greater confidence in the capacity for enlightened individuals to assert an active control over demographic outcomes through probabilistic strategies. It also marks the emergence of a more positive attitude towards risk itself, now regarded as offering the possibility of improvement or gain rather than simply vulnerability to loss.

Rosenhaft identifies the decade of the 1770s as the moment when a demographic calculus was decisively embraced by the framers and members of life insurance societies, at least within the territory of Hanover. But in her view the application of actuarial logic to life insurance led to a more acute consciousness of risk-taking, since the security of a widow's pension was no longer seen to derive from pious motives or from presumed divine endorsement but from the aleatory character of the investment itself. This strategic embrace of risk counts against Lorraine Daston's influential thesis that the eighteenth-century insurance market exhibited a staged progress from risk-aversive to risk-taking motives, a development that she contends was consonant with the rise of a bourgeois culture that prized thrift and precaution, of which insurance was emblematic. Rosenhaft demonstrates instead that firmer actuarial understandings of insurance in the later eighteenth century actually accentuated the riskiness of insurance as a potentially lucrative but definitely experimental investment. The risk-aversive aspects of insurance were therefore balanced by a countervailing taste for risk that was everywhere apparent in the capitalist economies of Europe.

Adam Smith appealed to the simultaneity of these impulses when he argued that the modest profits commonly made in the insurance business, when compared to the great popularity of lotteries, especially those with small odds of large prizes, revealed the public's juvenile 'contempt of risk and the presumptuous hope of success.'[4] A century earlier that delusive tendency to undervalue the chances of loss was compounded by strong moral objections to insurance as an impious interference in divine providence. In their survey of Gottfried Wilhelm Leibniz' work on insurance, J.-Mattias Graf von der Schulenburg and Christian Thomann note that attempts to establish municipal fire insurance offices in Oldenburg and Hanover during the seventeenth century were opposed or thwarted on religious grounds, even after the chastening conflagrations of 1666 in London and 1676 in Oldenburg. While Leibniz made important contributions to the mathematical calculation of life rents and urged the formation of fire insurance mutuals, he nonetheless exhibited the reluctance so characteristic of his age in applying probability theory and demographic or other statistical data directly to the business of insurance. In any case, Leibniz favoured public and compulsory forms of risk pooling, believing that insurance could not be established on a sufficiently wide basis by private entrepreneurs who were themselves averse to the size of the risks involved. Schulenburg and Thomann demonstrate by applying formal economic theory to Leibniz' design for a fire insurance cooperative that a public, redistributive form of insurance based on mutual contribution was entirely sound and could, as Leibniz argued, be expected to advance public welfare.

That insurance promoted the general good was nowhere more controversial than in the case of the English transatlantic slave trade, discussed in Geoffrey Clark's essay, 'The Slave's Appeal: Insurance and the Rise of Commercial Property.' Although instances of insuring the lives of slaves can be found as far back as the fifteenth century, the development of the American plantation system and the concomitant rise in the demand for African slave labour led to the routine use of insurance to cover slave cargoes plying the Middle Passage. Through an examination of a cluster of legal cases involving insurance and slavery from the 1770s and 1780s, Clark argues that the increase of insurance on human chattels in the eighteenth century, together with the multiplying uses of life insurance on free persons, posed a stark challenge to established common law understandings about the nature and extent of human property as well as to the social hierarchy built upon those property relations. Life insurance policies and closely related life-contingent contracts and wagers offered wives and children the means to invert the social order by transforming their husbands and fathers into commodities.

The economic and political ethos of self-possession so characteristic of English constitutional thinking in the eighteenth century therefore encountered a thorny paradox as the freedom of economic subjects to make commercial contracts at times compromised the personal integrity of political subjects. The conversion of African slaves via insurance into property pure and simple represented the extreme case of a worrying process to which all economic actors were liable. Consequently, the gradual truncation of slave owners' rights in Britain as a result of the Thomas Lewis and Somerset cases (1771), the outlaw of speculative life insurance by the Gambling Act (1774), the infamous case of the *Zong* (1781), and the subsequent limitations on the recovery of insured losses from slave cargoes that were imposed by William Dolben's Act (1788) may all be seen as appealing to a redefinition of the kinds of proprietary claims that one individual could make on another.

Robin Pearson's essay on fire and perceptions of risk in eighteenth-century Britain examines another instance of epistemological transition, this one having to do with evolving attitudes towards fire and strategies for containing its ever-present threat. The emotions aroused by fire were multiple and contradictory: dread of uncontrolled flame or explosion, anxiety over the consequent loss to property, the excitement of a dangerous spectacle, fatalism in the face of its natural inevitability or as a just punishment by God. But how did the individual imagination or the cultural discourses surrounding fire translate into strategies for reducing its risk? Pearson, like Rosenhaft and Clark, identifies the third quarter of the eighteenth century as a critical period. Those years saw both a crescendo in the frequency and severity of fires and a rejoining of the battle to contain fire and to minimize its financial consequences. This effort was visible in, for example, the London building acts (which regulated, among other things, the thickness of party walls and foundations and the use of wood around hearths), in better means of fire-fighting and fire-proofing, and in a rapid increase through much of the country in the value of property insured against fire. These developments were mutually reinforcing, since by rebuilding in stone and tile and organizing better fire-fighting, towns became more attractive markets for fire insurers, while insurers conversely tried to raise awareness of fire hazards by educating the public and lobbying Parliament.

Pearson finds, however, that the impact of these public and private measures on individuals' thinking and behaviour was limited, ambiguous, and slow. Even though insurance in the eighteenth century made increasingly explicit appeals to probabilistic thinking and statistical data, risk (and its legal definition) remained for many an unquantifiable uncertainty, or simply a realm ruled by providence and beyond the ken of humankind. Pearson finds scant if any evidence that people became more prudential even as they accustomed themselves to the insurance habit. Instead, he observes, householders often quelled their anxiety about fire by purchasing an insurance policy, but persisted in carelessly handling fire or incendiary materials. Something more is involved here than a moral hazard created by insurance. The failure to act prudentially reflects a continued mental adherence to providential or fatalistic ideas. Indeed, Kafka saw in the very practice of insurance a kind of ritual 'like the religions of primitive peoples who believe they can ward off evil by all kinds of manipulations.'[5] Kafka's percipience has recently been confirmed by psychologists who have shown that purchasers of insurance commonly believe themselves less likely to suffer insured losses simply for having taken out a policy, a clear indication of magical thinking.[6] It therefore seems that Pearson's epistemological transition to statistical thinking is an ongoing process.

The aleatory nature of insurance contracts has always made them morally suspect as vehicles for gaming. English law tried to remove this taint by imposing a standard of 'insurable interest' according to the terms of the Gambling Act, which demarcated licit, indemnifying insurance from illicit, speculative policies in which there existed no capacity for loss. In his essay 'A License to Bet: Life Insurance and the Gambling Act in the British Courts,' Tim Alborn traces the legal aftermath of the Gambling Act into the nineteenth century as insurance companies, their (mostly upper-class) customers, and the courts adjusted to the new legal strictures by, eventually, ignoring them. But with the spread after 1850 of 'industrial life insurance,' which consisted of low-cost policies mainly intended to cover a relative's funeral expenses and which was marketed specially to the working classes, the 'unruly' behaviour of working people speculating by means of technically illegal forms of third-party insurance again embroiled the courts in the problem of determining, as Alborn puts it, a 'boundary between legitimate and illegitimate insurance, in an insurance market that appealed to all social classes because of – not in spite of – the fact that it often shaded imperceptibly into gambling.'

In working-class communities it is no surprise that insurance shaded over into gambling, since here the industrial insurance companies had to compete with the appeal of mainstream gambling. Although Ramsay McDonald, later the first Labour prime minister, argued that working-class betting was 'a disease which spread downwards to the industrious poor from the idle rich,' gambling was firmly and independently established in British working-class culture by the late-nineteenth century.[7] Ross McKibbin provides support for Alborn's thesis about the unruly nature of working-class behaviour in respect of life insurance and has argued that gambling fitted more securely into the 'harum-scarum' social economy of the working class and was more compatible with their mental culture than either saving or insurance, apart, that is, from the life (i.e., death) policies, which covered basic funeral expenses.[8] Even though industrial insurance companies sought to associate insurance with prudence rather than with gaming, a calculated approach to life insurance prevailed among many working-class clients for whom such insurance may have accounted for 10 per cent of the household budget. Against this background there was fierce competition between the companies for market share, which in turn led to hard and questionable selling by agents who also sometimes connived with policyholders in their insurance frauds. As a result, the companies often fell well short of fulfilling their self-proclaimed mission of cultivating sober, prudential behaviour in the labouring classes. And because such policies were in the end legally unenforceable, policyholders who concluded that their past premium payments now outweighed the value of an expected claim could turn the tables on the company and sue for the return of premiums. Bringing these cross-currents of interest and strategy into greater confluence had to await, first, the passage of the Assurance Companies Act of 1909, which relaxed the insurable interest standard in certain respects, and then the reorganization of the industrial insurance business by introducing such features of middle-class insurance as bonuses and endowment policies, which financially rewarded policyholders of long standing. Alborn thus provides another example of a process, described by Clark in connection with gambling and slave insurance, of an attempt by legal authorities and underwriters to regulate the motives and control the strategies at work in the insurance market.

The way insurance has acted as a means of political governance and social discipline is directly addressed in Liz McFall's 'The Rules of Prudence: Political Liberalism and Life Assurance in the Nineteenth Century.' By decoding the political messages embedded in the promotional literature of Victorian life insurance firms and placing those ideas within a history of discourse about prudence, McFall argues that the practice and rhetoric of insurance advanced a particular vision of liberal governance that joined market freedom to a 'rule-bound formalism' and an accent on personal responsibility. According to this strain of liberalism, true freedom was only possible once prudence had been cultivated, and insurance was both the soil and the fruit of that ethiculture.

But if Victorian life insurance acted as a liberal technology of private governance, insurance was not thereby constrained always to serve that political master. McFall's claim that insurance is sufficiently malleable as a technology of governance to be applied in a variety of political contexts joins an ongoing debate about the role insurance has played as supplying a new basis of justice and political rationality. That the Victorian insurance project sat uneasily within some variants of liberal ideology argues against the assertions of François Ewald and Jacques Donzelot that the insurance technique increasingly dominated twentieth-century governance owing to its superior efficiency in regulating populations. Instead, McFall sides with Pat O'Malley in seeing the technique of insurance as itself being shaped according to the logic of ascendant political rationalities, most clearly exemplified in the neoliberal program of privatized risk management in the 1980s and 1990s.

The ways in which, as McFall notes, insurance both adapted to and in turn shaped rule-based systems to the economics of the market and the moral imperatives underlying personal responsibility resonate with some of the issues explored by Gregory Anderson in his account of the growth of the fidelity insurance business in nineteenth-century Britain. This essay provides a vivid example of how insurance was utilized by firms attempting to enforce the faithful service of their employees. As firms grew larger and more bureaucratic and anonymous, the older system of private suretyship, a personal bond extended by kith or kin providing a guarantee against fraud or defalcation, no longer suited the demands of corporate management. With the gradual withering of surety bonds, fidelity insurance companies stepped into the breach with techniques that enforced the good behaviour of employees and monitored their performance. Anderson notes that in the 1840s fidelity companies were even enlisted by railway companies to vet applicants for staff positions, while staff members who were denied cover after being investigated by the fidelity company likely faced dismissal. As the fidelity business developed, however, it became steadily less concerned with the individual employee and his particular culpability, and more focused on collective policies that subsumed acts of fraud and embezzlement under the rubric of 'accident,' in a compelling illustration of Ewald's point about the insurance principle leading to the emergence of a new redistributive system of justice.

Eventually the 'corporatist' nature of fidelity insurance even attracted the interest of the state, which replaced surety bonds with insurance contracts as a prophylactic against the financial malfeasance of its subalterns who were entrusted with the administration of the estates of children and the mentally ill. But whether applied in a public or private context, the business of fidelity insurance declined in the late nineteenth and early twentieth centuries as internal investigative, auditing, and accounting units within corporations or government assumed responsibility for the surveillance and control of their servants that they had formerly ceded to fidelity insurers. Although fidelity insurance would not endure as a distinct branch of insurance, its apogee in the mid-nineteenth century marked a crucial watershed in the movement from a commercial and administrative world welded together with personal bonds of obligation to one where the costs of fraud and embezzlement were assumed and factored into the cost of doing business by means of risk pooling.

In all but one of the remaining essays the links between the growth of insurance and the rise of the 'corporate state' are more pronounced, with state responsibility and intervention in the area of social insurance growing rapidly from the late-nineteenth century, first competing with and then absorbing the activities of private agencies. Martin Lengwiler's 'Competing Appeals: The Rise of Mixed Welfare Economies in Europe, 1850–1945' takes up the theme of shifting institutional responsibilities by looking at the provision of state-sponsored and private insurance in a continental context. Recognizing that the study of insurance and of social welfare systems has traditionally been divided between economic and social historians respectively, Lengwiler draws upon Peter Baldwin's pioneering work on integrating these approaches to argue that the development of life and health insurance systems in Europe can best be understood as the outcome of competition between public plans on the one hand and private or mutual insurers on the other. Throughout Switzerland, Germany, and Britain the later decades of the nineteenth century saw a massive expansion in the working-class market for life insurance, previously a product targeted for the middle class. Health insurance, conversely, emerged out of the mutual funds created by fraternal associations and then moved up the social ladder into the middle class on an individualized basis through private insurance, while more activist states like Bismarck's Germany intervened directly to establish more comprehensive and sometimes compulsory coverage.

The mix of public/private or local/national institutions providing insurance benefits shifted over the course of the late nineteenth and early twentieth centuries, reflecting, Lengwiler argues, not just the relative strength of local, provincial, or national political authorities, but also the degree to which a social solidarity could be forged across classes, regions, and cultures that could serve as a basis for a more limited or a more expansive socialization of risk. The structure of insurance provision in the various countries of Europe therefore stands as an index of a nation's political ambitions, social structure, religious endowments, and economic development. This history thus echoes not only Gregory Anderson's essay on fidelity insurance but also Liz Mcfall's more theoretical discussion of insurance in the context of liberal and neoliberal governance.

Jerònia Pons Pons explores some of the same ideas in her essay on the development of accident insurance in Spain during the twentieth century, following the passage in 1900 of legislation holding employers responsible for accidents suffered by their workers in the industrial, mining, and construction sectors. Now held financially accountable for accident, employers voluntarily formed mutual associations to insure against the losses for which they were liable. By forming accident insurance on this basis, employers maintained control over the underwriting and so could better control the terms and costs of insurance. By the same token, they could exercise greater control over their own workforce by scrutinizing suspect claims of injury and adjusting benefits to remove temptations of goldbricking. Through insurance they also acquired a valuable means of battling strikes or other workers' actions by suspending insurance benefits. This paternalism – and the continued dependency of the workforce – was replicated in the countryside once accident insurance was extended to the agricultural sector in 1931.

From initially resisting even a voluntary accident insurance system, therefore, employers found in insurance provision a means of fortifying their own economic and political power. Partly for this reason, they tried to stave off the day when legislation would nationalize accident insurance as part of a comprehensive social insurance system, as finally happened in 1963, even though industrial accident mutuals managed for still obscure reasons to stay in business. Other accident mutuals became indistinguishable from commercial firms, becoming the powerful international firms they are today. Whatever the trajectory of individual firms, the history of Spanish accident insurance in general reinforces Mcfall's point that regimes of quite different ideological characters have adapted the technology of insurance as their own political reasons have dictated.

Finally, Aaron Doyle and Richard Ericson question the insurance industry's appeal as a means of promoting fair and beneficial economic and social outcomes. Building on their earlier work on insurance as forming a new layer of governance outside direct state control, they explore five ironies of modern insurance practice. By 'irony,' Doyle and Ericson mean an unintended, contrary, or perverse consequence of the stated aims or purpose of insurance. Insurance companies, for example, tend to individualize risk through special ratings groups even as risk is generally pooled. In addition, the adaptation of medical and legal actors to the incentives provided by stated insurance benefits leads to the unwitting creation of new risks that are themselves predicated on insurantial strategies of risk reduction. Doyle and Ericson further point out that the profit motive and the widely used commission system operating within the insurance industry have commonly led to deceptive or dishonest practices that directly contradict the morally elevating claims of the companies themselves, whereas incentives are similarly created for customers to stretch the truth beyond the breaking point in making claims.

The sudden death of Richard Ericson as this volume was coming together was a major blow to the emerging cross-disciplinary study of insurance, just as it was a huge loss to sociology and criminology. Like Ericson's other pioneering books and articles on insurance, the 'Five Ironies of Insurance' shows that the appeal of insurance, considered in both its magnetic and hortatory aspects, continues to be, as it has been for the past three hundred years, contradictory, controversial, and sometimes even chimerical. In common with the other essays presented here, it points the way to further research in a still developing field and indicates the complexity of the task society has set itself in giving no hostages to fortune as it tries to ransom fortune by means of insurance.

## NOTES

1 Quoted in Ernst Pawel, *The Nightmare of Reason* (New York: Schocken Books, 1984), 177.
2 Insurance Information Institute, *International Insurance Fact Book*, http://www.iii.org/international/overview, accessed 27 March 2008. CEA, *European Insurance in Figures*, CEA Statistics no. 31 (August 2007).
3 Kenneth S. Abraham, *The Liability Century: Insurance and Tort Law from the Progressive Era to 9/11* (Cambridge, MA: Harvard University Press, 2008).
4 Adam Smith, *An Inquiry into the Nature and Causes of the Wealth of Nations*, vol. 1 (Philadelphia, 1789), 141–3.
5 Max Brod, *Franz Kafka: A Biography* (New York: Schocken Books, 1963), 74, 84.
6 Orit E. Tykocinski, 'Insurance, Risk, and Magical Thinking,' *Personality and Social Psychology Bulletin* 34, no. 10 (October 2008), 1346–56.
7 Roderick Floud, *The People and the British Economy 1830–1914* (Oxford: Oxford University Press, 1997), 38.
8 Ross McKibbin, 'Working-Class Gambling in Britain 1880–1939,' *Past and Present*, no. 82, 1978.

# 1 How to Tame Chance: Evolving Languages of Risk, Trust, and Expertise in Eighteenth-Century German Proto-Insurances

EVE ROSENHAFT

This essay re-examines the contradictory relationship between the emergence of 'classical probability' as a body of expertise and a style of thought and the modern market in life insurance, through a study of schemes for widows' pensions (proto-life insurances) in eighteenth-century Germany. It focuses on the public debates touched off by the failure of two generations of pension schemes, the latter of which gave a critical impulse to the German reception of statistical probabilism. It argues that the distinction between risk-aversive and risk-taking behaviour that informs the vision of a historic 'taming of chance' is overdrawn and that lay, juridical, and mathematical notions of risk developed in relation to one another. At the same time, it confirms a shift over the century in the balance between providentialism, individual calculation, and acknowledgment of the authority of experts.

## The Problem of Life Insurance in the History of Risk and Probability

Recent sociological literature on risk tends to define it in terms of dangers, or negative outcomes. As Mary Douglas (among others) has commented, such definitions diverge somewhat from the term's original sense of an enterprise consciously undertaken in the hope of gain and in the awareness that one may lose.[1] (The term 'hazard' has undergone the same transformation, even more radically.) Risk in this original sense defines gambling (gaming) behaviour, in which the inherent uncertainty and uncontrollability of the outcome itself increases the prospect of gain. But it is present, too, in any act of social or technological innovation. A new venture attracts investment (of money, time, or affection) by virtue of promising improvement, but the very fact of its being new implies the danger that it may fail. From this point of view, the *ambivalent* or complex meaning of risk survives implicitly (at least) in accounts of perceptions of technologically induced environmental hazards in the late twentieth century, and its dimensions can be described in the terms in which the theorists of 'risk society' have characterized modernity.[2] The notion of 'risk society' is rooted equally in a qualitative distinction between the 'first modernity' and our own, and in a presumption that one difference lies in the relative success that earlier generations had in conquering 'naturally occurring' risk. Nineteenth- and twentieth-century schemes for social security are presented as effective versions of complex expert systems – effective both in displacing local and personal relationships as objects of trust and in compensating for the loss of security (or increase in individual life-risks) involved in the loosening of family and community ties. This illustrates a defining feature of modernity itself, and particularly of the drive to innovation and complex systems that characterizes it. Partaking of its benefits involves entering routinely into relationships with strangers, and indeed relying on others: on the designers of new systems, whether mechanical or organizational, and on those who can make them work – in short, on experts. But this is not an unproblematic move, either psychologically or in terms of its possible consequences. It is in the nature of technical expertise that it is not subject to test by the immediate experience of the lay individual, and systems that rely on deploying a number of kinds of expertise are still less transparent. Well-informed though it may be, then, reliance on expert systems is not simply a displacement of trust but an act of faith; there is always the possibility that trust will prove to have been *misplaced*.

The historical literature on the development of life insurance has paid close attention to the relationship between risk-taking and risk avoidance in the transition to economic and social modernity. A central puzzle in the history of life insurance is this: the market in life insurance emerged in England early in the eighteenth century, *before* the calculus was developed that would make it possible to apply known mortality rates to the calculation of premiums and benefits. After mid-century, a second wave of foundings of life insurance and pension funds coincided with the existence of more or less reliable systems of calculation, but their founders ignored them, often defying good advice. So what ought to have been systems for the 'taming of chance'[3] in everyday life resisted the influence of the scientific discourses – statistics and probability – that would have made them effective. A very influential answer to this paradox has been offered by Lorraine Daston: at its beginnings life insurance was essentially a speculative activity, indulged in in a gambling spirit; it was a pastime for risk-takers, with uncertainty increasing the return. Certainty, and science, became relevant only with a change in underlying values, namely the adoption of domesticity and thrift as defining qualities of middle-class life. Geoffrey Clark challenged this view in his work on early English life insurance, which persuasively argues that the insurers' reliance on common sense and rule-of-thumb calculations was dictated by caution in the face of a plethora of information and lack of consensus among the experts. Betting on lives there certainly was, and in other ways life insurance practice displayed the elements of fantasy and consumerism inherent in an emerging commercial culture, but Clark's evidence disposes of the idea that gambling was ever *all* that was going on.[4]

In order to make the argument about a crucial conjuncture between middle-class values and probabilism, Daston dismissed a significant part of the history of life insurance, namely the proto-insurance schemes known as widows' funds. These were created as early as the seventeenth century in the Netherlands and from the beginning of the eighteenth century in Britain and Germany.[5] They were founded on the initiative of middle-class men, often clergymen, with the express purpose of providing survivors' benefits for their widows and orphans. A second wave of foundings took place from the mid-eighteenth century onwards all over Europe, and in the German case we can reasonably speak of a fashion and even a passion for widows' pensions. The foundations of the 1750s and 1760s went further than the turn-of-the-century funds in extending their recruitment base, opening membership to the general public, and many that had begun by setting a maximum number of subscribers dropped the restriction in favour of apparently unlimited expansion. The most adventurous of these funds was the Calenbergische Witwenversorgungs-Gesellschaft, based in Hannover; from its foundation in 1767, the Calenberg set out to recruit as many subscribers as possible, welcoming members not only from all over Germany but from all over Europe. Between 1767 and 1780, more than five thousand married couples joined the Calenberg. Since the Calenberg, though the largest, was not the only such fund in existence, these numbers allow us to describe the purchase of widows' pensions as a mass phenomenon (bearing in mind that the funds addressed themselves to the relatively small constituency of the educated professional middle class); other funds had subscriber numbers in the upper hundreds.[6]

Daston acknowledged the involvement of non-gambling clerics with prudential motives in such schemes, as 'sentiment without mathematics,'[7] but she argued that those schemes did not qualify as life insurance, in order to insist on a change in values in the last quarter of the century. I would argue (as Geoffrey Clark does) that pre-premium schemes are part of a continuous development of 'life-insurance culture'; we might better see the 'gaming' forms of insurance as the historical byway. In the German case, it is clear that the *objects* of these schemes — the preservation of middle-class families and indeed the enforcement of one or another form of patriarchal family structure – remained constant over the century, although their evolving practice reflects changing possibilities for envisaging relations within the family, applied with an increasing degree of self-consciousness from the middle of the century. Moreover, while the term insurance (*Assecuranz*) was rarely applied to German widows' funds at the time, the Calenberg's founders were self-consciously extending the principles of property insurance to securing the futures of families in their scheme for a widows' fund. The practices of the Calenberg were closely modelled on the fire insurance scheme introduced in the Hanoverian lands in 1750.[8] It was certainly in the context of these schemes for family welfare that the refinement of probabilistic methods by expert mathematicians took off in the 1770s. If anything, though, the most radical applications of statistical thinking emerged among Enlightenment thinkers who were prepared to *question* the truisms of the bourgeois gender order. The best example of this is the approach of George Christian von Oeder, whose actuarial calculations formed the basis for the operations of the Hamburgische Allgemeine Versorgungsanstalt (HAVA). Founded in 1778, the HAVA is generally credited with being the first modern German insurance institution because of Oeder's application of principles recognizable as those of modern premium insurance, and it was the only eighteenth-century German foundation to survive into the twentieth century.[9]

While the objects of the funds remained broadly the same, it is clear that the readiness of the *managers* of German widows' funds (from the start not experts but more or less educated amateurs) to consider mathematical techniques of one kind or another increased from the middle of the century onwards. This resulted from a combination of what might be called endogenous and exogenous impulses. The uneven but intensifying circulation of knowledge about techniques for calculating annuities on the basis of vital statistics and their reception by a generation of men who had a nose for technological projects certainly constituted an exogenous factor. The endogenous impulses that led fund managers to seek new technical solutions to familiar problems were less a matter of changing values than of the need to increase the funds' recruitment base in the face of growing competition. This was particularly true in the case of the funds created after the middle of the century, which increasingly sought to boost recruitment by underselling one another – offering unrealistically high pensions against unrealistically low contributions. The drive for expansion that was inherent in the logic of the 'business' accordingly incurred a significant risk of failure. A particularly urgent impulse to the adoption of new techniques thus emerged in the late 1770s, when a number of interlinked funds found themselves unable to meet their pension commitments because of insufficient income, previous failings were acknowledged, and technical solutions were actively sought. The Calenberg, being the most ambitious, had the most spectacular fall; at the point when its deficits became too large to be overlooked, it had about 3,700 married couples on its books and owed pensions to over 700 widows. The resolution of the crisis – the reform of the fund – took four years and touched off a chain of lawsuits that went on for a decade.[10] The HAVA grew out of a parallel crisis in Hamburg widows' funds, which involved some of the same actors as those implicated in the fate of the Calenberg. Thus while we find evidence of a reception of probabilistic principles as early as the 1760s, in the form of the application of mortality statistics and the reliance on some version of the law of large numbers, it is in the following decade that the application of calculus and the technical language of probability and risk enter into the practices of the widows' funds.

At the same time, the distinction between risk-taking and risk-aversive behaviour that underlies the vision of an epochal shift in values driving the diffusion of technical innovation seems overdrawn when we pay attention to the evidence for the expectations of the men who bought insurance (or widows' pensions). While (on the one hand) their motivations were consistently prudential rather than gaming, there is plenty of evidence (on the other) that they were aware of the possibility that the enterprise might fail, and in that sense conscious that they were taking a risk. If by investing a relatively small amount in a pension rather than pursuing the more familiar (and arduous) path of accumulating savings for their widows to invest after their death they succeeded in securing peace of mind in life and security for their survivors, the risk would have paid off handsomely. The failure of the experiment, of course, might leave them and their widows destitute. In view of the experimental nature of the widows' funds, it may be appropriate here to speak of 'uncertainty' rather than 'risk,' bearing in mind the distinction that some economists and economic historians have made between the two when considering investment behaviour in 'emerging markets' (or innovations in financial practice).[11] What we can see changing are the terms in which the nature of the uncertainty was articulated. In this respect, the 1770s were indeed critical for the development of forms of understanding that allowed for a positive and productive notion of risk to replace the negative and passive one of uncertainty. The significance of that development becomes clear when we compare the events of the last quarter of the century with the fate of a turn-of-the-century widows' fund. The Christliche Gesellschaft zu Versorgung der Witwen und Waysen, founded by Lüneburg clergymen in 1700, entered into a five-year process of liquidation in June 1720 with 122 married couples and 55 widows on its books. Here it is worth pointing out the tenacity with which eighteenth-century men and women prosecuted the insurance experiment; in the town and duchy of Lüneburg, the grandchildren of the men who had failed in the 1720s invested heavily in the Calenberg and had even brought forward a plan for their own regional widows' fund at the point when the Calenberg opened for business. [12] The events of 1720–25 were very similar to those of the last decades of the century; in both cases subscribers and widows took action to defend their interests against the fund managers and against each other. But the lessons drawn were quite different. The reflections of the men and women who lost out in successive crises bespeak their awareness of having entered into an uncertain enterprise; they also narrate a mental search for reassurance. Articulated in the context of crisis, this narrative was often cast in terms of notions of trust and blame. The question of where trust should be placed and where blame for failure should lie implies an understanding of what is and is not possible in the context of human agency, and here it is indeed possible to identify a series of changes that took place over the course of the century and were accelerated by developments in the 1770s. Over three generations of the same social formation and even the same families, we can observe how confidence in the possibility of 'taming chance' replaced explicitly providential or fatalistic thinking, and how by the same token confidence in expert systems, and in particular mathematics, began to displace other forms of trust. The words and actions of the actors in the second crisis also throw some light on the way in which both vernacular and expert languages of risk and probability emerged out of the confluence of juridical and mathematical discourses with new social and cultural practices.

## The Lüneburg Case

As its name implies, the Christliche Gesellschaft zur Versorgung von Witwen und Waysen (Christian Society for the Maintenance of Widows and Orphans) was not only a clerical foundation but one whose guiding ethos was Christian and providential. From start to finish, its business was couched in religious terms: the founders, invoking the biblical injunction to care for widows and orphans and the duty of charity as their rationale, placed their trust in God and invited both God's and the public's acknowledgment of their own *good intentions* as guarantees for the success of the fund.[13]

To be sure, this was not sufficient to win official approval for the scheme in the first instance. The Lüneburg city council raised objections to the draft constitution that precipitated an appeal to the Faculty of Law at the University of Leipzig. But the hazards anticipated at this stage were of a political and ethical kind, referring broadly to problems of social order. The councillors wondered whether it was not a usurpation of state prerogatives for the proposers to draft a 'constitution' and publish it in advance of official approval; whether the proposed scaled penalties for late payment of contributions did not constitute a form of compound interest or usury; and whether an association of private persons could legitimately forbid its members to bring suit against the association. They were also troubled by the provision that threatened that any member who might demand the return of his money on resigning from the society would forfeit his reputation as an honourable man. The

Leipzig lawyers dismissed the council's objections (on the grounds that the constitution was in the nature of a private contract, and no one who objected to its terms was obliged to join the fund). They acknowledged, though, that the size of the association was a consideration. The initial proposal cited 50 potential subscribers already recruited, while the constitution as drafted (and finally approved) envisaged a maximum membership of 100. In fact, this maximum was reached in September 1705, and recruitment nevertheless continued, peaking at 174 couples in the summer of 1710. An annual meeting of as many as 100, however, was regarded as a sufficient source of potential disorder to warrant an application for approval from the highest authority (the Crown). [14]

There is no evidence that there was any discussion of the danger that the scheme might simply not work. The fund's creators showed themselves to be aware of the potential for routine corruption and mismanagement. Their constitution provided for regular accounting and the liability of the fund administrators in case of inadvertent loss of money or accounting errors, enjoined 'all the caution humanly possible' in the handling of cash, and specified who should keep the keys to the cash box. Provision was made for levying supplementary contributions in case income did not cover the pension outgoings in any given quarter, but only on a one-off basis. They did not address the possibility of collective incompetence, technical error, or a systemic failure of the kind that finally occurred, in which the mechanisms originally set up for generating income proved inadequate to the demographics of the fund. The principal hazard envisaged by their constitution was a natural one: epidemic disease. The terms in which this prospect was invoked are characteristic, in the association between natural hazard and divine providence, in the confidence they reflect that a crisis could be weathered (somehow or other), and in the rhetorical balancing of a hypothetical misfortune against a comparable good fortune:

> We also reserve the right, should God bless our project and the fund, to increase the widows' annual pensions (subject to the Society's agreement), the which will be considered annually and an increase fixed according to the fund's resources. And should God punish us with pestilence – which however we heartily pray may be averted – [we reserve the further right] to provide for the conservation of this Society through emergency measures [*eine Interims-Verordnung*].[15]

When the fund collapsed, the same vocabulary was deployed not only to allocate blame but to set the parameters of responsibility. In June 1720, the fund managers proposed its dissolution, realizing that there was no hope of the contributions of a dwindling number of subscribers ever covering the pensions owed to 55 widows. There ensued a conflict over whether and on what basis the fund should be re-established and what claims the pensioner widows and subscribers respectively could make against the remaining capital; the parties to the dispute included widows, subscribers, and fund managers. The Lüneburg city council (most of whose patrician and burgher members were themselves involved in the fund, personally or through kin), the Crown, and the High Court in Celle also became involved as a formal enquiry was initiated and, in parallel, the parties proceeded to litigate against one another.

As befitted their desperate situation, the widows deployed all the arguments available in their petitions against the subscribers who were proposing that the fund should be wound up and their investments returned to them. These included appeals to practical interest, the letter of the constitution, and moral principle, but the terms in which they were couched were Christian and providential. They advised subscribers that if they were prepared to keep the fund going, their capital would be 'nowhere better or more securely invested, and if not it would probably be lost through God's dispensation, having been taken from the widows in a manner both illegitimate [*unbillig*] and un-Christian.' The widows characterized the men's actions as 'irresponsible' and motivated by 'untimely fear,' but also as displaying 'un-Christian lack of trust [*unchristliches Mißtrauen*].'[16]

This phrase invokes the theological sense of the term 'trust' (*Vertrauen*), which was current in early eighteenth-century Germany, and referred specifically to trust in God. In the Protestant reading of scripture, with which these clerical widows would have been familiar, men were enjoined to place their trust in God whatever the circumstances; lack of trust in God was a breach of the first commandment. Trust in one's fellow men – the expectation of help – was a lesser form of trust, and could even be regarded as weakness, since in the case of human beings there was no assurance (as there was with God) that they both could and would come to one's aid. That is, trust in men had to be based on evidence, but this evidence could never be perfectly reliable; trust in God, being based on revelation and the certainty rooted in faith, could not be subject to test or overturned by any (imagined) evidence. In the faithful, this kind of trust engendered peace of mind, whose outward and visible sign was patience in adversity. At the same time, individuals should not look to God for miraculous intervention. On the one hand, they should be content to acknowledge God's purpose in nature and the vicissitudes of daily life. On the other, they should use the resources provided by God to help themselves.[17] The widows' reproaches implied that the subscribers' spiritual transgression in acting hastily in anticipation of disaster was of a piece with their material breach of contract and the dictates of decency.

The events of 1720–25 suggest that where trust was something placed in God and not subject to being tested by circumstance, blame and explanation were equally difficult to articulate. References in the sources to responsibility and irresponsibility, and even to loss of credit and reputation, are not systematically linked to any account of what had gone wrong or whose fault it was. Called upon to adjudicate, the High Court in Celle invoked no general principle that would constitute a definition of the fund's status or imply any presumptions about how it should operate. The judges ordered that subscribers who wished to resign be allowed to do so and take their capital with them, since the rule prohibiting that was premised on the fund's pension guarantee; in the light of the fact that that guarantee could not be fulfilled, the rules were no longer binding. They *implicitly* imputed bad faith (mis-selling) to the fund's founders and managers by stating that the subscribers had been 'misled' into joining.[18] Nor did the responses of the subscribers draw on any discourse of shared responsibility – in spite of the fact that the fund was in law and in practice a 'civil society' association whose administrators were not slow to challenge the authority of the city council when it asked them to open their books. Rather, the uncertainty about how to account for what had happened extended to an ambivalence about the very legitimacy of individual claims to agency, whether practical or moral. In keeping with the terms on which the widows' fund was founded, the parties to its crisis could appeal to no authority apart from God and the government. The comment of a fifty-two-year-old clergyman from Braunschweig is striking in its lack of point:

> The widows and their fatherless children will surely not thank those who are to blame for the fact that this admirable project has had to be ended. I thank God that I carry no responsibility for this, for I must otherwise fear that the tears and sighs of the widows would do me and mine no

> good in the eyes of God. If, in my humble opinion, the gentlemen in Lüneburg want to preserve their credit, they could do no better than set up a new widows' fund, but it would have to be placed on a completely different footing, and everything that produced such base practices and disorder be completely removed. But my humble opinion would probably not help the matter much, so the safest thing for me will be to go along with the majority, as it must be all the same to me whether the fund is continued or dissolved; but if I have a choice, I would choose continuation above all things.[19]

What 'different footing' was available, or who exactly was 'to blame,' or what the source of 'base practices and disorder' was, remain carefully unspecified here. Another pastor (aged fifty-five) suggested, in support of a compromise solution, that keeping the fund going might persuade God to grant the subscribers longer life, because it would be done 'in fulfilment of God's will and for the preservation of the widows,' adding: 'We need not plan everything according to the measure of reason, but must entrust most things to God's providence.'[20]

## The Calenberg and Its Crisis

The principle of trust in God would be invoked again nearer to the end of the century, in a context in which all the values associated with the Lüneburg experiment were explicitly inverted in the service of the same proximate ends. In a publication of 1788 composed to advertise the virtues and services of the HAVA, J.F. Günther (a HAVA director) invited his readers to share his amazement at the idea that less than one hundred years before, the principle of mutual funds had been attacked with arguments about 'blind trust in God's help and men's transgression of divine providence, such as even in our day are sometimes dragged out of the broom-closet of superstition for priestly attacks on lightning rods and inoculation.'[21] By this time, it was not trust in God but the certain knowledge that a man's family would not fall into poverty after his death that was being promoted as a source of 'peace of mind – energy in business – and satisfaction,' even by clergymen.[22] And that certainty depended on trust or confidence in the worldly institution of the widows' fund and the men who operated it; it is characteristic that Günther's encomium on the HAVA used the language of 'reliability' and 'solidity' to recommend it to his readers.

As earnest of its solidity, moreover, he invoked an entirely secular set of authorities: sound mathematical principles, many years' careful assembly and analysis of data, and the fact that the institute had been set up by a man of acknowledged competence in the field and carefully checked by experts.[23]

By the 1770s reference to God had almost disappeared. The rhetoric of Christian charity persisted in writings that set out the rationale for new funds or defended the principle of the fund, but usually in combination with the secular language of preventing poverty – an object of good policy (or *Polizey*). The royal decree of 1767 that called the Calenberg into being cited both the divine injunction to relieve the poor and the state's interest in promoting marriage as guiding principles. In the crisis, opponents of reform often had resort to a pious appeal to Christian duty towards widows and orphans, but this was easily dismissed as sheer bluster. Characteristically, when it became apparent that if the Calenberg was to survive at all the widows' pensions would need to be reduced, the fund managers worried not about the widows' tears incurring divine judgment but about the effect their complaints would have on public opinion.[24] The debates around the crisis of the Calenberg and other contemporary funds invested agency and responsibility fully in human actors. What remained unresolved was whose agency was the most reliable guarantor of security.

Even the founding and first years of the Calenberg were dominated by secular and technical discourses. The Göttingen Scientific Society sponsored a public competition for proposals and set out guidelines that insisted that any scheme submitted for consideration be firmly grounded in relevant facts and figures. The newly established fund made a point of insisting in its publicity and demonstrating in its published semi-annual statements that its operations were based on careful and systematic calculations; the Calenberg's founders went so far as to suggest that their scheme was so sophisticated as to be beyond the comprehension of ordinary men: 'Those who are perhaps unfamiliar with this kind of calculation will not take it amiss if we expect that they place more confidence in the judgement of men who have more knowledge of the business, and who join the society with them, than in their own.'[25]

By the same token, the key concerns that were voiced about the Calenberg in the run-up to its opening and in the years that followed were specifically about its viability in the light of its design. Even into the 1780s it was possible to find challenges to the whole principle of widows' funds rooted in a suspicion of innovation, in moral objections to a system that seemed the obverse of thrift, or in pious indignation at the flouting of divine providence that was implicit in any kind of insurance scheme.[26] But around the ambitions of the Calenberg there clustered warnings of another kind: predictions that the fund was bound to collapse because in the long run it would not be able to meet its pension obligations. These predictions were made in private to the civil servants charged with setting up the fund, and they had to be refuted before the scheme could gain royal assent. The chief critic of the Calenberg was Johann Augustin Kritter, and he based his comments on a claim to technical expertise: he had studied the relevant data – principally the existing evidence for mortality in comparable populations – and had a clear view on what kinds of calculations should be applied in order to determine how many widows a fund would need to be able to support and what it would cost. When his private advice was ignored, he proceeded to publish his doubts, forcing the fund managers into a campaign of counter-publicity in the north German periodical press.[27]

By 1779 it was becoming apparent that Kritter had been right in predicting that the pensions commitment was bound to outstrip income. The crisis broke when a group of subscribers in Hamburg refused to pay the semi-annual contribution; creeping increases in the contribution rate had alerted them to the problem. A letter from Hamburg of March 1781 contains most of the key discursive elements that would be in evidence in subsequent debates. It includes a strong element of self-reproach:

> The plan lay before us; we could check and calculate; joining was the most voluntary act in the world. But for our part we failed to see what we see now, our eyes having been opened by the [increase in] contributions, and what should and could have been clear to us given the nature of the fund itself ... The contribution was so small at the beginning ... And there was the example of many well-respected men, who were known to be of a critical cast of mind. And the reputation of the Calenberg Estates, whose dependability was so well and rightly trusted ... We were warned, we cannot deny it, but often in that nagging tone that we dislike in others, and that made us suspicious of the intentions behind it. Where this wasn't the case, Hope went before Scrutiny; either it took too great an effort to check and calculate, or we chose not to for the sake of our ease

> of mind; in short, as too often happens to people, our hearts ran away with our heads.[28]

Here, the subscribers acknowledge that they are aware of having taken a risk, in that they deliberately ignored warnings that it would have been in their power to acknowledge and test. Their words bespeak a presumption that the success of a fund did depend on particular knowledge and skills, but also that these were available to every member of the fund – or at least to those who, like the signatories to the letter, were educated men. Shared competence implied shared responsibility. In this low-tech vision, trust seems almost unnecessary; indeed, disaster had been the consequence of trusting others *rather than* doing the brainwork oneself.

As the rest of the letter reveals, however, this particular group of men had access to a more sophisticated understanding of the technology necessary to make a widows' fund work than that possessed by the ordinary educated man. In the letter, a formulaic reassertion of continued confidence in the competence and good faith of the fund managers is followed by a critique of the operating principles of the Calenberg:

> But there is a fundamental error in the ... very nature of our institute. *Give* and *take* must exist in the correct relation to one another. During his probable years of marriage, each provider [i.e., subscriber] must pay in as much in contributions as will permit the fund to pay his widow the pension [he] has stipulated for her probable years of widowhood. Let us use Euler's words ... If his widow lives beyond her probable life expectancy, another widow who dies sooner thereby secures the first widow's pension, and this by the very nature of the arrangement.

This betrays the authors' familiarity with the most up-to-date probabilistic principles, and that is not surprising. One of the signatories to the letter was Johann Georg Büsch (professor at the Commercial Academy in Hamburg). Büsch had already been closely involved in the formation of the HAVA. The use of 'probable' in this passage, like the reference to the Swiss mathematician Leonhard Euler,[29] takes the letter beyond a statement that income must match expenditure, and bespeaks the influence of Georg Christian von Oeder in particular. The key move here is from a crude principle of restitution and mutuality modelled on fire insurance, in which the contributions of living subscribers actually paid the pensions of current widows, to one in which (as the Hamburg protestors went on to assert) 'each member actually invests for himself and for his own widow's probable needs, and absolutely not for others.'

Büsch and Philip Gabriel Hensler (city physician in Altona), went on to act as authorized spokesmen for some 1300 Calenberg subscribers organized in regional associations. In this context, they worked in association with the Kiel philosopher and mathematician Johann Nicolaus Tetens to devise reform proposals of their own in active and aggressive negotiation with the Calenberg administrators. The openness and complexity of the consultation process that developed in the Calenberg crisis is notable by contrast with the Lüneburg case. The involvement of subscribers was not only on a different scale but also took on a different quality through the deployment by both subscribers and fund managers of the periodical and pamphlet press. Still more significant is the extent to which technical expertise was employed on both sides. While Tetens deployed his developing understanding of actuarial principles on behalf of the subscribers, the Calenberg managers formally commissioned four university-based mathematicians to advise them. They also turned to their chief critic, Johann Augustin Kritter, as a consultant.[30]

The debates among academics, committed amateurs (like Kritter), and members of an educated public that emerged from the general crisis of the widows' funds and came to a head in the Calenberg crisis constitute a watershed in the development of modern notions of risk and probability in the German lands. In the widows' fund literature the term '*Risico*' (risk) itself was used almost exclusively to mean the danger of financial loss to the fund inherent in the enterprise or in a particular policy or technique. This was, of course, directly related to another form of 'risk,' the one inherent in the uncertainty of human life. What funds could do in the case of individuals was attempt to assess and accommodate risks that fell within the range of the normal and to exclude high-risk individuals; from a very early stage publicly recruiting funds required proof of good health and imposed higher premiums on older men and men with dangerous occupations.

In the 1760s, the element of uncertainty that always provided the rationale for the funds began to be articulated systematically in terms that implied an actuarial notion of risk. A properly operating fund allowed individual risks to cancel one another out by incurring a collective risk that was spread over (or shared by) a number of individuals. And this limited the danger of loss to both the fund and the individual subscriber. The principle of abnormally long lives balancing out abnormally short ones was expressed as early as the founding of the Calenberg in terms that paraphrase (though without citing) the Law of Large Numbers:[31]

> Since by its nature the number of subscribers must be very great, we have the right to assume that we cannot be much in error in respect of the life expectancy which we attribute to each member when he joins; for to the extent that we overestimate in one case, we will underestimate in others, so that in the end we will find that it works out as well as if each man had reached exactly the exact the goal set for him [i.e., the anticipated age of death].[32]

In the case of the Calenberg the 'exact goal set' for each husband and wife was established by reference to the tables of mortality first published by Johann David Süßmilch in 1741, and contributions were nominally fixed according to a calculus that took into account the respective ages (and hence life expectancies) of the marriage partners. This was in keeping with the advice of the Göttingen Scientific Society in its original call for suggestions for the design of a widows' fund in 1764. Indeed:

> [The Society] suspects that if we are to assess correctly the probability [*Wahrscheinlichkeit*] of the sentence 'Tita, who is this old, will outlive Titius, who is this old, by this many years,' some practice in mathematics will be necessary, and the algebraists may need to be called on for help ... But its concern is less with algebra than with calculations that are correct and grounded in facts.[33]

The limited sense in which 'probability' is being used here, and in particular the agnosticism about the role of mathematical analysis, are characteristic of a still inchoate approach to the calculation of risk. In the everyday work of the Calenberg, these gestures at statistical probabilism were overshadowed by more primitive practices of projection and accounting.

We have seen the Hamburg subscribers to the Calenberg, with George Christian von Oeder and Johann Nicolaus Tetens in the background, challenging those practices from a probabilistic standpoint.

From the late 1770s onwards, an explicit discourse of risk and aleatory probability was developing around the operation of the widows' funds. Oeder's public and private writings reflect a growing insight into basic statistical techniques (such as the random sample) and the mathematical principle of *distributing* risk in a population. As early as 1778 he was using the term *Wahrscheinlichkeitsregel* (rule of probability) in its modern sense to characterize 'ideal typical' mortality patterns. And he assessed the viability of pension funds in terms of whether their subscribers were sufficiently numerous for 'favourable and unfavourable cases to compensate one another,' a circumstance he characterized with the concept of the free play of chance (*Hasard*).[34] By 1791 the directors of the HAVA would be referring to each of the eight subscription classes into which the pension fund was divided as a body of individuals held together by a 'shared risk' (*gemeinschaftliches Risico*).[35] It was in the Calenberg crisis that other German mathematicians began to use *wagen* (in the verbal sense of 'hazard') and associated expressions of risk – notably *aufs Spiel setzen* – in ways that echoed the language of gamblers. But, as Johann Nicolaus Tetens put it in the treatise on annuities that emerged out of his engagement with the Calenberg crisis, they now understood that life insurance, properly designed, was a gamble in which even the loser (the policyholder who lived a long life in certainty that his survivors were well provided for) had nothing to complain of.[36]

A tetchy aside in that same treatise reflects how firmly the character of life-contingent pensions was established as a problem for the experts by the end of the crisis. Tetens wrote: 'Who were the inventors of all those plans for widows' ... funds and the like, by which the public was cheated? Mere adders-up, but not algebraists, who could have made a general calculation of the business.'[37] However, it would be a mistake to take the increasing use of probabilistic language and the sophistication of statistical techniques in this generation for the practical triumph of mathematical thinking. Well into the nineteenth century, even successful life insurance practitioners continued to use essentially arithmetical, or summative, methods in drawing up their life tables and calculating premiums. If even the experts tended to remain on familiar ground when it came to practical applications, it is perhaps not surprising that the public remained sceptical. Indeed, the more refined the thinking of the experts became, the more remote it became from common sense, or public understanding: the experts and the reformed funds operated with the new concept of the 'probable length of a marriage.' To explain that the probability of any two people both continuing to live for a particular period of time (the marriage's probable length, or 'life expectancy') was different from the probability of survival of either of them as individuals (individual life expectancy) required reference to a body of theory and a style of thought that even the experts had trouble grasping.

This did not prevent members of the public from entering the debate, though, and indeed the terms in which the experts argued were sometimes formulated in direct response to the *public* and controversial use of the language of risk by lay people. In this sense, the discursive ground had shifted. Where the generation of 1700 appealed to divine providence against rigid human systems, it was against the claims of *mathematics* that even sceptics among their grandchildren invoked the inherent uncertainty of life and death: 'Talk as much as you like about reliable calculations of the possible number of deaths [wrote one subscriber]; the business itself is by its very nature a matter of uncertainty.'[38] This quote alone shows how problematic it was for the fund managers to appeal to mathematics as a 'technology of trust'[39] in order to resolve the political impasse, for while its author acknowledged the availability of expertise he explicitly rejected its authority. But most subscribers did not challenge the mathematicians, because the claim of the experts that certainty was possible provided a kind of validation of the subscribers' insistence that they had had every right to expect that the fund would not collapse. In effect, they argued that they had not knowingly taken a risk in joining the fund; on the contrary, they had acted on the guarantee of security provided by the fund managers. If they had ignored critical expert voices before, they were now prepared to accept the general arguments of the mathematicians. These were particularly plausible when they were able to demonstrate that the pensions received by the surviving widows were 'excessive' or 'disproportionate' – as the conflict between subscribers and widows over who was to pay the cost of rescuing the fund developed into an exercise in mutual blame-laying.

The organized widows responded with a set of arguments calculated to minimize their own liability by inflating the risk involved in joining the fund; this involved the explicit rejection of the claims of statistical probabilism. The key to their arguments was to insist that the fund was based on an aleatory contract, or gambling agreement whose outcome was subject entirely to chance. They argued that each of the subscribers (both their own husbands and the current ones, who were now demanding the right to withdraw from the fund at the widows' expense) had 'knowingly [entered into] an insecure transaction in which he could win and [i.e., or] lose'[40] when he joined. The widows had an interest in this reading of the situation, because they were in the position of having *gained* from their husbands' joining the fund, while the living subscribers (and their potential widows) stood to lose by the same act; their construction of the widows' fund as a gamble meant that in equity neither the fund managers nor the subscribers could demand compensation from them. This interest presumably outweighed the moral risk they took in declaring that their late husbands, most of them respectable schoolmasters and ministers of the gospel, had gambled with their families' future.

In making this claim, what the widows were doing was to deploy the expertise that suited their purpose, namely the legal definition of justice. For the Calenberg directors had consulted four law faculties as well as four mathematicians. Jurisprudence was better established than mathematics as a body of expertise, of course, with much more explicit claims to set the parameters for trust and blame. The jurists, though, struggled to locate the widows' fund within existing categories – or to find ways of accommodating the new terms in which certainty and risk were being defined in the public debate in their account of the situation. All insurance contracts were defined *a priori* in continental law as aleatory contracts. When invited to extend this principle retrospectively to a new institution, the German lawyers showed themselves uncertain about what was meant by uncertainty; some of them proved unable to distinguish between a possibility of collapse inherent and anticipatable from the start and the characterization of the collapse as an accident or a catastrophe that was 'really nobody's fault.' The jurists at the University of Leipzig came closest to a technically 'clean' definition, and also explained what it was that made the funds a gamble: they ruled that a widows' fund depended 'on the length of human life, and so on a completely uncertain outcome.'[41] The submissions of the widows themselves translated this bland statement into a direct attack on the expertise of the mathematicians who claimed that a widows' fund *could* be other than a gamble: the Calenberg, the widows argued, was 'an essentially insecure and uncertain enterprise ... *because* everything depends on the calculation of mortality.'[42] It was to this challenge that Tetens's assertion that insurance was indeed a gamble, but one that benefited even the 'loser,' cited above, was a direct response.

The very document that contained this testimony to lack of faith in calculation seized the opportunity to cast blame back on the subscribers for having failed to heed expert warnings. This is a reminder that the purpose of all the statements made by the protagonists in the crisis of the widows' funds was forensic, or polemical, but this is not a reason to see their testimony as inauthentic. Even instrumental uses of language draw on underlying value systems, as their deployment itself constitutes a test of those systems and prompts reflection and reformulation. The conflict between widows and subscribers generated exaggerated claims on both sides. They were agreed in the prudential, or risk-aversive, character of the underlying intentions; every man who joined was looking for a way individually to guard *against* the likelihood that he would die before he had accumulated enough capital to see his widow provided for.[43] On the nature of the act itself, there seemed no middle ground between those who insisted that subscribers were not knowingly taking any risk in joining and those who insisted that the risk had been total. This ground was claimed by the expert mathematicians, whose perception of the initial risk rested on the conviction that calculation could have eliminated it.

Objectively, though, all had been taking a more or less calculated risk, and many of them (at least) understood that. The spirit of experimentation that characterized this generation, and the increasing range of moral and technical calculi that they applied when assessing which experiments to buy into, may be illustrated by the nearest thing we have to a 'focus group' discussion about widows' funds in the 1780s.[44] At the height of the Calenberg crisis, in 1783, a minor civil servant in the kingdom of Hannover hatched a scheme for a widows' fund whose membership would be restricted to servants of the Crown. He canvassed support for this by circularizing the Crown servants posted in all the towns and villages of the kingdom, inviting them to express their support in principle. The responses of 181 of them survive.[45] Of these, only 5 gave an outright 'no,' and 13 an unqualified 'yes.' The majority wanted to know what they were getting into: 57 simply said they would wait to see a full plan while 84 were slightly more positive, indicating that they would join if the plan, once presented, offered the prospect of security, permanence, reliability, effectiveness, affordability, and/or 'proportionality.'[46] Most of these men wanted to subject the scheme at least to their own judgment, and the responses of seven of them showed that they considered themselves to have some understanding of the technology of pension funds. As for external sources of confidence: 1 was satisfied to put his trust in the proposer of the plan, as a man of good intentions; 1 thought he would join if everybody else did; fully 13 said they would join if the plan had royal approval (thus ceding scrutiny to a political authority); and 7 explicitly or implicitly cited the approval of expert mathematicians as a precondition for their commitment. By this time, clearly, some lessons – and a new vocabulary – had been learned from the crisis. People were not yet prepared to give up, though. Nothing came of the 1783 scheme, but a year later one of the civil servants originally canvassed wrote to the Crown authorities urging them to approve the plan – not *in spite of* his experience of the crisis, but *because* he had lost the equivalent of more than a year's income in the collapse of the Calenberg.[47]

We may compare the tone and content of these men's statements with the clergymen's comments of 1725, in the light of Brian Wynne's observation that 'credibility' and 'trust' – ostensibly manifest in varying degrees in public responses to risks and scientific knowledge – 'are themselves analytical artefacts which represent underlying tacit processes of social identity negotiation.'[48] The practised humility and programmatic fatalism that appear as vagueness and bafflement in the earlier generation have given way to implicit and explicit claims to competence, understanding, and real-world agency. The men of the 1780s display a positive orientation to technical expertise as part of their self-presentation, or identity. In the wider debate around the reform of the Calenberg, too, even those who questioned the legitimacy of technical solutions expressed their challenge in a shared language of risk, exploiting its instability for their purposes or consciously setting the language of the lawyers against that of the mathematicians. The men who had the power and responsibility to carry out reforms, the fund managers, were generally persuaded of the need for expert solutions, though whose expertise was most reliable remained an open question for a long time. And among those who claimed expertise, competition proceeded within a consensus that the 'taming of chance' was a genuine possibility.

NOTES

1 Mary Douglas, *Risk and Blame* (London: Routledge, 1992), 22ff. For a good overview of the changing meanings, see Deborah Lupton, *Risk* (London: Routledge, 1999), 5–13.

2 Reference here is to the work of Ulrich Beck, Niklas Luhmann, and Anthony Giddens.

3 The term is that of Ian Hacking, *The Taming of Chance* (Cambridge: Cambridge University Press, 1990).

4 Lorraine Daston, *Classical Probability in the Enlightenment* (Princeton: Princeton University Press, 1988) and 'The Domestication of Risk: Mathematical Probability and Insurance 1650–1830," in *The Probabilistic Revolution*, Vol. 1: *Ideas in History*, ed. Lorenz Krüger et al. (Cambridge, MA: MIT Press, 1987), 237–60; Geoffrey Wilson Clark, *Betting on Lives: The Culture of Life Insurance in England 1695–1775* (Manchester: Manchester University Press, 1999). See also Robin Pearson, 'Thrift or Dissipation? The Business of Life Assurance in the Early Nineteenth Century,' *Economic History Review*, 2nd ser., 43 (1990), 236–54.

5 Cf. Bernd Wunder, 'Pfarrwitwenkassen und Beamtenwitwen-Anstalten vom 16.–19. Jahrhundert. Die Entstehung der staatlichen Hinterbliebenenversorgung in Deutschland,' *Zeitschrift für historische Forschung* 12 (1985), 429–98; J.C. Riley, '"That Your Widows May be Rich": Providing for Widowhood in Old Regime Europe,' *Economisch- en sociaal-historisch jaarboek* 45 (1982), 58–76.

6 For the Calenberg, see *Nachricht von der Situation der Calenbergischen allgemeinen Witwen-Verpflegungs-Gesellschaft im 24ten und 25ten Termin* (August 1779), Niedersächsisches Hauptstaatsarchiv Hannover [hereafter cited as HStAHann], Hann 93, vol. 3706, 358; *Verzeichnis sämtlicher recipirten und verstorbenen Männer der Calenbergischen Witwenpflegegesellschaft nach dem Alter zur Zeit der Aufnahme* (November 1783), HStAHann, Dep 7B, vol. 358, 208–64. For a contemporary survey, see Johann Augustin Kritter, *Sammlung wichtiger Erfahrungen bey den zu Grunde gegangenen Wittwen- und Waisen-Kassen* (Leipzig: Hilscher, 1780).

7 Daston, *Classical Probability*, 174.

8 Friedrich-Edmund Horstmann, *Versicherungseinrichtungen in der Stadt Hannover in der Zeit von 1728 bis 1885: Eine rechtshistorische Studie* (Hannover: Hahnsche Buchhandlung, 1966). See *Verordnung, d.d. 16/17 Mart. 1750, Die Brand-Assecurations-Societaet betreffend*, in Klosterbibliothek Loccum, XXII, 16 Acta betreffend Brandkasse Kataster des Stifts Loccum und des

Kantons Rehburg. A key agent of 'technology transfer' here seems to have been Georg Ebell, Abbot of Loccum from 1732 to 1770. He spent time in London before joining the clergy, and once appointed abbot was *ex officio* chairman of the Treasury Committee of the Calenberg Estates under whose auspices both the fire insurance scheme and the widows' fund were set up; cf. *Zum Jubiläum des Klosters Loccum* (Hannover: Buchdruckerei des Stephansstifts, 1913), 152. Some contemporaries noted that from a financial point of view the model of a form of insurance whose purpose was to compensate for one-off losses was entirely inappropriate to a pension fund, but their objections were not taken seriously; this reinforces the impression of a high degree of actuarial naivety and/or wishful thinking on the part of the founders of the fund; see *Unvorgreifliche Gedanken über den von Hochlöbl. Calenbergischer Landschaft publicirten Plan einer Allg. Witwen Pflegschaft* (undated MS, probably December 1766), HstAHann, Dep 7B, vol. 327, 179–203, and other correspondence in the same volume.

9 See Eve Rosenhaft, 'Did Women Invent Life Insurance? Widows and the Demand for Financial Services in Eighteenth-Century Germany,' in David R. Green and Alastair Owens, eds., *Family Welfare: Gender, Property and Inheritance since the Seventeenth Century* (Contributions to Family Studies, no. 18) (London: Praeger, 2004), 163–94.

10 The most detailed account of these events in the literature is provided by Reinhard Oberschelp, *Niedersachsen 1760–1820*, 2 vols. (Hildesheim: Lax, 1982), vol. 1, 230ff. The records are deposited in HstAHann. For analogous developments in Hamburg, see *Sammlung verschiedener Aufsätze die Hamburgische beeidigte Christen-Mäckler Wittwen- und Waysen-Casse betreffend zum Besten sämmtlicher Interessenten und Pensionisten zum öffentlichen Druck befördert von den jetzigen Vorstehern gedachter Casse* (Hamburg: Reuss, 1777); William Boehart, *'Nicht brothlos und nothleidend zu hinterlassen'* (Hamburg: Verein für Hamburgische Geschichte 1985). For an account of the crisis that emphasises the gender politics of the public debate, see my '"But the Heart Must Speak for the Widows": The Origins of Life Insurance in Germany and the Gender Implications of Actuarial Science,' in Marion Gray and Ulrike Gleixner (eds.), *Gender in Transition: Breaks and Continuities in German-Speaking Europe 1750–1830* (Ann Arbor: Michigan University Press, 2007), 90–113. The moment of crisis or anticipated crisis plays an important role in the historiography of life insurance and actuarial accounting, since it provokes the articulation of values and expectations, whether courts are called on to intervene between disputing parties or public bodies address the question of regulation; see, for example, Theodore M. Porter, 'Precision and Trust: Early Victorian

Insurance and the Politics of Calculation,' in M. Norton Wise, ed., *The Values of Precision* (Princeton: Princeton University Press, 1995), 173–97.

11 Larry Neal, 'The Money Pitt: Lord Londonderry and the South Sea Bubble; or How to Manage Risk in an Emerging Market,' *Enterprise & Society* 1 (December 2000), 673.

12 For the 1767 proposal: HStaHann, Dep 7B, vol. 372II, 479–508.

13 *Ordnung der Christlichen Gesellschaft zu Versorgung der Witwen und Waysen* (Lüneburg, 1700).

14 *Acta die Confirmation der christlichen Gesellschaft zu Versorgung der Witwen und Waysen aufgerichtet betreffend*, Stadtarchiv Lüneburg (hereafter cited as StALü), Rep 102, I, 6/6.

15 *Ordnung der Christlichen Gesellschaft zu Versorgung der Witwen und Waysen*, art. 31.

16 Widows (unnamed) to fund administrators, 3 July 1720; *Allerunterthänigste Vorstellung und Bitte um Verordnung einer Commission [...] von Seiten der Prediger und anderer Wittwen wieder die jetzt lebenden Interessenten der in Anno 1700 errichteten Lüneburgischen Wittwen Casse*, both documents StALü, Rep 102, I, 12/1.

17 This is based on the extensive discussion of the terms *Mißtrauen*, *Mißtrauen gegen Gott*, *Vertrauen*, and *Vertrauen in Gott* in Johann Heinrich Zedler, *Großes Universal-Lexicon aller Wissenschaften und Künste* (Halle and Leipzig: Zedler, 1728–35), vol. 21, column [Spalte] 501, vol. 48, columns 19–33. Cf. Ute Frevert, 'Vertrauen. Eine historische Spurensuche,' in Ute Frevert, ed., *Vertrauen. Historische Annäherungen* (Göttingen: Vandenhoeck & Ruprecht, 2003), 14f.

18 High Court (*Justizkanzlei*) Celle to the King, enclosing order to the Mayor and Council of Lüneburg, 15 June 1724, HStAHann, Hann 70, no. 976.

19 Letter of H. Petri, Braunschweig, 19.6.1720, StALü, Rep 102, I, 13 (no pagination).

20 Letter of M.G. Kiliani, Bleckede, 5.7.1720, StALü, Rep 102, I, 13 (no pagination).

21 [J.F. Günther], *Ueber Leibrenten, Witwen-Cassen und ähnliche Anstalten, und besonders über die im Jahr 1778 zu Hamburg errichtete allgemeine Versorgungs-Anstalt. Zum Unterricht fur Leser, denen die bisherigen Nachrichten von diesem Institut nicht bekannt oder nicht deutlich genug sind* (Hamburg: Hofmann, 1788), 4.

22 Carl Daniel Küster, *Der Wittwen- und Waisenversorger, oder Grundsätze, nach welchen dauerhafte Wittwen- und Waisensocietäten gestiftet werden können. Zum nutzen unbelehrter Leser, welche Aufseher oder Glieder dieser*

*wohlthätigen Anstalten sind* (Leipzig: Junius, 1772), 2. Küster was a minister and officer of the Reformed Church in Magdeburg.

23 [Günther], *Ueber Leibrenten, Witwen-Cassen und ähnliche Anstalten*, 10.

24 Landsyndicus Meyer to J.G. Büsch, 21 March 1781, HStAHann, Dep 7B, vol. 370 (no pagination); minutes of a meeting of the Schatz-Collegium on 22 November 1781, ibid., vol. 369, 2–7.

25 Untitled, undated manuscript, HstAHann Dep 7B, vol. 326I, 1–6. The following account of debates around the founding of the Calenberg is based on other documents of 1766 and 1767 included in this volume.

26 See for example Johann Peter Süßmilch, *Die göttliche Ordnung in den Veränderungen des menschlichen Geschlechts, aus der Geburt, dem Tode, und der Fortpflanzung desselben erwiesen*, Part 3, ed. Christian Jacob Baumann (Berlin: Buchhandlung der Realschule, 1787), 465f. (editor's comment).

27 Johann Augustin Kritter, *Sammlung von dreyen Aufsätzen über die Calenbergischen, Preussichen und Dänischen Wittwenversorgungsanstalten* (Hamburg: Reuss, 1777); 'Gedancken über die Calenbergische Witwen-Verpflegungs-Gesellschaft,' *Göttingische Gelehrte Beyträge* 1768, 37. Stück (17.12.68), 464–5; [A.C.] v[on] W[üllen], 'Über die Gedanken, so das Calenbergische Institutum einer allgemeinen Wittwenverpflegungsgesellschaft betreffen,' *Hannoverisches Magazin* 1769, 22. Stück (17.03.1769), 337–51. On Kritter, see *Deutsches Biographisches Archiv*, 215–31; Hans-Jürgen Gerhard, *Diensteinkommen der Göttinger Officianten 1750–1850* (Göttingen: Vandenhoeck & Ruprecht, 1978).

28 Letter from Holstein, Matthiesen, Hensler, Cropp, Dusch, Eberwein, Büsch, Winthen, Fulda to Calenberg administrtion, 24 March 1781, HstAHann Dep 37B, vol. 335, 37–43.

29 For traces of the reception of Euler in Germany, see, e.g., Leonhard Euler, 'Des Herrn Leonhard Eulers nöthige Berechnung zur Einrichtung einer Witwencasse,' *Neues Hamburgisches Magazin* 43, no. 2 (1770), 1–13.

30 Correspondence between Calenberg managers and mathematicians, in HStAHann, Dep 7B, vol. 343; Kritter to Calenberg administration, 17 December 1787, HStAHann, Dep 7B, vol. 359, 49.

31 The Law of Large Numbers is the foundational theorem in probability theory proposed by Jacob Bernoulli in his *Ars Conjectandi* of 1713. It holds that the larger the number of observations of a particular phenomenon the more likely the average observed outcome is to equate to the average of the totality of possible instances of the phenomenon.

32 MS publicity material for Calenberg, n.d. (filed among founding documents), HstAHann Dep. 7B, vol. 326I, 1–6.

33 Johann David Michaelis, *Nöthige Aufmerksamkeit, die man bey Vorschlägen*

*zu Einlegung guter Witwencassen beobachten muss: ein Aufsatz, der im Nahmen der Kön. Societät der Wissenschaften zu Göttingen abgefasset, und am 21ten Sept 1764 bekannt gemacht ist*, in *Vermischte Schriften*, 2 vols, Frankfurt a.m.: Garbe, 1766–69, II. Theil, 103.

34 Oeder to Graf Holmer, 5 March 1778, Niedersächsisches Staatsarchiv Oldenburg, 31, 2-46-41, 536–40; see also G.C. Oeder, *Consilium* (MS sent to Calenberg directors), 19 August 1782, HstAHann Dep. 7B, vol. 343, 265–74.

35 *Convention zwischen Löbl. Kammerei der Stadt Hamburg und der Direction der Hochobrigkeitlich bestätigten Hamburgischen allg. VA* (January 1791), Archives of Hamburg-Mannheimer Versicherungs AG, Hamburg, F0001-00019, vol. 2.

36 Johann Nicolaus Tetens, *Einleitung zur Berechnung der Leibrenten und Anwartschaften, die vom Leben und Tode einer oder mehrer Personen abhängen*, 2 vols. (Leipzig: Weidmanns Erben und Ruch, 1785–6), vol. 1, iv. Cf. Daston, *Classical Probability*, 166. Compare also the consultant paper provided by Hindenburg to the Calenberg in August 1782, HstAHann Dep. 7B, vol. 343, 109–57, which characterizes a subscriber whose age is close to or lower than that of his wife as someone who 'takes a risk against the dictates of probability, and so places [his money] at stake in the expectation of losing' [*wider die Wahrscheinlichkeit wagt, und so gleichsam als verlohren aufs Spiel sezt*]. For the vision of 'losers' as 'winners,' see also [Günther], *Ueber Leibrenten, Witwen-Cassen und ähnliche Anstalten*, 3.

37 Tetens, *Einleitung*, vol. 1, xvii.

38 *Sammlung verschiedener Aufsätze*, 97.

39 The term is that of Theodore M. Porter, *Trust in Numbers: The Pursuit of Objectivity in Science and Public Life* (Princeton: Princeton University Press, 1995).

40 *Replicae, nisi quid novi, submissivae cum petitis an Seiten der in actis genannten Wittwen, Klägerinnen [...]* (26 March 1789), HStAHann, Dep 7B, vol. 360, 233.

41 Report of Leipzig Law Faculty, November 1781, HStAHann, Dep 7B, vol. 342, 43. Cf. Daston's critique of Hacking on 'epistemic' versus 'aleatory' senses of probability, and her proposition that juridical discourse with its notions of equity and expectation critically shapes 'classical probability.'

42 *Replicae, nisi quid novi*, 233 (emphasis mine).

43 It should be noted, though, that this could itself be seen as a licence for taking risks in life; the purchase of contributory pensions was widely perceived in the eighteenth and nineteenth centuries as the *opposite* of thrift.

44 For an example of the use of focus groups to assess late twentieth-century attitudes to financial services in the context of 'risk,' see Peter

Lunt and Justine Blundell, 'Public Understanding of Financial Risk: The Challenge to Regulation,' in Peter Taylor-Gooby, ed., *Risk, Trust and Welfare* (Basingstoke: Macmillan, 2000), 114–30.

45 HStAHann, Hann 93, no. 3704, 53–102.

46 The terms used to name the desiderata included *Sicherheit, auf sicherem Fuß, Bestand, begründete Dauer, Festigkeit, dauerhaft, standhaltend, zuverlässig, auf sichere und proportionierte Art eingerichtet,* and *verhältnismässiger Beitrag.*

47 Letter of A.J. von Reinbek, 11 December 1784, HStAHann, Hann 93, no. 3704,64f.

48 Brian Wynne, 'Misunderstood Misunderstandings: Social Identities and Public Uptake of Science,' in Alan Irwin and Brian Wynne (eds.), *Misunderstanding Science? The Public Reconstruction of Science and Technology* (Cambridge: Cambridge University Press, 1996), 41.

# 2 Gottfried Wilhelm Leibniz's Work on Insurance

J.-MATTHIAS GRAF VON DER SCHULENBURG
AND CHRISTIAN THOMANN

The appeal of insurance is not to be limited to insurance companies' attempts to persuade potential customers to purchase their products or the desire of the new bourgeois class to ensure a certain standard of living even beyond the life of the breadwinner. Insurance also appealed to one of the most prominent scientists of the late seventeenth century: Gottfried Wilhelm Leibniz. It may therefore be no coincidence that the conference on insurance history with the wonderful title *The Appeal of Insurance* took place in Hanover in the Leibniz house, the former house of this great scientist, which belongs now to the Leibniz University of Hanover. In this chapter we discuss how the different fields of insurance sciences, spanning from actuarial considerations to insurance economics, were treated by this scholar. After introductory remarks we briefly describe Leibniz's written contributions to insurance, provide some insights on the historical background of his work on insurance, and, in the final two sections, deal with special aspects of his insurance mathematical work and the economic rationale for his call to found a public insurance company.

## Introduction

There is no doubt that Gottfried Wilhelm Leibniz, who lived in Hanover for almost forty years and who died there in 1716, was one of the greatest polymaths of modern times. He invented the integral and the integral sign $\int$, the binary number system that is the basis for our modern digital world, and worked on probabilities and life tables (or, more properly, mortality tables). In addition, he invented a mechanical calculating machine (which never worked perfectly), built new street lighting in Vienna, and constructed machines to pump out the water of silver mines located in the Harz mountains south of Hanover. Leibniz maintained a correspondence with more than three thousand scientists and politicians, which was possible after the introduction of a functioning mail system in Europe. Among many other subjects, he was very interested in the development of institutions for risk-sharing. The focus of this chapter is his contribution to insurance regulation, politics, and theory. Our analysis is based on a recently published volume containing Leibniz's manuscripts on insurance and financial mathematics, with commentary by Eberhard Knobloch, Ivo Schneider, Edgar Neuburger, and Walter Karten.[1]

## Leibniz's Writings on Insurance

Which of the very many papers of Gottfried Wilhelm Leibniz do we consider as a contribution to insurance theory? Firstly, there are the general papers, in which Leibniz claims that the government has to install public insurance companies because the welfare of the people is increased if certain risks are securely covered by a public scheme. Leibniz did not believe that sensible (today we would call them risk-averse) private entrepreneurs would found insurance companies that were large enough to serve a great part of the population. His position can probably be justified in a time of limited data and little knowledge of calculating probabilities; writing an insurance contract would have appeared to be a gamble more suitable for speculators than for serious business men. We group the following papers under the first category of basic papers on the need for insurance protection:

- Letter to Duke Johann Friedrich of Hanover written in September 1678
- Memorandum to the Emperor Leopold of Habsburg of the Holy Roman Empire of the German Nation written in July 1680
- A paper on public insurance companies also written in July 1680
- A paper on the foundation of Insurance Funds (*Versicherungs Caßa*) written in 1688
- Memorandum on installing a 'Societas Scientiarum et Artium' in Berlin from 26 March 1700, probably written for Jablonski and Leibniz's friends in Berlin

Another group of papers deals with the methods of discounting and interest calculation of long-term payments (like pensions) and long-term loans and credits. Modern premium calculation of long-term insurance contracts in life and health insurance is based on concepts that have their roots in the work of Leibniz and other scientists of the late seventeenth century. We have identified twenty-four papers and pieces of correspondence by Leibniz on these topics, written between 1680 and 1683.

A third group of papers discuss questions about pension calculation, life insurance, and life expectancy. Seventeen papers are published in the volume on Leibniz's contributions to this topic of insurance science. Leibniz wrote them between 1675 and 1683.

The last group of papers is on business financial transactions, a topic that has no direct link to insurance. However, these papers not only provide basic insights into financial business but deal with business risks and the management of those risks. Just as in modern times, institutions managing financial funds and allowing for a diversification of financial risks are crucial for the development of an economy based upon a division of labour. The volume on Leibniz's contribution to insurance and financing contains four papers that cover a wide range of subjects: the use of logarithmic tables, money credits, and management of lending houses (*Pfandhäuser*). Again, these papers were written between 1680 and 1883.

Most of Leibniz's papers on insurance are also dated between 1680 and 1683. It is noticeable that the content of the majority of these papers is very little influenced by probability theory, although Leibniz must have known that the insurance business is closely related to the ability to calculate expected losses by employing probabilities. Leibniz was in close contact with Jacob Bernoulli, the father of mathematical probability theory, and so was aware of probability theory. He may have ignored the advances in this field because he was a strong critic of Bernoulli's probability measure, which Bernoulli had developed from Hughes's expected value theorem. Perhaps Leibniz also did not believe in the possibility of calculating expected losses at a time when data collection and processing was still a problem. We see that Leibniz's view of insurance was far from the image that Adam Smith would draw in 1776. In *The Wealth of Nations*, published a little more than sixty years after Leibniz's death, Smith provides a very accurate description of a modern insurance company: 'In order to make insurance … a trade at all, the common premium must be sufficient to compensate the common losses, to pay the expense of management, and to afford such a profit as might have been drawn from an equal capital employed in common trade.'[2]

## Historical Context of Leibniz's Work on Insurance

The letters exchanged by Gottfried Wilhelm Leibniz and Jacob Bernoulli allow for a better understanding of Leibniz's knowledge of probability theory and mortality research. In 1697 Leibniz received a letter from Jacob's younger brother Johann. Johann reported on his brother's development of a theorem that was later called the law of large numbers. Yet Leibniz remained sceptical and considered that these ideas of Jacob Bernoulli were not applicable to real-life problems, especially in the context of legal cases. Leibniz was also aware of the advances in mortality research at the time. In a letter to Jacob Bernoulli in 1703, Leibniz refers to the mortality tables of Johan de Witt in a book that was written in Dutch to help Dutch investors calculate life pension contracts. Yet when Jacob Bernoulli died in 1705, there was no agreement between these two famous scientists on whether the laws on the calculation of probabilities by means of selecting a random sample were at all useful. It is interesting to notice that the brilliant scientist Leibniz, who so favoured the foundation of insurance companies, did not realize the benefit of probability theory and mortality tables for the insurance business. A possible explanation of why we do not find any of Leibniz's works on insurance that build upon the developments of probability theory and mortality is that he seems to have lost interest in insurance in 1683, years before he learned more about these new theoretical concepts.

Leibniz is certainly the greatest scientist of his day who dealt much with the public's new desire to protect itself against risks with the help of insurance. This desire was the consequence of the catastrophic experience of the Thirty Years War from 1618 till 1648, which destroyed houses and cities, and of the great plague of 1635. Another catastrophic event was the Great Fire of London in 1666. This fire destroyed about thirteen thousand houses, and many Londoners lost all their property. The Great Fire led to different activities aimed at providing protection and coverage. The Rebuilding Act of 1667, for instance, was designed to reduce vulnerability to fire, stipulating that houses be built out of stone instead of wood. To protect people against future loss of home and property by fire, the merchant Nicholas Barbon in 1667 developed an insurance plan proposing that each house owner pay a small contribution to build a fund that would cover losses by fire. Following on Barbon's plan, Christopher Wren, one of England's leading architects, opened an insurance office in 1667 in London; this office began to sell fire policies in 1670. By the end of the seventeenth century a number of independent insurance companies had been founded, among them the Friendly Society, founded in 1683, and the Amicable Contributors, which obtained its licence in 1696. These newly founded insurance companies organized private fire services that became responsible for fire protection until 1865.

Leibniz visited London six years after the Great Fire. He saw the damage with his own eyes and unquestionably heard of the fire insurance and loss prevention initiatives. In addition, Leibniz certainly knew about the fire in the town of Oldenburg in 1676, about one hundred miles from Hanover, which destroyed two thirds of the houses and left three thousand people homeless. In Oldenburg there was no fire insurance to cover these losses, because the governing Count Anton Günther of Oldenburg-Delmenhorst had rejected a plan by Wilhelm Stiell, a Hamburger merchant, in 1609 to found a fire insurance company. The count's reasoning for rejecting this scheme reflects the religious and moral sentiments at the time: 'a fire insurance company is an act against God's right of his Providence.' Stiell's proposal of 1609 was interesting not only in its timeliness with respect to the Oldenburg fire of 1676 but also in that it was one of the earliest proposals for founding a fire insurance company. According to Stiell's proposal only houses – not furniture and other belongings – could be insured. The premium was set at one per centof the insured value, if certain security standards were met.

The absence of fire insurance protection proved, not surprisingly, to be a disaster for the people. Oldenburg, which became Danish after the death of the Count of Oldenburg-Delmenhorst, recovered very slowly. Twenty-five years after the fire of 1676 not even half of the houses of Oldenburg had been rebuilt.

Another event that Leibniz must also have been aware of was the merger, in 1676, of the forty-six fire contracts in Hamburg, which were united in the General Fire Funds. It was thus straightforward and rational for Leibniz to call for the founding of a fire insurance company by the Duke of Hanover (1678) and the Emperor of the Holy Roman Empire of the German Nation (1680). This call was in stark contrast to the opinion of a number representatives of the churches, who still considered fire as God's instrument and insurance as amoral.

### Leibniz's Mathematical Contribution to Insurance

The core of Leibniz's insurance mathematical work is the calculation of life-long pension contracts (*aestimatio redituum ad vitam*), that is, the calculation of the present value (*reditus temporalis*) of a life-long pension or a pension for a given number of years. The problem has two aspects: the method of discounting and the estimation of the survival probabilities of the pensioner.

Leibniz's ideas were based on a criticism of the method of discounting brought forward by Benedikt Carpzov in 1670. Carpzov's method leads to false results, and the magnitude of the error increases with the length of the pension contract. Leibniz suggested his method, which he called 'calculus popularior' or 'regula legistica,' *and* discussed this topic again and again in a number of papers. Taking numerical examples, he shows the shortcomings of the methods used at his time. What Leibniz really proposes is the calculation of a premium with an increasing safety loading.

For the calculation of the survival probabilities Leibniz uses a model in which the age distribution is constant over time and where every person who dies is replaced by a newborn. He also studies the survival probabilities of combined lives, that is, in cases where the time of a pension payment period is determined by the longest-lived member of a group of persons. All these considerations are the basis of our modern insurance premium calculation in life, pension, health, and nursing insurance.

## Leibniz's Proposal for a Public Insurance Company

Leibniz's most important manuscript is the one on public insurance companies. As in his other manuscripts, he argues in the spirit of mercantilism, the leading economic philosophy at that time: the state has the obligation to increase the wealth and well-being of its citizens. In addition, the state should take measures to increase population, which was a popular policy after the disastrous Thirty Years War.

Expressed in modern terms, Leibniz believed in an obligatory (social) insurance scheme that was financed by ex-post assessment (pay as you go) rather than a fully funded system working with actuarial premiums anticipating the expected losses. He argued that such an arrangement for sharing risks would increase the welfare of the population. In fact, in the light of modern expected utility theory he was quite right. This can be shown by a simple model.[3] Assume two individuals, Jacob and Johann, each owning identical houses, each having a property value $\overline{w}$. If a fire breaks – out the damage will be $L$, leaving the owner with a wealth of $\overline{w} - L$. The probability that the fire breaks out is $p$, the probability that a house is spared is $1 - p$. Both individuals are risk averse and have a utility function $U(w)$ The risks of each house catching fire are independent.

The expected utility of each individual without insurance is given by:

$$E\big(U(w \mid without\ insurance)\big) = (1 - p) \cdot U(\overline{w}) + p \cdot U(\overline{w} - L)$$

If both individuals make an agreement that both will cover all risks together and split the loss at the end of a period, the probabilities will be as follows:

- The probability that both are without a loss is $(1 - p)^2$.
- The probability that both have a loss is $p^2$.
- The probability that only Jacob has a loss is $p \cdot (1 - p)$.
- The probability that only Johann has a loss is $(1 - p) \cdot p$.

The payment to the mutual insurance fund will be either 0, $\frac{L}{2}$, or $L$ for each individual. The expected utility for each of them is:

$$E\big(U(w \mid with\ insurance)\big) = (1 - p)^2 \cdot U(\overline{w}) + (1 - p) \cdot p \cdot U\left(\overline{w} - \frac{L}{2}\right) + p \cdot (1 - p) \cdot U\left(\overline{w} - \frac{L}{2}\right) + p^2 \cdot U(\overline{w} - L)$$

The expected utility is constant if $p = 0$, $p = 1$, and/or $L - 0$.
In all other cases, we may ask if forming a mutual insurance company may increase the expected utility of Johann and Jacob:

$$E\big(U(w \mid \text{without insurance})\big) < E\big(U(w \mid \text{with insurance})\big)$$

or

$$(1 - p) \cdot U(\overline{w}) + p \cdot U(\overline{w} - L) < (1 - p)^2 \cdot U(\overline{w}) + 2 \cdot (1 - p) \cdot p \cdot U\left(\overline{w} - \frac{L}{2}\right) + p^2 \cdot U(\overline{w} - L)$$

By transforming this inequality we get:

$$\big((1 - p) - (1 - p)^2\big) \cdot U(\overline{w}) + (p - p^2) \cdot U(\overline{w} - L) - 2 \cdot (1 - p) \cdot p \cdot U\left(\overline{w} - \frac{L}{2}\right) \leq 0$$

or

$$(p - p^2) \cdot U(\overline{w}) + (p - p^2) \cdot U(\overline{w} - L) - 2 \cdot (p - p^2) \cdot p \cdot U\left(\overline{w} - \frac{L}{2}\right) \leq 0$$

or

$$U(\overline{w}) + U(\overline{w} - L) - 2 \cdot U\left(\overline{w} - \frac{L}{2}\right) \leq 0 .$$

If $U(\overline{w})$ is concave, which is characteristic for risk-averse individuals, $2 \cdot U\left(\overline{w} - \frac{L}{2}\right)$ is greater than $U(\overline{w}) + U(\overline{w} - L)$. This is demonstrated by Figure 2.1.

Figure 2.1: Benefits of Risk Sharing

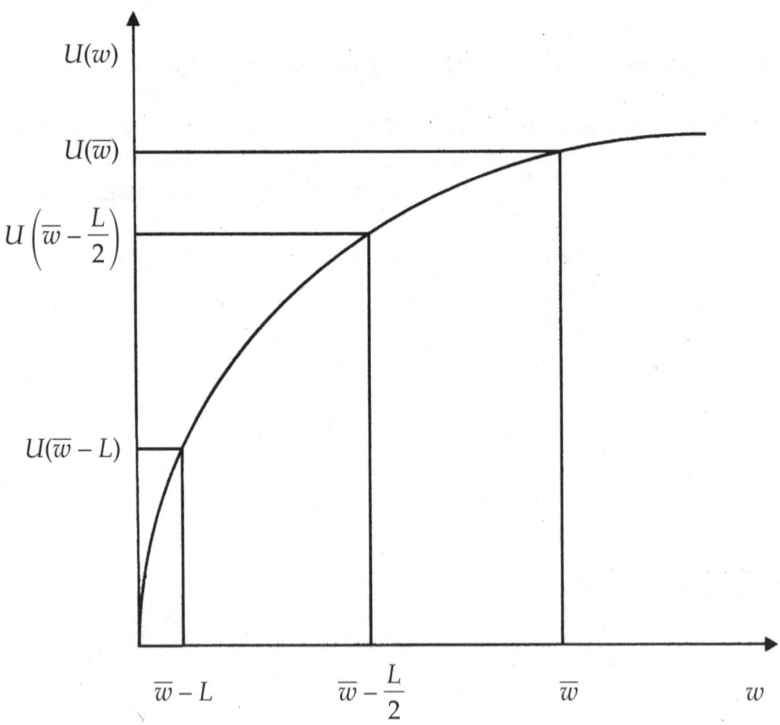

Therefore, Leibniz was right in assuming that the welfare of all members of society increases if they mutually finance the losses of fire. However, this will hold only if the risks are identical and there is no moral hazard behaviour.

Our brief description shows that Leibniz and his contemporaries were aware of the questions that needed to be asked in order to develop arrangements for collective risk-sharing. It would take more research in the different fields of insurance sciences to generate the proliferation of insurance as we know it today. Adam Smith's description of an insurance market was a further step in this direction. Yet Smith's estimates of only one household out of twenty purchasing insurance shows that even more efforts by insurance theorists and businessmen would be necessary for insurance to appeal to a more general public.[4]

## NOTES

1 Eberhard Knobloch and J.-Matthias Graf von der Schulenburg, eds., *Gottfried Wilhelm Leibniz – Versicherungswissenschaftliche und Finanzmathematische Schriften* (Berlin: Akademie Verlag, 2000).

2 Adam Smith, *An Inquiry into the Nature and Causes of the Wealth of Nations* (New York: P.F. Collier & Son Company, 1776; repr. 1909), book 1, chap. 10.

3 J.-Matthias Graf von der Schulenburg, *Versicherungsökonomik* (Karlsruhe: Verlag Versicherungswirtschaft, 2005), 34–6.

4 Smith, *Wealth of Nations*, 76.

# 3 The Slave's Appeal: Insurance and the Rise of Commercial Property

GEOFFREY CLARK

> There is something extremely offensive to humanity in the idea of any part of the human species becoming property, and a subject of commerce, capable of being bought and sold like beasts of burthen. And yet it is to be lamented that this traffic has existed in all ages, even amongst the most polished nations of the world, and where moral refinements were the most highly cultivated.

So wrote Samuel Marshall in the second edition of his *A Treatise on the Law of Insurance* (1808) in the year following parliament's abolition of the slave trade.[1] Whatever congratulations Marshall felt were due to the enlightened action of 'the British legislature, roused by the calls of humanity' was surely tempered by the uncomfortable knowledge that the nation's commerce, and the insurance industry in particular, had profited handsomely from the slave trade up to that moment. Jurists like Marshall were caught in an ethical and legal predicament during the final decades of the licit slave trade, torn on the one hand by their veneration of open and vigorous commerce – widely recognized as the basis of British power – and on the other by a decent regard for the economic and political liberties of their petitioners. The rapid growth of the slave trade and the more frequent entry of slaves into Britain in the second half of the eighteenth century exposed this incongruity to be sure, but the dilemma was made more acute and threatening by the proliferating forms of commercial property that in some degree transformed human life into a commodity. The slave ship was just the most extreme example of a more general threat that certain kinds of commercial contracts, not least insurance policies, posed to personal self-possession and liberty.

It has recently been argued that the slaves shipped across the Atlantic occupied an ambiguous legal position 'somewhere between personhood and property,' and that the insurance of slave cargoes therefore marked an intermediate stage in the 'progress from insurance on goods to insurance on persons.'[2] This historical analysis echoes the contemporaneous moral criticism levelled by the abolitionists themselves that the slave trade hopelessly conflated goods and persons. Yet both these interpretations fail to recognize that, as a legal matter and a social fact, individuals had long been construed as property. Subsuming individuals under title of property was nothing new to the eighteenth century generally or to the transatlantic slave system in particular. The almost complete lack of ethical hand-wringing by traders of slaves or their insurers implies that they accepted this settled state of affairs and saw their own business as in no way inconsistent with polished manners or moral refinement, even if the ruthless rationalization of the Atlantic slavery system quickly stripped away the norms that previously had governed legal relationships involving human property.

By the start of the nineteenth century Marshall and his ilk had distanced themselves from the conventional views of the generation before and acknowledged that 'the unfortunate objects of this cruel traffic were formerly too much considered as mere merchandise.'[3] That earlier and allegedly alien attitude was no more shockingly illustrated than in a notorious incident that had occurred aboard a slave ship a quarter century before.

### The *Zong*

On 18 August 1781 a Dutch prize, the *Zong* (originally, *Zorgue*) departed the African coast laden with 442 slaves bound for the West Indies. As was commonplace, especially in summer, disease broke out so that, by the time the *Zong* reached the Caribbean fifteen weeks later, more than 60 slaves and 7 of the 17 original crew members had already died.[4] Ominously, dozens more were seriously ill and likely to die. As was later alleged, the *Zong*'s captain, Luke Collingwood, then made a navigational error in mistaking Jamaica for Hispaniola, which resulted in a forced continuation of the voyage. Faced, as he claimed, with a disastrous shortage of drinking water, Collingwood determined to save what he could of his crew and human cargo by instructing his men to select the sickest slaves and jettison them. Accordingly, though not without some protest by the chief mate, 133 slaves were brought on deck, divided into batches, and, over the course of three days, flung into the sea.[5]

News of this atrocious act aroused little public notice at the time, nor two years later when the circumstances of the *Zong*'s voyage and the motivations of its captain were interrogated in court and reported in the papers. Despite this general lack of concern, the *Zong* case did have a galvanizing effect on the small circle of British abolitionists centred on Granville Sharp, who would with time succeed in holding the horrors of the slave trade up to the nation's conscience. James Walvin punningly observes of the case, the 'line of dissent from the *Zong* to the successful campaign for abolition was direct and unbroken, however protracted and uneven.'[6]

Despite its lack of contemporary notoriety or even its significance in purely legal terms, the *Zong* episode became in the hands of abolitionists and later cultural critics a shorthand for the manifold horrors of the slave trade.[7] J.M. Turner's *Slavers Throwing Overboard the Dead and Dying, Typhon Coming On* (1840) cemented the *Zong*'s iconic status by elevating it, in the judgment of Marcus Wood, to 'the only indisputably great work of Western art ever made to commemorate the Atlantic slave trade.'[8] Turner's painting is, he argues, nothing less than an 'artistic salvage' in which the sacrifice of the victims is redeemed in the destruction of Atlantic slavery. Ian Baucom concurs that Turner's painting is the most important 'meditation on the trans-Atlantic slave trade' and argues further that the *Zong* case itself represents *the* seminal modern event.[9] The *Zong* 'haunts' the present, says Baucom, adverting to Walter Benjamin, because the long twentieth century 'inherits or continues' the eighteenth century, the century that made 'sovereign the value form legally secured in the *Zong*'s marine insurance contract.'[10] For, stripped of its wider philosophical and humanitarian implications, the *Zong* case essentially concerned insurance.

Indeed, the actions of Luke Collingwood are intelligible only by reference to the routine insurance coverage of slave cargoes, the terms of which were thoroughly familiar to slavers. Marine insurance policies on slave cargoes typically excluded claims resulting from the 'natural' mortality of Africans aboard ship, such as from disease or suicide. But losses due to an emergency jettison of cargo to save the ship or crew *were* subject to claim. The *Zong* case (or more formally, *Gregson v. Gilbert*) came before the Court of King's Bench owing to a dispute between the *Zong*'s owners and the underwriters over a claim lodged by the owners for the value of the jettisoned cargo, 132 slaves, computed at £30 per head. (132 rather than 133 because, astoundingly, one African thrown overboard managed to grab one of the ship's trailing lines in the water and pull himself out of the sea and into a porthole, where he secreted himself among the other captives and apparently survived the voyage.)

Although Collingwood himself died within days of the *Zong*'s landing in Jamaica, when the case landed in court in March 1783 counsel for the shipowners steadfastly maintained Collingwood's original claim that low reserves of water had required that the slaves be thrown overboard. That justification was contradicted by testimony offered in court that no water rationing had been imposed prior to the first group of slaves being thrown into the sea, and that on the day the second group was dispatched a steady rain had allowed no fewer than six casks of rainwater to be collected, clearly eliminating the need for emergency action. The real motivation behind Collingwood's decision was instead coldly calculating. While Collingwood was employed to serve the financial interests of the *Zong*'s shipowners, he as captain was also entitled to a share of the profits, and so had a direct economic interest in the success of the voyage. Diseased slaves dying aboard ship were straight losses to both Collingwood and the shipowners. On the other hand, the value of slaves jettisoned in order to safeguard the ship was a recoverable loss. Hence the pretense that a dire water shortage existed aboard the *Zong*.

The jury quickly delivered a verdict in favor of the shipowners, but the underwriters applied for a second trial to revisit their allegation that the jettison of slaves had not resulted from a genuine emergency. The application was heard in May 1783 before Justices Mansfield, Willes, and Buller, who decided in favour of a retrial based on the dubious evidence presented in court of the ship's having been in peril. In a nice piece of understatement Chief Justice Mansfield pronounced the case to be 'very uncommon,' a reference not only to the evidentiary deficiencies of the shipowners' case but also to the extraordinary callousness of Collingwood's actions, a callousness also reflected in the legal argumentation presented by the shipowners. Their attorney, John Lee, frankly asserted the objective character of the *Zong*'s cargo:

> What is all this vast declamation of human people being thrown overboard? The question after all is, Was it voluntary, or an act of necessity? *This is a case of chattels or goods.* It is really so: it is the case of throwing over

> goods; for to this purpose, and the purpose of the insurance, *they are goods and property: whether right or wrong, we have nothing to do with it.*[11]

The outcome of the second trial, if one was in fact ever held, is lost to history since it was not reported. But the court's narrow legal question over the validity of the insurance claim and the willingness of the initial jury to decide the case within that frame, made clear the futility of Granville Sharp's hope that murder charges might eventually be brought against the crew. A century of slave trading had seemingly done nothing to alter a solicitor-general's proclamation of 1677 that 'negroes ought to be esteemed goods and commodities within the Acts of Trade and Navigation.'[12] From a legal standpoint, therefore, the Africans loaded onto a slave ship were indistinguishable from rum or molasses or timber. Indeed, the slang term for embarked slaves – 'logs' – testifies to that reification.[13]

That embarked slaves clearly had the legal status of chattels, at least until the close of the eighteenth century, seems well established. But Tim Armstrong has recently argued that terms routinely inserted into the insurance policies on slave ships implicitly recognized that these captive Africans were in fact *not* equivalent to other kinds of cargoes. Armstrong contends that the inclusion of averaging clauses, which freed insurers from claims arising from insurrections aboard ship if amounting to less than 5 or 10 per cent of total value of the cargo, ship, and outfit, suggests that insurers hedged against what they saw as a significant probability of slave revolt. 'But insurrection implies agency,' he continues, 'making slaves something more than goods.'[14]

In answer to this line of analysis it may first be pointed out that contemporary fears of insurrection aboard ship were probably inflated.[15] Estimates of the frequency of slave outbreaks on the transatlantic passage vary from 10 per cent for the eighteenth century as a whole to a low of under 2 per cent experienced by Rhode Island slavers.[16] However terrifying the prospect of revolt for captain and crew, insurrections were in fact usually contained and the resulting number of slave deaths quite limited. This reality was reflected in John Weskett's guidebook, *Complete Digest of the Theory, Laws, and Practice of Insurance* (1781), under the entry for 'commodity,' in which a number of goods are grouped according to risk of carriage, from 'least hazardous' through 'common hazardous' and 'more hazardous' to 'most hazardous.' Cattle, hogs, slaves, and tobacco pipes are among those commodities categorized as being 'common hazardous,' indicating that slaves, while admittedly prone to revolt, posed a relatively low risk of loss.[17] Indeed, one expert has concluded that insurance of slave cargoes was taken out primarily against ordinary perils of the sea rather than against the special contingency of slave revolt.[18]

A more telling point, however, turns on the issue of agency, which Armstrong regards as a uniquely human trait. The treatment of livestock losses at sea, though, closely adheres to the compensation rules that governed slave cargoes: deaths due to disease or other natural causes were excluded, but losses due to the perils of the sea or directly caused by those perils were covered. James Oldham has identified, for example, two early nineteenth-century policies in which insurers were held liable for deaths of livestock due to their panic during oceanic tempests.[19] Of course sheer panic falls well short of the mental faculties required for conspiracy, but agency – whether animal or human – is involved just the same. Consequently, the possession of agency does not in itself supply an analytical distinction that might have presented a paradox in the law's otherwise consistent treatment of slaves as goods.

The law's alleged incapacity to treat a human being both as a person and as an article of property serves as the basis of Armstrong's claim that the practice of insuring slaves marked an anomalous moment in the development of maritime law, when slaves occupied a 'middle position in the progress from insurance on goods to insurance on persons.'[20] This serial view of insurance as latching first onto things and then moving on to people fails to account, though, for the fact that from its origins in the late middle ages insurance on things and insurance on people developed in tandem. While the drama of the *Zong* case raises the problematic nature and limits of the concept of commercial property confronting eighteenth-century jurists, the conflation of 'personhood and property' was not itself legally confounding.[21] Understanding just how and why the insurance of the slave trade proved so legally vexatious requires instead an appreciation of the deep historical relationship between insurance and slavery, the legal norms regulating property in people, and the ways in which commercial innovations of the eighteenth century were steadily undermining that older legal regime.

## Insurance of Human Property

The historical association of insurance and slavery long antedates the heyday of the slave trade in the late seventeenth and eighteenth centuries.[22] In fact, insurance on slaves appeared strikingly early in the history of insurance, and these early usages provide important points of contrast when assessing the later commoditization of slaves in the Atlantic trade.

By the end of the fourteenth century, less than a century after the invention of the modern insurance contract, insurers at Genoa, Venice, and Barcelona were issuing marine policies on the survival of individual slaves on voyages around the Mediterranean.[23] Policies were applied to terra firma by the early fifteenth century when the Generalidad of Catalonia instituted an insurance scheme to compensate slave owners for losses stemming from the desertion of their slaves. Instances can also be found in early records of particular slave owners insuring their slaves for a given term of life, as when in 1501 Bartholomew Campmaior, a Barcelona mat maker, insured a teenager named Francisco against natural death for one year.[24] A much less familiar use of insurance, though one that may well have been the most common form of insurance on slaves in the late medieval period, involved the strange practice of insuring the life of a female slave made pregnant by her owner or some other man. Ordinances in force at Genoa, Rome, and Barcelona all addressed this contingency although they seem to have treated the matter in rather different ways. At Genoa and Rome, for example, a fine was assessed on a slave owner regardless of whether he was responsible for impregnating his slave, and the fine was doubled in the event she died during pregnancy or childbirth. At Barcelona, by contrast, legal liability was created only if the slave was impregnated by someone other than her owner and a fine was imposed only in the event of her death. However the statutes were formulated, they all created an incentive to insure a slave's life for the term of her pregnancy and delivery. Thus at Barcelona in 1467 a thirty-five-year-old slave named Maria, already five months pregnant, was insured by her owner, Bernat dez Lor, a physician. Two underwriters each assumed half the risk, charging 8 per cent to pay £50 in case she died in childbirth or from other natural causes.[25]

What could have been the state's interest in so discouraging the pregnancy of slaves? Economic damage seems not to have been at the root of concern. The Italian statutes were designed to punish the owners of pregnant slaves, not to protect their financial interest. In Barcelona, compensation for the death of a pregnant slave should properly have been paid not to the state but the owner himself. And a man impregnating his own slave could hardly be expected to answer for damage done himself. Although the precise rationale for these ordinances remains obscure, it seems that moral rather than strictly proprietary considerations were uppermost in the minds of legislators. The preservation of a domestic sphere of licensed matrimonial sex mandated that men refrain from sexual contact with their household slaves. As for a slave's impregnation by another man, the state might legitimately construe that as a form of trespass against the slave owner, an infringement of his property rights. That the state made this a matter of public rather than private injury, however, suggests something about the assumed dominion of patriarchs under whose authority and protection the household operated. Making another man's slave pregnant was fundamentally an affront to the hierarchical system of social relations and property-holding upon which public order was built. Understood this way, an enslaved woman's death owing to pregnancy or childbirth represented the very worst outcome of a social and moral transgression, an eventuality that warranted punitive intervention by the state. Ironically, life insurance, the contractual means by which men indemnified themselves against the financial liability of impregnating a slave and thereby evidencing a trespass on the property of others, would later become the very means by which incursions on the self-possession of others would be facilitated.

These early instances of life insurance policies on slaves, together with the statutory incentives for taking out coverage on female slaves, reveal that slavery in the late medieval Mediterranean was embedded in a system of reciprocal social and moral norms that prevented slaves from being treated as property *tout court*. But as claims to property, especially commercial property, became more insistent and exclusive in succeeding centuries, insurance acquired an increasing, perhaps unique, capacity to alienate property from unwilling subjects, and in the most extreme cases to register and reinforce the complete destruction of personal self-possession.

## The Perils of Insurance and Commercial Contracts

Writers on insurance in the early modern period rehearsed a familiar list of ways insurance could grease the skids of commerce, mobilize landed wealth, widen investment horizons for the propertied, and relieve anxieties over the security of one's own fortune and family. In the early seventeenth century Gerard Malynes marvelled that 'men cannot invent or imagine any thing, but the value of it may be assured.'[26] A century and a half later the Scottish jurist John Millar noted with approval the wider benefits of insurance: 'Insurance is no less advantageous to the public than to individuals, by moderating and diffusing the profits of trade, and by preventing accidental misfortunes from operating to the ruin of individuals, or companies of merchants, which might obstruct the uniform progress of commerce, and endanger public credit.'[27] To these benefits the economic writer Corbyn Morris added a psychological dimension, observing that insurers 'take the whole Risk upon themselves, leaving the Merchant at liberty to urge his Commerce, with Quiet of Mind, with steady Pursuit, and with solid Credit.'[28] In particular, the 'advantages resulting from [life] insurances are many and obvious,' glowed the late eighteenth-century jurist Sir James Allan Park, who then enumerated their benefits 'to persons possessed of places or employments for life; to masters of families; ... to married persons; ... to dependents upon any other person; ... [and] to persons wanting to borrow money.'[29] Across the Channel, the author of the French commercial manual known popularly as *Le Guidon* enviously described the way life insurance in other nations was utilized to cover the risk of death on voyages, to collateralize debts, or to benefit heirs. But life insurance having been proscribed in France as a practice 'against good morals and customs,' these benefits were not available to those under French rule.[30]

The French prohibition was one instance of the nearly total outlaw of life insurance across Europe from the sixteenth to the nineteenth centuries. Yet in France the ban could not be consistently maintained in the face of the enormous profits to be won in the transatlantic slave trade and the clamour of French merchants wishing to insure their valuable cargoes of slaves. Insurance was too vital to overseas trade to be forsworn on moral grounds, and French jurists obligingly supplied a rationale, however tortured, to permit policies on slaves.

French law forbidding life insurance contracts was confirmed in 1681 by Louis XIV's *Ordonnance de la Marine*, which stated flatly, 'We prohibit any insurance to be made on the life of persons.'[31] Despite the apparent finality of the statute's wording, life insurance was considered legally valid within the special circumstances of a ransom insurance contract. Ransom insurance was commonly taken out by Europeans sailing the Mediterranean who sought to hedge against the possibility of being taken captive by Moorish or Turkish pirates and held hostage. Ordinarily, if the insured hostage died before being ransomed or on the voyage home, the contract was nullified on the theory that the insured contingency was captivity, not death. Under French law, however, insurers were required to honour claims in cases where the redeemed captive 'is retaken, killed, drowned, or perishes by any other means than by natural death.'[32] In his commentary on the *Ordonnance* of 1714, René-Josué Valin acknowledged that this provision of the *Ordonnance* plainly contradicted the blanket prohibition against life insurance it enacted elsewhere, but Valin deferred to the will of the king: 'It seemed right to the legislator, and that suffices.'[33]

Valin recognized that the *Ordonnance*'s treatment of insurance against death defied logic. He nevertheless followed that illogic by rejecting the validity of life insurance, which he pronounced as 'null of law and by its nature,' while endorsing the legitimacy of life insurance in cases of death resulting from violent or unnatural causes in the context of ransom insurance. Something less than high legal principle was involved here. Valin's object was to reconcile the *Ordonnance*'s wholesale condemnation of life insurance with a justification of its use in covering slave cargoes, since French merchants needed a legal basis to insure their slaves on the Middle Passage. Ransom insurance provided the loophole. By recasting the parties to the contract, insurers treated the Africans loaded aboard ship as hostages of French slavers, who now assumed the role previously played by the Turks, while the underwriters and shipowners indulged in the legal fiction that the price slaves fetched in the West Indies equaled their 'ransom.' This legal legerdemain allowed the human cargo to be insured, at least within the established limitations of a ransom insurance policy. As a consequence, the lives of slaves lost through 'natural' processes such as sickness or suicide, 'as happens very often,' could not be claimed. But if the slaves went down with the ship, or were killed or thrown into the sea as the direct result of a revolt, the insurers had to answer for the loss.[34]

The challenge to settled norms posed by this necessary adjunct to the Atlantic trade was repeated in rather different legal and cultural circumstances north of the Channel. In England the enormous expansion of the slave trade in the eighteenth century paralleled London's emergence as a major centre of insurance. It appears that in the late seventeenth century the Royal African Company made only limited use of insurance on its cargoes of gold, silver, and sugar, and seems not to have insured its shipments of slaves at all.[35] This relative lack of insurance cover probably reflected both the relatively undeveloped state of the English underwriting market at that time and, perhaps more importantly, the wealth and diversified holdings of the proprietors of the company, who could effectively insure themselves because their investments were already sufficiently diversified.[36] Once the slave trade was opened to all comers in 1698, however, the smaller fry understandably availed themselves of insurance protection.[37] By the late eighteenth century, a time when some eighty thousand Africans were being shipped annually to the Americas, Lord Mansfield could advise a jury deciding a law suit having to do with insurance on a slave ship that the 'policy is in the common form,' suggesting that the slave trade and the insurance of it had grown in tandem.[38] Although the evidence is fragmentary, it seems safe to conclude that the insurance of slave cargoes was so pervasive that policies on the heads of Africans during their transport to the New World far outnumbered policies made at the time on English men and women, who then comprised by far the largest life insurance market in the world.[39]

As important as the insurance of slave ships was to the Atlantic trade, it did not constitute the mainstay of the British marine insurance business, as has recently been claimed.[40] Yet the increasing numbers of Africans caught up in the net of the Atlantic slave system and their growing visibility in England as they accompanied their nabob masters for stays at home, presented a nettlesome set of legal questions about the validity of slavery in Britain. The implications of domestic slavery went beyond the political and moral issues raised by the treatment of humans as chattel property – the spectre so darkly raised by the massacre aboard the *Zong*. For the problem of slavery constituted but one example, however important and dramatic, of a diverse set of disruptions caused by insurance and other novel forms of commercial contract to established property relationships and the social order. How far English law was prepared to countenance slavery within the kingdom was inextricably linked to questions about the manner and degree to which property in otherwise legally free people could be created through the operation of contract.

The turbid state of English law with respect to the status of slaves in the kingdom began slowly to clear in the 1770s through a series of celebrated, though frequently misunderstood, court decisions. The first of these, the case of Thomas Lewis (*Rex v. Stapylton*), came before the Court of King's Bench in 1771. Lewis, a slave residing in Chelsea, petitioned the court to prevent his forcible removal from the country at the hands of a Captain Seward, to whom he had supposedly been sold by a man named Stapylton. Lord Mansfield, being doubtful about the defendant Stapylton's evidence of his ownership of Lewis, left the matter to the jury to determine whether Lewis had in fact been Stapylton's slave. When the jury returned a verdict declaring Lewis to be outside his alleged master's power to compel his return to the West Indies, the courtroom rang to cheers of 'No Property! No Property!'[41] Despite the sweeping view of the jury's verdict by Lewis's supporters, however, the decision was in fact made on exceedingly narrow legal grounds and, as the Chief Justice himself later explained, turned on the question of Stapylton's ownership of Lewis, not on whether slaves in general had the right not to be taken out of the kingdom.[42]

That more expansive question came up just a few months later in December 1771 when James Somerset, a slave of Charles Stewart, asked the Court of King's Bench to prevent Stewart from sending him to the West Indies to be sold. The famous Somerset case, heard the following year, was also decided against the slave master, a verdict that was widely (though, again, incorrectly) interpreted as having abolished slavery within Britain. Mansfield was painfully aware of the potentially devastating economic consequences of suddenly extinguishing the property Englishmen and women then possessed in some fifteen thousand slaves residing in the kingdom, and he therefore tried his best to have Stewart free Somerset prior to trial so as to prevent such a test case from being heard. Once the case did arrive in court, Mansfield characteristically decided it as narrowly as possible. He subsequently described his judicial decision as a 'determination [that] got no further than that the master cannot by force compel him [the alleged slave] to go out of the Kingdom.'[43] Mansfield drew his precedent from established usages of servants or slaves in England: 'No master ever was allowed here to take a slave by force to be sold abroad because he deserted from his service, or for any other reason whatever – therefore the man must be discharged.'[44]

Given the limited scope of Mansfield's ruling, the status of slavery remained uncertain even after the Somerset case. To understand the law's particular difficulty in handling these cases of domestic slavery requires that we focus on a critical issue contained in both the Lewis and Somerset cases: the *alienability* of human property. English law had long recognized an inalienable kind of property in people who constituted objects of personal dominion, that is, being neither chattels nor fully autonomous individuals.[45] Personal dominion originated as an appurtenance of real property and of householding, so that wives, children, servants, apprentices and other bound labourers or bondsmen were in some measure the property of their lords and masters. The common law understood this form of property-holding as having regulative norms and reciprocal, though unequal, obligations. But it did not contemplate or recognize the ability to buy or sell such people. So, as Teresa Michals explains: 'While commercial legislation simply opposed the class of persons, who by definition have certain rights, to the class of things, which by definition do not, the common law's emphasis on status traditionally presented another, mixed category, that of a right-bearing subject who is also the property of another.'[46]

This insight makes comprehensible Blackstone's otherwise baffling pronouncement made in the 1760s, despite clear evidence to the contrary, that 'pure and proper slavery does not, nay cannot, subsist in England: such I mean, whereby an absolute and unlimited power is given to the master over the life and fortune of the slave.'[47] That may have been a widely shared understanding among English jurists, but that judgment did not thereby assume that by being considered freemen slaves were therefore liberated from their masters. For freemen included those who lived in a state of perpetual servitude.[48] Blackstone resolved the apparent paradox this way:

> A slave or negro, the instant he lands in England, becomes a freeman; that is, the law will protect him in the enjoyment of his person, and his property. Yet, with regard to any right which the master may have lawfully acquired to the perpetual service of John or Thomas, this will remain exactly in the same state as before: for this is no more than the same state of subjection for life, which every apprentice submits to for the space of seven years, or sometimes for a longer term.[49]

Blackstone thereby assimilated slavery into the established institution of apprenticeship, and though the term of service might be anomalous in its indefinite length, the law would not interfere in the arrangement. What were mere chattels on the high seas became in England servants different in degree but not in kind from millions of others subject to the private dominion of others.

This status brought with it a form of condign liberty consisting of protection by the servant's more powerful master. Blackstone described the mutual bond between master and servant this way: 'A master ... may justify an assault in defence of his servant, and servant in defence of his master: the master, because he has an interest in his servant, not to be deprived of his service; the servant, because it is part of his duty, for which he receives his wages, to stand by and defend his master.'[50] This passage is remarkable in the way an archaic feudal sensibility is imported into contemporary social and economic conceptions of the reciprocal interests joining master and servant. The servant must support and defend his master in order to secure his continued employment and protection, but the master actually has an *interest* in his servant. According to Blackstone, 'the inferior hath no kind of property in the company, care, or assistance of the superior, as the superior is held to have in those of the inferior ... The child hath no property in his father or guardian; as they have in him ... [the servant] had no property in his master.' As Michals observes of these relationships, the 'element of ownership goes only one way.'[51]

This proprietary asymmetry provides a key to appreciating the offence and scandal raised by a series of insurance and gambling cases heard before Lord Mansfield and the King's Bench in the very same years that the Lewis and Somerset cases were tried. The first of these cases arose over the disputed outcome of a wager contracted over dinner at Newmarket one evening in 1770 by two aristocrats, Robert Pigot and Lord March. The bet was of a sort commonly made by insurance brokers as well as mere gamblers, and turned on whether Pigot's father or Sir William Codrington's would live longer. By a remarkable coincidence, Pigot's father had in fact died earlier that very day in Shropshire, 150 miles distant. Upon learning of his father's death, Pigot claimed that the bet, as a contract *in futuro*, was invalid since the assumed preconditions no longer existed at the time of the wager. March took Pigot to court and won the case, but the notoriety it created led to a storm of public criticism about the impropriety of sons making sport on the lives of their fathers. After all, to make a bet of this type was impiously to create a property in the life of a father, and thereby to violate a parent's authority and control.

Another instance of a commercial contract seen at least by some as corroding the supports of the social hierarchy involved the rampant speculation on the true sex of Charles de Beaumont, the Chevalier d'Eon. D'Eon was widely rumoured to be a woman who had disguised herself as a man as a diplomatic ruse in the service of Louis XV.[52] By 1770 D'Eon was residing in London attired as a woman, lending credibility to the story and giving rise to a flurry of speculation around town and especially in London's insurance brokerages and betting houses, where several hundred thousands of pounds were staked on whether D'Eon was really male or female. All such wagers were held in abeyance until proof could be offered one way or the other. The matter finally came to a head in 1777 when D'Eon quarrelled with a friend, who then disclosed publicly that D'Eon had privately confessed three years earlier to being a woman.[53] Policyholders on D'Eon's sex predictably seized upon this new evidence and brought suit against underwriters to pay the claims on their policies. On 1 July 1777 a suit brought by Mr Hayes, a London surgeon, against an underwriter known as Jacques was heard before Lord Mansfield at Guildhall. Mansfield expressed reservations about the propriety of such bets, but he did not hold the contract to be illegal. After hearing testimony from Mr Le Goux, a surgeon who claimed to have examined D'Eon's genitals, the jury found in favour of the plaintiff.[54] Yet the following year a similar case (*Da Costa v. Jones*) brought before Mansfield led the Chief Justice to lose his patience with such suits, which he said created scandalous public inquiry about frivolous questions of a private nature.[55]

Yet it would be wrong to see Mansfield's irritation as prompted solely by a wish to maintain a seemly distinction between private and public affairs. After all, in the eighteenth century insurance firms commonly invited prospective customers to examine their policy registers in order to assay the strength of their business, revealing a blithe disregard for matters we would today consider as highly confidential. Rather, the insurance policies and bets on D'Eon's sex represented a kind of trespass on his property, his own self-possession. As an aristocrat, D'Eon took great affront at wagers being made on the subject of his body. Not only was this commercial activity degrading, it also subverted the social order by enabling commoners and mere money-men to create and deal in the property of a social superior.

The difficulties of maintaining social hierarchy against the fluid effects of insurance are also illustrated, this time within a domestic setting, in Mary Spencer's case, heard by Justices Mansfield, Dunning, and Wallace at Guildhall in 1777. Mary Spencer's husband owned a large estate, of which his sister was heir, when he sailed for the West Indies to join a military detachment there. Prior to his departure, Mr Spencer bought a £500 annuity to be paid to Mary should he die during his tour of duty. But on her own initiative, and presumably unbeknownst to her husband, Mary Spencer purchased an insurance policy on her husband's life for the considerable sum of £5,000. Mr Spencer did in fact die abroad but the underwriters refused to honour

Mary's claim, arguing that as her husband had already provided for his widow with an annuity commensurate to her station, she had no further economic interest in his life for which she could legally recover. Counsel for the underwriters cited the new Gambling Act of 1774, passed in the wake of the public outcry over *March v. Pigot* and other perceived insurance abuses, which imposed the economic standard of 'insurable interest' in the making of all life insurance. But how would such a standard apply within the context of a marital relationship? The justices were divided in their opinions. Wallace opined that 'the *interest* mentioned in the [Gambling] act, an object of insurance, must be capable of being estimated and *ascertained*; and, not an *imaginary* interest, like that set up in the present case.' Dunning on the other hand argued that the contract was valid because, legally speaking, a woman's interest in her husband's life was indistinguishable from his interest in his own life, and the legitimacy of that interest could not be denied. The underwriters tried to refute that view by implicitly invoking the law of necessaries, arguing that Mr Spencer's provision of an annuity for his wife in an amount proportional to her social status removed any remaining '*natural* interest' she might have in his life.[56] But Mansfield sided with Dunning in holding the contract to be valid, and the court decided in favour of Mary Spencer.[57]

The Spencer case highlighted the legal uncertainty of treating husbands and wives as legally one (as under the common law) or as two (as under civil law), and whether wives might legitimately exercise through means of commercial contract the kind of economic initiative that would subject their own husbands to a kind of subordinate proprietary status. Mary Spencer provides another example of the increasing latitude of action afforded by insurance that has been explored in a German context by Eve Rosenhaft.[58] Access to commercial contracts like insurance allowed women to fashion their own economic strategies and to express their own interests besides and beyond their husbands'. This greater freedom carried with it, however, the worrisome possibility that the dominion of husbands over wives and the moral stability of the whole family might be undermined in the process.

Insurance was one of several types of commercial contracts that knit economic actors together in novel ways and in so doing established various forms of proprietary claims on the contracting parties. 'In the late eighteenth century,' Robert W. Gordon observes, 'property in contracts, property in hopes and expectations, was becoming the prevalent form of commercial property,' and lists among these 'paper money, shares of the public debt, certificates of stock in land or insurance companies, mortgages on land or inventory, bills of exchange, promissory notes, accounts receivable, and ... the unsecured but contracted-for performance of executory commercial promises.'[59] The proliferation and heritability of debt instruments extended commercial horizons but also threatened to entrap landed gentlemen – the paragons of independence – in the snares of a humiliating dependency. Thomas Jefferson complained, for example, that the endlessly revolving debts owed by Virginia planters to British merchants 'had become hereditary from father to son, for many generations, so that the planters were a species of property annexed to certain mercantile houses in Britain.'[60] Such socially degrading commercial contracts threatened not only to upend the established social hierarchy, but also to curtail the economic liberty of the self due to husbands, fathers, and masters. This danger was particularly acute in the case of insurance, which had the potential to create property willy-nilly through a rarified trade in abstract contingencies.

In this way, the growth of transatlantic slavery and the proliferation of commercial contract intersected in the insurance policy, the contract most emblematic of reified human life. It is not surprising, therefore, to find contemporaneous efforts at reform in the last quarter of the eighteenth century directed to limiting the capacity of insurance contracts to wantonly transform human life into property pure and simple, and also to transforming plantation slavery into a more traditional form of servitude comporting with historic English legal norms and usages. Those who advocated reform of West Indian slavery rather than its outright abolition typically urged the transmutation of chattel status into something akin to the villeinage existing in medieval England. Anglo-Saxon or Norman laws, it was argued, would profitably tie slaves to the land and prevent the despair that attended their sale, after which they tended to 'languish and die.'[61] The plantation economy would itself be bolstered economically, improved morally, human property restored to a close correspondence with a stable social hierarchy, and the slaves themselves set on the same gradual path to political liberty travelled by the English themselves over the previous five hundred years.[62]

With respect to insurance regulation, the Gambling Act of 1774 eliminated with tolerable success the element of wagering from the insurance business by demanding a demonstrable economic interest in the subject of a policy. In theory anyway, this requirement limited property-holding via insurance to those who could apply an existing economic measure to their policy and forestalled morally suspect or socially subversive uses of the contract. A parallel curtailment in the commoditization of slaves occurred fourteen years later with the passage in 1788 of William Dolben's Act, which provided that in policies on slave cargoes 'no loss or damage shall be recoverable on account of the mortality of slaves by natural death or ill treatment, or against loss by throwing overboard of slaves on any account whatsoever.'[63] Henceforth, insured 'emergencies' aboard ship could not be construed under any circumstances as justifying the sacrifice of embarked slaves, as subsequently happened in 1796 when a shipload of slaves was starved owing to a shortage of food.[64] Insurance of slaves was made entirely illegal as a logical concomitant to the abolition of the slave trade in 1806.[65]

## Natural Law and Civil Contract

The expanse of ocean across which slave traders sailed in the eighteenth century demarcated the most dynamic and improvisational economic zone in the world. As David Hancock has pointed out, the essential characteristic of the Atlantic world 'in the early modern period is not the particular body of water, but instead its emphasis on contexts, on linkages among peoples, places and activities, on boundary crossing and interpenetration.'[66] Those boundary crossings not only disrupted economic and social relations all along the Atlantic littoral, they also provoked a rethinking and rearrangement of the philosophical, legal, and moral categories according to which the leading European powers operated the burgeoning system of global commerce.

That system depended heavily for its growth upon multiplying forms of commercial contract, but as we have seen, those contracts often corroded legal doctrines of dominion, political assumptions about the necessity of subservience, and a traditional social order based on patriarchy and land-holding. This commercial challenge was augmented by a new legitimating rhetoric about nature and the laws it sanctioned. And more explicitly than in any other line of business, practitioners of insurance invoked a new and powerful natural 'science of man': political arithmetic. An amalgam of statistics and demography, political arithmetic removed human and civil affairs from direct providential superintendence and subsumed them under the new authority of natural law. Following an identical epistemological trajectory, history itself became naturalized as biology increasingly took its place alongside physics as a site for systematic and mathematical analysis. Similarly, the analysis of wealth – what had been the domain of moral philosophy – reached out to biology in order to supply the generative metaphors utilized by the physiocrats (who prized agriculture as the ultimate source of wealth) and by the classical political economists who abandoned the stasis of mercantilist accounting for the fruitful outcomes engendered by mutually beneficial exchange. Insurance united economics and biology by capitalizing on knowledge about the underlying regularities disclosed by morbidity and mortality data in order to hedge against the financial liabilities of death.

The increasing sway of natural law in the century of the Enlightenment is of course a commonplace. Less remarked on is another boundary crossing in which nature, having asserted a certain legal command over human affairs, was then reintegrated into the civil world. Thus Corbyn Morris, in discoursing about the amount of insurance proper to cover a voyage, computed the value of the lost cargo, the policy premium, and brokerage fee, but also the 'Sea's Share,' as if the sea itself was a party to the contract and demanded its due profit from commerce. 'And it is probable,' Morris explained, 'from the great Number of Insurers, that the Rate of Insurance, or the Premium, is reduced very low, so as that the Insurer has no more than a small Profit over and above what he is responsible for to the Sea.'[67] Turner's famous painting of the *Zong* portrays the same interpenetration of the civil and natural in its depiction of the sea as both an elemental natural power devouring the hapless victims of the Middle Passage *and* an accessory to a monstrous crime made possible by regarding humans as nothing more than natural resources in a great profit-making system, as commodities pure and simple, insurable at £30 a head.

## NOTES

I owe thanks to Tom Baker and the members of the Insurance and Society Workshop for their valuable comments and criticisms of an earlier version of this essay. Discussions with my colleagues Jim German, M.J. Heisey, and Sheila McIntyre also advanced the ideas presented here. Suzanne Smith made her usual editorial improvements, and filial indulgence for this project was generously provided by Charlotte, Daniel, Peter, and Frances.

1 By 47 Geo. III c. 36. The act also prohibited insurance being taken out on embarked slaves. Samuel Marshall, *A Treatise on the Law of Insurance*, 2 vols. (London, 1808), vol. 1, 93. In the first edition of 1802 Marshall expressed the same moral reservations about the slave trade but assuaged his conscience and that of his readers by citing the humane provisions of William Dolben's Act of 1788, discussed below.

2 Tim Armstrong, 'Slavery, Insurance, and Sacrifice in the Black Atlantic,' in Bernhard Klein and Gesa Mackenthun, eds., *Sea Changes: Historicizing the Ocean* (New York: Routledge, 2004); Jane Webster, 'The *Zong* in the Context of the Eighteenth-Century Slave Trade, *The Journal of Legal History* 28, no. 3, 296.

3 Marshall, *Treatise*, vol. 1, 216.

4 This loss was somewhat above the level of mortality usually encountered on the Middle Passage, but because rates of mortality on slaving voyages varied widely, 'average' mortality is not an especially meaningful datum. Mortality rates for slaves in transit fell steadily during the eighteenth century, but those for crews did not and by century's end were actually higher than for the slaves themselves. Philip D. Curtin, *The Atlantic Slave Trade: A Census* (Madison: University of Wisconsin Press, 1969), 282–3; Herbert S. Kline, *The Middle Passage* (Princeton: Princeton University Press, 1978), passim; Joseph C. Miller, *Way of Death: Merchant Capitalism and the Angolan Slave Trade 1730–1830* (Madison: University of Wisconsin Press, 1988), 427–37.

5 The fullest account of the *Zong* case is to be found in F.O. Shyllon, *Black Slaves in Britain* (London: Oxford University Press, 1974), 184–209.

6 James Walvin, *Black Ivory: A History of British Slavery* (London: Fontana, 1993), 19.

7 The best discussion of the early cultural impact of the *Zong* is provided by Anita Rupprecht, '"A Very Uncommon Case": Representations of the *Zong* and the British Campaign to Abolish the Slave Trade,' *Journal of Legal History* 28, no. 3, 329–46.

8 Marcus Wood, *Blind Memory: Visual Representations of Slavery in England and America 1780–1865* (New York: Routledge, 2000), 41–68.

9 Ian Baucom, *Spectres of the Atlantic: Finance, Capital, Slavery, and the Philosophy of History* (Durham: Duke University Press, 2005), 212.

10 Baucom, *Specters*, 17, 18.

11 Quoted in Shyllon, *Black Slaves*, 190.

12 Quoted in Teresa Michals, '"That Sole and Despotic Dominion": Slaves, Wives, and Game in Blackstone's Commentaries,' *Eighteenth-Century Studies* 27, no. 2 (Winter 1993–94), 195–216.

13 Eric Williams, 'The Golden Age of the Slave System in Britain,' *Journal of Negro History* 25, no. 1 (January 1940), 98.

14 Armstrong, 'Slavery, Insurance, and Sacrifice,' 171.

15 This is not to say that security aboard ship was at all light. Crews on slave ships were some 50 per cent larger than on other kinds of vessels in order to ensure that the slaves were kept under control. Indeed, so much was expended on shackles and armaments that one historian has described the slave ship as a 'floating Alcatraz': Okon E. Uya, quoted in Emma Christopher, *Slave Ship Sailors and Their Captive Cargoes, 1730–1807* (Cambridge: Cambridge University Press, 2006), 182–3. The point being made here is that the measures taken to ensure the safety of the ship and crew against the possibility of slave revolt were usually equal to the task, and rendered the objective risk of slave revolt below the risks commonly assumed in the carriage of many other commodities.

16 James Oldham, 'Insurance Litigation Involving the *Zong* and Other British Slave Ships, 1780–1807,' and Michael Lobban, 'Slavery, Insurance, and the Law,' both in *Journal of Legal History* 28, no. 3, 299–318 and 319–28.

17 John Weskett, *A Complete Digest of the Theory, Laws, and Practice of Insurance* (London, 1781), 105–6.

18 Lobban, 'Slavery, Insurance, and the Law,' 322.

19 Oldham, 'Insurance Litigation,' 308.

20 Armstrong, 'Slavery, Insurance, and Sacrifice,' 170.

21 In an otherwise excellent article on the *Zong*, Jane Webster follows Tim Armstrong's analysis on these points. Jane Webster, 'The *Zong* in the Context of the Eighteenth-Century Slave Trade,' *Journal of Legal History* 28, no. 3, 296–7.

22 See for example the many life insurance policies made on free and slave lives in late medieval and early modern Barcelona contained in José María Madurell Marimón, *Los Seguros de Vida de Esclavos en Barcelona (1453–1523)* (Madrid: Ministerio de Justicia y Consejo Superior de Investigaciones Científicas, 1955), and idem, *Los Antiguos Seguros de Vida en Barcelona (1427–1764)* (Madrid: Instituto Nacional de Estudios Juridicos, 1958).

23 Giuseppe Stefani, *Insurance in Venice from the Origins to the End of the Serenissima*, 2 vols. (Trieste: Assicurazioni Generali di Trieste e Venezia, 1958), vol. 1, 118–19; Enrico Bensa, *Histoire du contrat d'assurance au moyen âge* (Paris: Thorin et Fils, 1897), 90; Frederigo Melis, *Origini e sviluppi della assicurazioni in Italia (secoli XIV–XVI)* (Rome: Istituto Nazionale delle Assicurazioni, 1975), vol. 1: *Le fonti*, 210.

24 Robert Sidney Smith, 'Life Insurance in Fifteenth-Century Barcelona,' *Journal of Economic History* 1, no. 1 (May 1941), 57.

25 Bensa, *Histoire*, 90–3; Melis, *Origini*, vol. 1, 211–12; Smith, 'Life Insurance,' 57–8.

26 Gerard Malynes, *Consuetudo, uel Lex Mercatoria, or The Ancient Law Merchant* (London, 1629), 149.

27 John Millar, *Elements of the Law Relating to Insurances* (Edinburgh, 1787), 2.

28 Corbyn Morris, *An Essay Towards Illustrating the Science of Insurance* (London, 1747), 1.

29 James Allan Park, *A System of the Law of Marine Insurances, with Three Chapters on Bottomry; on Insurances on Lives; and on Insurances against Fire* (London, 1787), 488.

30 *Guidon Stile et Usance des Marchands qui mettent à la Mer* (Rouen, 1619), 64.

31 René-Josué Valin, *Commentaire sur l'ordonnance de la marine du mois d'aout 1681* (Poitiers, 1828), book 3, 255.

32 Valin, *Commentaire*, book 3, 257 and sec. 6, art. 11.

33 Valin, *Commentaire*, book 3, 258.

34 Valin, *Commentaire*, book 3, 258–9.

35 K.G. Davies, *The Royal African Company* (London: Longmans, Green, 1957), 208.

36 Lucy Stuart Sutherland, *A London Merchant 1695–1774* (London: Oxford University Press, 1933), 43 and n. 3.

37 Hugh Thomas, *The Slave Trade* (New York: Simon & Schuster, 1997), 205.

38 Walvin, *Black Ivory*, 318; James Allan Park, *A System of the Law of Marine Insurances* (Philadelphia, 1789), 65.

39 It is worth noting that English commentators never mentioned among the benefits of life insurance the coverage of slave cargoes. No doubt they would have wished to consider policies on slaves as a form of marine rather than life insurance. On the other hand, the French resort to ransom insurance in order to insure slaves' lives while evading the legal prohibition on life insurance suggests that the classing of slave policies as marine insurance was not always assumed.

40 Baucom, *Specters*, 99–100. The respective values of imports, exports, and re-exports of the North Sea, Mediterranean, and Asian circuits of trade, when added together, greatly exceeded those of the Atlantic circuit in the first half of the eighteenth century and continued to do so at least until 1774. David Ormrod, *The Rise of Commercial Empires: England and the Netherlands in the Age of Mercantilism, 1650–1770* (Cambridge: Cambridge University Press, 2003), 68–70, 354.

41 Walvin, *Black Ivory*, 14–15.

42 James Oldham, 'New Light on Mansfield and Slavery,' *Journal of British Studies* 27, no. 1 (January 1988), 52.

43 Oldham, 'Mansfield and Slavery,' 54.

44 Walvin, *Black Ivory*, 15.
45 Michals, 'Sole and Despotic Dominion,' 195.
46 Michals, 'Sole and Despotic Dominion,' 201.
47 *Blackstone's Commentaries*, 5 vols. (Philadelphia, 1803), vol. 2, 423.
48 Michals, 'Sole and Despotic Dominion,' 198.
49 *Blackstone's Commentaries*, vol. 2, 424.
50 *Blackstone's Commentaries*, vol. 2, 428.
51 Blackstone quoted in Michals, 'Sole and Despotic Dominion,' 202.
52 Gary Kates, *Monsieur D'Eon Is a Woman* (Baltimore: Johns Hopkins University Press, 1995), 3–4, 65–76.
53 *The London Magazine*, September 1777, 445.
54 *The Gentleman's Magazine*, July 1777, 346–7.
55 *English Reports* (Abingdon, 1986), vol. 98, 1334.
56 Margot Finn, 'Women, Consumption and Coverture in England, *c.* 1760–1860,' *Historical Journal* 39, no. 3 (1996), 709.
57 John Weskett, *A Complete Digest of the Theory, Laws and Practice of Insurance* (London, 1781), 337–8.
58 Eve Rosenhaft, 'Did Women Invent Life Insurance? Widows and the Demand for Financial Services in Eighteenth-Century Germany,' in David R. Green and Alastair Owens, eds., *Family Welfare: Gender, Property, and Inheritance since the Seventeenth Century* (Westport, CT: Praeger, 2004), 163–94.
59 R.W. Gordon, 'Paradoxical Property,' in A. Bermingham and J. Brewer, eds., *The Consumption of Culture, 1600–1800* (London: Routledge, 1995), 99.
60 Quoted in Gordon, 'Paradoxical Property,' 99.
61 Philo-Xylon (pseud.), *Letters of Philo-Xylon first published in the Barbados gazettes, during the years 1787 and 1788* (Barbados: T. W. Perch, 1789), 17, 20–2.
62 Philo-Xylon, *Letters*, 22; Michals, 'Sole and Despotic Dominion,' 206–10.
63 Quoted in Shyllon, *Black Slaves*, 206.
64 Shyllon, *Black Slaves*, 207–8.
65 47 Geo. III c. 36 declared all insurance on the slave trade illegal, providing a penalty of £100 and triple the premium 'on any of his majesty's subjects who shall subscribe, effect, or make any such unlawful insurances.' Marshall, *Treatise*, 1, 217.
66 David Hancock, '"An Undiscovered Ocean of Commerce Laid Open": India, Wine and the Emerging Atlantic Economy, 1703–1813,' in H.V. Bowen, Margarette Lincoln, and Nigel Rigby, eds., *The Worlds of the East India Company* (Woodbridge, Suffolk: Boydell, 2002), 154.
67 Morris, *Essay*, xii, 14–21, 25.

# 4 Fire, Property Insurance, and Perceptions of Risk in Eighteenth-Century Britain

ROBIN PEARSON

During the early modern period, the common response to natural disasters was a religious one. Catastrophic events had a didactic function as revelations of divine judgment on sin and human frailty, and as a 'summons to the Cross.'[1] Epidemics, storms, floods, fires, and earthquakes were hailed as acts of God, with moral lessons to be drawn from them. A lapse in religious devotion, as well as imprudence in daily life, could lead to one downfall.[2] By the beginning of the twentieth century, however, 'scientific approaches' to natural hazards had largely triumphed in the Western world. The pulpit language of calamity and providence had been supplanted by 'disaster experts,' by the arithmetic and rhetoric of probability, by safety regulations, design and 'risk management,' and by scientific experimentation to forecast, reduce, or eliminate hazards.[3] There is general agreement, or at least a widespread assumption, among historians that this epistemological transition took place before a range of deadlier hazards and apocalyptic events undermined the basis of the new 'risk society' during the course of the twentieth century.[4] Yet we know little about why, when, how, or at what pace the original transition occurred.

This chapter argues that a critical phase in this transition took place in Britain during the long eighteenth century. This was the site of the first mass insurance industry and the location, though by no means the only one in Europe, of important developments in scientific method, including actuarial science, inductive logic, and the laws of probability.[5] Building upon my previous research, here I explore the relationship between the growth of fire insurance and its meaning in terms of changing popular perceptions of risk.[6] The first part of the chapter surveys the extent and nature of the fire hazard in Britain and examines the multivalent popular responses to fire and to risk more gener-

Table 2.1
Recorded fires in England, Wales, and Scotland, 1730–79

| | No. of fires | Houses destroyed | Average size of fires x houses destroyed |
|---|---|---|---|
| 1730–9 | 90 | 1587 | 18 |
| 1740–9 | 78 | 1755 | 23 |
| 1750–9 | 210 | 847 | 4 |
| 1760–9 | 423 | 2443 | 6 |
| 1770–9 | 139 | 1000 | 7 |

Source: Adapted from Robin Pearson, *Insuring the Industrial Revolution: Fire Insurance in Great Britain 1700–1850* (Aldershot, 2004), table 1.6

ally. In the second part I outline the development of fire prevention and insurance. The final two sections assess the evidence that a transition in British attitudes towards risk took place at this time, and examine the role in this transition ascribed to insurance.

## Fire Hazards and Attitudes to Risk

'Of the numerous calamities to which mankind are liable,' wrote George Stonestreet in 1790, 'there is none which excites more uneasy sensations or to which persons of all ranks are more equally exposed.'[7] Chimneys caught fire, coals fell out of hearths, ovens and copper wash tubs overheated, tar kettles boiled over, lids of stills blew off, burning candles scorched bed sheets, linen, and curtains and toppled into casks of oil and spirits or onto straw and hay in stables, hot ashes thrown into back yards set household rubbish alight, and sparks from burning warehouses blew across docks to set alight the rigging of ships. The losses can only be guessed, but they were certainly enormous. Fires recorded in newspapers totalled 940 between 1730 and 1779 (see table 4.1), and destroyed over 8,300 houses and other buildings, burnt an incalculable amount of agricultural produce and livestock, and caused at least 376 human fatalities. And these figures account for only a fraction of the real toll of destruction, which must have run into tens of thousands of properties in this period alone.[8]

This data on urban and large rural fires lends support to the thesis that the 1760s marked a watershed, for numbers peaked in that decade, with 2,443 houses destroyed in 423 fires. The average size of fires, measured by the number of houses destroyed, fell substantially after 1750, but fire remained a dangerous source of death and destruction, especially in the docklands and the less solidly built parts of London, and in the large villages of southern England.

The region most blighted by fire was the southwest of England, stretching from Totnes in Devon through Dorset as far east as Blandford and Poole. Eight of the nineteen provincial towns that suffered most from large fires were found in this region.[9] Tiverton was the worst hit. Only Wapping in east London had a comparable record of destruction. Tiverton's biggest fire occurred in 1731, when nearly 300 houses were destroyed and the damage was estimated at 4,000. Goods salvaged from burning buildings were thrown into churches and meeting houses, or into nearby fields where, a contemporary observed, 'a great many hundred poor persons lay for want of beds.'[10] In total over 530 houses were destroyed in Tiverton fires during the course of the century, a figure that amounted to 44 per cent of the town's (inhabited) housing stock in 1801. Other towns in the region also faced staggering levels of destruction. Fires in Crediton and Honiton destroyed at least three-quarters of the houses in each town. In 1743 around 460 houses burned down in Crediton at a cost of about £50,000. Twelve years earlier, 337 houses were incinerated in Blandford at a cost of over £44,000, leaving just 26 houses standing in the town. At Shipwash, Devon, in 1743 the 'whole town was consumed except a few houses at the lower end' in a fire which left two dead. The entire village of Frampton, Dorset, consisting of 43 houses, burned down in 1796, though these had all been rebuilt by the time of the population census five years later.[11] Elsewhere, among the smaller towns and larger villages, the destruction was less complete but still on a terrible scale. It can be estimated that up to 40 per cent of the housing stock in Dorchester, Wareham, Abbotsbury, and Bere Regis in Dorset and Great Torrington in Devon and up to 25 per cent of houses in Sturminster Newton, Bridport, and Beaminster in Dorset and Chumleigh in Devon were destroyed by fire during the eighteenth century.[12]

The aggregate losses by fire could understate the devastating way that fire scarred individual lives, sometimes repeatedly. It cast a long shadow, for example, over the life of the artist William Hogarth that was reflected in his work. It burnt down one of his favourite haunts, White's coffee house, in 1733, depicted in plate six of the *Rake's Progress*. It killed his mother, Anne, who died of shock during a fire at her house in Cranbourn Street in June 1735. It destroyed the original paintings of the *Harlot's Progress* in 1755. It was central to his portrayal of *Night* (1738), a scene 'full of pain, fire and misrule.' It was also the focus of plate one of *The Times* (1762), where the Earl of Bute was pictured as a fireman of the Union Fire Office trying to put out the blaze of the Seven Years War, while being obstructed by his political opponents.[13]

For many, the fear of fire was never far from consciousness. Some Londoners slept with rattles by their beds in case of the need to raise an alarm.[14] A detailed reading of numerous fire events in the Georgian capital suggests a city of insomniacs, with many leaping out of their beds within minutes at the smell of smoke or the sight of flames, escaping into the streets dressed only in their nightshirts, waking up neighbours, alerting watchmen and firemen, and carrying what they could of their linen and goods.[15] There are numerous examples of the individual and collective fright induced by a false fire alarm or the report of a real fire. When guns were fired and bells rung in the Berkshire village of East Hendred in September 1758 to celebrate the British victory at Louisburgh, the noise alarmed the neighbouring villages, whose residents, unaware of the news, 'thought the town was on fire, and were coming up in great numbers to our assistance.'[16] The immediacy of such fears was a recurrent motif in contemporary fiction. In *Tom Jones*, when 'news' of the 'French invasion' reached the prodigal daughter Sophia Western, she was relieved that the alarm was not announcing the arrival of her angry father. Fielding tried to convey her relief through a cumbersome reference to the fear of fire:

> As a miser, who hath in some well-built city a cottage value twenty shillings, when at a distance he is alarmed with the news of a fire, turns pale and trembles at his loss; but when he finds the beautiful palaces only are burnt, and his own cottage remains safe, he comes instantly to himself and smiles at his good fortune.[17]

The shock of an alarm could, in Fielding words, put a man 'out of himself.' This shock was greater still in a real fire event. Big fires were frightful, not only because of their destructiveness, but also because they could be rapid, unpredictable, and extremely difficult to extinguish. The great fire at Tiverton in 1794 burned for twenty-four hours before it was brought under control. Fires at Crediton in 1743 and at Ottery St Mary in 1767 each lasted about ten hours, while the Honiton fire of 1747 began on a July afternoon, while many were in church, and burned until four o'clock the following morning.[18] Fire-fighting was often ineffective in saving lives and property, even where the flames were confined to just a few buildings. In Exeter, freezing water made it difficult to put out several fires that broke out there in February 1740.[19] Another winter fire that burned down one of Exeter's lodging houses in 1775

> broke out so suddenly that a number of the travelling poor, who lodged in the upper part of the house, perished in the flames; ten of their bodies were found and the remains of some others; but several were burnt to ashes. In a few hours the fire was extinguished, after burning two houses only and damaging some others.[20]

In London and many provincial towns water shortages were a problem. The Dorchester fire of 1775, which began in a soap boiler's workshop opposite the jail

> raged for several hours taking very irregular directions, making great havock among the thatched houses and passing those that were roofed with tiles or slates; water was so scarce for some time that one of the engines, in a narrow lane, was obliged to be abandoned by the men who worked it, and by means of the falling thatch caught fire, was totally destroyed.[21]

A wind could add to the unpredictability of flames. In Ottery St Mary in 1767, a high wind helped a fire burn more than fifty houses and shops, and 'it was with the greatest difficulty prevented from destroying the town.' In the Abbotsbury fire of 1764 it was believed that 'had not the wind changed ... it would have burnt down the whole town.'[22] In the smaller towns, where there was little equipment to fight a fire, the residents sometimes had to improvise quickly. A fire in the Devon town of Moreton-Hampstead, which destroyed six houses in 1757,

> spread so fast that the inhabitants were terribly alarmed with the apprehension of the whole town being destroyed; but by the unwearied endeavours of the people in covering their houses with hides and other things, to prevent the flames catching the thatch, the fire was providentially extinguished.[23]

Terror for those caught up in a large fire, and a more widespread fear of sudden, unpredictable destruction, were common reactions. At Blandford in 1731,

> the consternation of the people was so great and the fire so quick that few saved any goods; near 300 houses were laid in ashes, and the Town in such confusion that 'twas difficult to find a road through it.[24]

The misery of those who had lost their homes and goods in such fires was considerable, resembling the effects of the civil war battles of the previous century. The Crediton fire of 1743 reduced

> more than 2,000 Persons ... to the most melancholy Circumstances; the far greater Part of whom being not only destitute of Lodgings, Cloaths and Victuals, but even of the Means of providing for any by the loss of their Looms and working Materials.

A victim of another fire in Crediton in 1769 wrote that 'we have scarce saved anything and what little we have is broken in pieces. We have lain an orchard two days and one night.' As Blandford burned in 1731,

> near 3,000 persons lay in the open field without cloaths or victuals; 150 of whom had the smallpox upon them, and were carried out of their beds into the meadows, and several dy'd and remain unbury'd.[25]

Donations for the relief of the victims came not only from local patrons, but also from neighbouring communities who knew just what such a fire could mean. Tiverton was the first of several towns in the southwest to contribute to the relief of Crediton in 1743, while Blandford and Poole each sent two cart loads of provisions to Wareham to help those who suffered in the fire of 1762.[26]

For those with substantial property, the threat was increased not only by the capriciousness of fire itself, but also by the negligence or wilful attitude towards the hazard of many of their social inferiors. The torch was the weapon of choice for many disgruntled employees and burglars, who started fires to punish an employer or to effect an escape.[27] Throughout the eighteenth century domestic servants were warned about the risks of carelessly handling uncovered candles. The act of 1707, to punish 'any menial or other servant' convicted of causing a fire in any house or outbuilding through 'negligence and carelessness,' was reprinted many times and circulated as handbills by several insurance offices.[28] Such publicity impressed those of a nervous disposition. The poet Thomas Gray, upon reading about several London fires in 1759, remarked to a friend:

> 'Tis strange that we all of us (here in town) lay ourselves down every night on our funereal pile, ready made, and compose ourselves to rest, while every drunken footman and drowsy old woman has a candle ready to light it before the morning.[29]

Outside the home, the carelessness of workers, the wilfulness of children, or the absent-mindedness of the elderly could indeed result in destruction. In 1758, for example, the pews and gallery of a new church at Wolverhampton caught fire, 'occasioned by the carelessness of the workmen who left a fire to dry their work.' At Kettering in 1766 some boys playing with squibs burnt down seventeen houses plus outhouses and corn ricks, at a cost of £4,000.[30]

Where life was cheap and expectations low, the consequences of mishandling fire were not given undue attention. Even in a world where measurable patterns were being found in nature, fires were regarded by most as the products of divine will that could deliver moral lessons about prudence and conduct, but not data upon which to base probabilistic estimates of risk.[31] Negligence towards fire, however, was not the sole prerogative of the poor and the superstitious. In 1730 the Sun Fire Office sued 'two young gentlemen at Bury for firing their pistols among thatched houses and causing a fire.[32] The failure of even the wealthy to learn from experience was noted by Walpole in 1763 after the burning of Lady Molesworth and her family in their London home. Fire, declared Robert Southey, was 'a tremendous calamity which is every day occurring in England, and against which daily and dreadful experience has not yet taught them to adopt any general means of prevention.'[33] Such impressions are supported by the evidence scattered in insurance records and newspapers of a persistent carelessness in the handling of dangerous materials, in the near ubiquity of wooden chimneys, candles, lanterns, torches, stoves; of combustibles including fireworks, gunpowder, and oil stored in house and street; of hazardous trades and open fires in workshops and shipyards; in the presence of children increasing the risk of accidents in the workplace; and in a devil-may-care attitude towards danger shared by all social classes, that can be associated with the general rumbustiousness for which eighteenth-century England was renowned.[34]

The terror and alarm of those caught up in conflagrations was contraposed by the carnivalesque humour of the crowds who turned out to watch the flames. Large fires and the efforts to extinguish them constituted a form of street theatre. According to his biographer, the miserly sculptor Joseph Nollekens usually neglected the chimneys in his London house:

> However, after having been several times annoyed by the fire-engines and their regular attendents, the mob, he was determined to have them more frequently cleaned; though some of them, for want of fires, yielded no soot.[35]

The novelist Tobias Smollett wrought some slapstick scenes out of fires and fire alarms, which reflected the familiarity of his readers with such events. In *Humphrey Clinker*, a chimney fire in a Harrogate lodging house induced panic among those trying to escape and some 'selfishly brutal' behaviour on the stairs. A false alarm at Sir Thomas Bullford's generated panic and mirth in equal measure as Lieutenant Lismahago clumsily tried to escape down a ladder from his bedroom window.[36] Just as the fear of fire was a democratic emotion, capable of affecting all social classes, there was also a subversive aspect to the way a conflagration could turn the world upside down, reducing the property of the wealthy to ruin and their families to homelessness, and converting figures of power and status to objects of pity, or in the case of Lismahago, to objects of ridicule.

The town houses of the rich were more likely to catch fire than their country residences, but the latter also burned down.[37] It has been estimated that fire damaged at least 10 per cent of all country houses in Hertfordshire every one hundred years.[38] In 1751 a fire at the seat of the Honourable Alexander Hume Campbell, at Colnbrook, Buckinghamshire, destroyed all the furniture, despite the efforts of three fire engines. Campbell, family, and guests had to wrap themselves in sheets and clamber for their lives down ladders placed outside their bedchamber windows.[39] Other notable fires included one at the French ambassador's house at Twickenham in 1734, costing £18,000; the fire at Sir William Richardson's house in Richmond Hill in 1749, which burnt all his furniture and two adjacent houses; the fire at the former hunting seat of the Prince of Wales in Epsom in 1755, which destroyed the house and furniture within two hours; the destruction of Lady Peters's house near Brentwood in 1757 through a fire caused by lightning; and the fires at Lord Craven's house at Beenham, near Newbury, in 1774, and at Lord Fortescue's house in Twickenham in 1780, the latter caused by overheated stoves.[40]

This proximity of the wealthy as well as the poor to fire hazards ensured that fear was mixed with familiarity throughout the social classes. Familiarity created a space for other emotional reactions, especially curiosity and fascination with the spectacle of fire events. At a fire in Old Street in 1771, for example, a wall fell down under the weight of spectators, killing one and injuring several others.[41] As usual, such aspects of everyday life spilled over into fiction. The final benefactor of Cleland's Fanny Hill died from a cold caught while watching a London fire.[42] Southey echoed a general feeling when he remarked that 'the traveller who is at London without seeing a fire ... is out of luck.'[43]

Closely following fascination came another emotion that could supercede more rational responses, namely the feeling that fire spectacles contained something of the sublime. Feelings of sublimity may also have been experienced by members of the lower classes – there is no reason to think that this was bounded by class – but the response was best articulated by the most literate among Georgian society. 'You know I cannot resist going to a fire,' Horace Walpole wrote to a correspondent in 1755, 'for it is certainly the only horrid sight that is fine.' With Walpole and others in mind, Bentham sardonically defined the purpose of the sublime as 'giving good reasons for unreasonable preferences.'[44] The sublime was viewed as a rapture or emotive transcendence caused by an external force or event, such as a landscape, or a great fire or other natural disaster. Alternatively, it was argued that rapture could be caused by an internal force, only indirectly related to an external event. One might, for example, view a great landscape from the top of a mountain without feeling the sublime, because it was not the landscape that generated sublimity but something within oneself. Whatever the origins of the sublime, there was widespread agreement about the range of emotional responses it gave rise to, including tranquillity, fear, terror, and a pain that in some minds was also a form of pleasure. In romantic literature, sublimity was commonly associated with the rapture of love that in turn was closely related to self-destruction – the standard text here was Goethe's *Young Werther*. In gothic literature the sublime took the form of terror, as in the novels of Ann Radcliffe and the poetry of Anna Barbauld. In his *Night Thoughts* the poet Edward Young connected it to the terrible empty vastness of the universe. Edmund Burke voiced approval of the concept in his *Philosophical Enquiry*, making the common link between pleasure and pain, and noting that obscurity and ignorance exerted a more powerful effect on the imagination than clarity and knowledge.[45]

But there was also condemnation. In her *Vindication of the Rights of Man*, for example, Mary Wollstonecroft argued that 'the cultivation of reason damps fancy,' while sublime rapture, especially in romantic love, was subversive of reason.[46] In the revolutionary 1790s, Burke himself was to reject violent passions and 'sublime speculations.'[47]

The relevant question here is, what was the impact of the sublime on eighteenth-century perceptions of risk, uncertainty, and fate? Sublime joy, fear, and terror are products in the first instance of individual imagination and memory, but they are also cultural artefacts, social constructions partly shaped by social norms and collective memory. As Bourke has put it, 'humanity could only fear within the context of the discourse of fear.'[48] Adam Smith argued that passions that derive from physical pain are soon forgotten, but the same is not true for those deriving from the imagination.

> Fear … is a passion derived altogether from the imagination, which represents, with an uncertainty and fluctuation that increases our anxiety, not what we really feel, but what we may hereafter possibly suffer.[49]

Sublime emotions such as fear, therefore, are not readily forgotten, because they pass through the individual's imagination and lodge in the memory. Thus, fear relates not to what we really feel in the present, but to the expectation of future suffering and, by extension, to a greater awareness of risk and the possibilities of risk avoidance. Smith and others believed that philosophy – 'the science of the connecting principles of nature' – could demystify unexpected events or objects by helping to identify the connections between them. By revealing the 'invisible chains' that bound together all the disjointed objects in nature, philosophy could help reduce fear and uncertainty and 'introduce order into this chaos of jarring and discordant appearances, to allay this tumult of the imagination.'[50]

A contemporary proverb held that fear was one part of prudence.[51] Both were socially constructed and placed in the balance, but the scales were often tipped in favour of the former, as Richardson's heroine, Pamela, noted:

> I have heard it said, *That here can be no prudence without apprehension*: but I am persuaded, that fear brings one into more dangers, than the caution, that goes along with it, delivers one from.[52]

The prudential response to fear was constantly undermined by other emotional responses to hazards, including resignation, denial, and the anticipated pleasures of excitement, thrill, and even rapture.[53] One well-known fictional example was Defoe's Moll Flanders, who, locked in Newgate and frightened by the prospects of the gallows, reproached herself

> with the many hints I had had ... from my own reason, ... and of the many dangers I had escaped, to leave off while I was well, and how I had withstood them all, and hardened my thoughts against all fear.

Only with the hindsight that she had mismeasured her stock of luck did Moll feel that she 'was hurried on by an inevitable and unseen fate to this day of misery.'[54] This theme of misjudging risk and imprudently challenging the goddess Fortuna was also taken up by Cleland's Fanny Hill, who observed that 'the greatest improbability is not always what we should most mistrust.'[55]

The eighteenth-century difficulty of assigning probabilities to events, by which future actions could be guided, derived from something more than the limitations of statistical knowledge or its popular diffusion. The difficulty also arose out of a deep ambivalence, experienced by all classes of society, about measurable risk and unmeasurable uncertainty, fortune and fate, fear and prudence, passion and reason. Fear was related to the expectation of future suffering, but, as argued above, not in a direct or uncomplicated way. The following section examines the consequences such ambivalence had for attitudes to fire prevention and insurance.

## Fire Prevention and Insurance

Attempts to regulate building, promote fire prevention, and support fire-fighting methods predate both the rise of the modern insurance industry and the conceptual developments discussed above. There had been frequent attempts, for example, to control and regulate new construction in London since the fifteenth century, but most legislation was evaded or ignored. Profits were to be made from patching up old buildings, digging cellars out of foundations, and constructing flimsy extensions to existing houses to accommodate more tenants. After the Great Fire a new type of legislation appeared that regulated party walls, limited the use of timber, and standardized the size and quality of bricks. Much of this also failed. The Brick Act of 1727 was widely ignored by members of the Company of Tilers and Brickmakers who were given the task of implementing it. Insurance offices complained that fire damage was greater than it should have been, because builders ignored the regulations requiring them to continue party walls up through the roofs of houses.[56] For the rest of the reign of George II little further was done to follow up earlier legislation.

After further major fires, public discussion of the problem resumed, a debate that culminated in the London building acts of 1764–74. These were part of a wider movement that comprised street widening, paving, and lighting in the City and Westminster, bridge building, and the rebuilding or repair of public buildings. The act of 1764 regulated the thickness and projection of party walls and the use of wood near hearths and chimneys, and introduced compulsory inspection for all new buildings. Builders who failed to comply faced a £50 fine or imprisonment. This act was amended two years later to extend penalties to the employees of master builders and to grant justices the right to issue warrants of entry to adjacent houses where a party wall needed repair or demolition.[57] The 1774 act was more adventurous than anything previously attempted.[58] Seven classes of building were categorized by value, floor area, height, distance from roads or other buildings, and type of use. A range of commercial and industrial property, as well as dwelling houses, were included in the act. The thickness of external and party walls and foundations was specified, almost all woodwork was banished from exteriors, and front walls were to be aligned with streets. District surveyors were appointed to enforce the legislation. Some improvements did follow, such as the increasing use of artificial, and less inflammable, materials for exterior ornamentation in fashionable west end houses. On the whole, however, parts of central London, the riverside, and the east continued to have large numbers of timber-built structures. Evidence from insurance records points to the increasing use of timber in the city's buildings before the 1780s, and to the persistence of timber structures – comprising between one-fifth and one-third of insured property – until at least the end of the century.[59] Here and there one glimpses the older wooden city in which many Londoners lived. In March 1773, for example, a maidservant in a house in Old Broad Street 'carelessly' hung up a sheet to dry before a kitchen fire. The sheet caught alight and the maid was suffocated to death by the fumes before her husband and several neighbours managed to extinguish the fire. Had they arrived a quarter of an hour later, it was reported, 'the whole neighbourhood might have been burnt, as the houses are very old and built chiefly of wood.'[60]

Fire prevention efforts dated back to at least the late Middle Ages. Many towns passed ordinances against thatched roofs, wooden chimneys, and dangerous kilns, the careless storage of combustible materials, and the carriage of fire in uncovered containers between buildings. By the early seventeenth century these concerns were receiving increasing attention as population expanded and urban property values rose. Fire-fighting equipment was common. At least sixty fire engines had been built by 1662.[61] During the half-century following the Great Fire of London there were increased attempts to improve facilities for fighting fire.[62] In London a system of parish brigades and night watchmen ('bellmen') was set up, with churchwardens being made legally responsible for the upkeep of buckets, ladders, engines, axes, hose, and squirts, and for installing stopcocks on water pipes in their parishes.[63] At the height of the War of the Spanish Succession, when the French were in virtual control of the Channel, an ordinance of 1707 provided up to thirty members of each brigade with highly valued admiralty exemptions from naval impressment.[64]

Several of the new London insurance offices established their own fire brigades. These company brigades at first complemented but soon became substitutes for the parish brigades. Despite the availability of legal sanctions and threats by insurance offices to prosecute parish officers who neglected their duties, parishes generally failed to keep their fire-fighting equipment and street pipes and plugs in good order and to provide a good supply of water at major fires. Moreover, the rapid rebuilding of London and many other towns destroyed by fire, such as Warwick in 1694, Gravesend in 1727, and Wareham in 1762, ensured that timber continued to be widely used in construction, notwithstanding legislation against this. The deterioration of parish fire-fighting equipment, the persistent lack of water in many places, and the continued use of timber in house-building indicated that earlier lessons about fire hazards had not been taken on board.[65]

Following the huge fire in Cornhill in 1748, and with increasing concern about arson and public disorder and the need to regulate construction and the storage of hazardous goods as a new construction boom in London got underway, greater public attention was given to fire prevention and fire-fighting matters. In 1755 Sir John Fielding called for more turncocks and an improved water supply for fire engines in London, and numerous other articles and pamphlets were published from the late 1740s advising on precautions to take against fire and making suggestions for better fire escapes and fire-fighting facilities in the capital.[66] In the early 1760s several artists, most notably Hogarth, turned to fire-fighting motives to make political points.[67] Fire engines were in place at George III's marriage and coronation in 1761, and fireworks were banned.[68] This sensitivity towards the fire hazard contrasted with the situation just twelve years before. Servandoni's giant fireworks display – 'Cracker Castle' – in St James's Park had exploded at the peace celebrations of April 1749, but the disaster did not dissuade the Duke of Richmond from putting on his own fireworks show at his house by the Thames just one month later.[69] The attitudes of at least some in society seemed to have changed rapidly in the following decades. The centenary of the Great Fire was marked by newspaper articles that reminded readers of the horrors of a major conflagration. Newspapers, journals, and pamphlets carried accounts of Ambrose Godfrey's fire-extinguishing experiments in 1760–61, the trials of the rival fire-proofing systems of David Hartley and Viscount Mahon in the 1770s, and several improved designs of the fire engine and water pump. These innovations were well received. Hartley's patented system, which consisted in covering the underside of wooden floors and timber parts in buildings with thin iron plates, was adopted in the royal naval stores at Portsmouth and Plymouth in 1777 following the arson attempts of John the Painter. In the same year Hartley was made a freeman of the City of London for his efforts.[70] Ten years later an Italian tourist was impressed by the column outside the house at Putney where Hartley's experiments had taken place, that had been erected 'with public ceremony in honour of him.' The inscription on the foundation stone noted that it was 'laid … one hundred and ten years after the fire of London, on the anniversary of that dreadful event, in memory of an invention for securing buildings against fire.'[71]

This surge in public attention directed to fire prevention and fire-fighting technologies during the third quarter of the eighteenth century was accompanied by an acceleration in the growth of fire insurance. The value of risks written by English fire insurance offices increased in real terms by nearly 90 per cent between the late 1750s and the mid-1770s.[72] There is also evidence that in particular areas of the country devastation by fire, or the fear of it, encouraged insurance sales. Huge fires in Potton and Biggleswade in 1783 and 1785, for instance, encouraged the expansion of the Sun Fire Office's business in

Bedfordshire. The Potton fire destroyed more than fifty dwellings, 'the greatest part of the town,' with damage estimated at £25,000. In Biggleswade the fire destroyed 120 houses – nearly half the town – within five hours, a rate of destruction that suggests that much of what went up in flames was timber and plaster.[73] The Sun was quick to donate three dozen fire buckets to Potton, plus £105 to the fund for the relief of the victims there, as well as twenty guineas to Biggleswade towards a new fire engine.[74] In 1789 the Sun opened a new agency at Potton that soon became the company's largest premium earner by head of population.[75] Similarly, a major factor contributing to the success of insurance sales at Exeter, the Sun's largest agency, was concern about the firestorms that repeatedly swept the cob, thatch, and timber towns and villages of east Devon.

As well as the direct impact of fire, it is evident that the growth of property values and incomes, especially in the south of England, was a factor in the expansion of insurance outside London. The proportion of risks written on property outside the capital was just 10 per cent in 1730, but 45 per cent by the end of the century. Much of this increase took place in the prosperous home counties. Calculations from the Sun's agency records suggest that the southeast of England generated three times more premiums per head of population than the industrializing northwest, even at the end of the century. The gap between the southeast and other regions of Britain was wider still.[76] Average property values and average sums insured against fire were up to 35 per cent higher in London than elsewhere, and the effect of metropolitan price levels also ensured that property values in the home counties were higher than in the midlands, the north, or Scotland. Large parts of the southeast prospered from the continual diffusion of the capital's wealth throughout the eighteenth century. Commercial centres on major transit nodes contained a range of banking, financial, professional, and personal services that enticed the wealthy to invest in property there. Businessmen, in their functions as local improvement commissioners or members of corporations, also invested in local infrastructures. Such towns were invariably well built and improved, and so offered attractive terrain for fire insurers. Between 1736 and 1799, 110 improvement acts were passed for the market towns and ports of the south of England compared to only 15 acts for towns in the industrial midlands and the north.[77] As well as rebuilding in brick or stone, improvement encompassed paving, lighting, and street cleaning and widening, and many of these measures also helped reduce fire

Figure 4.1: Middlesex building deeds and sums insured on London property, 1725–96

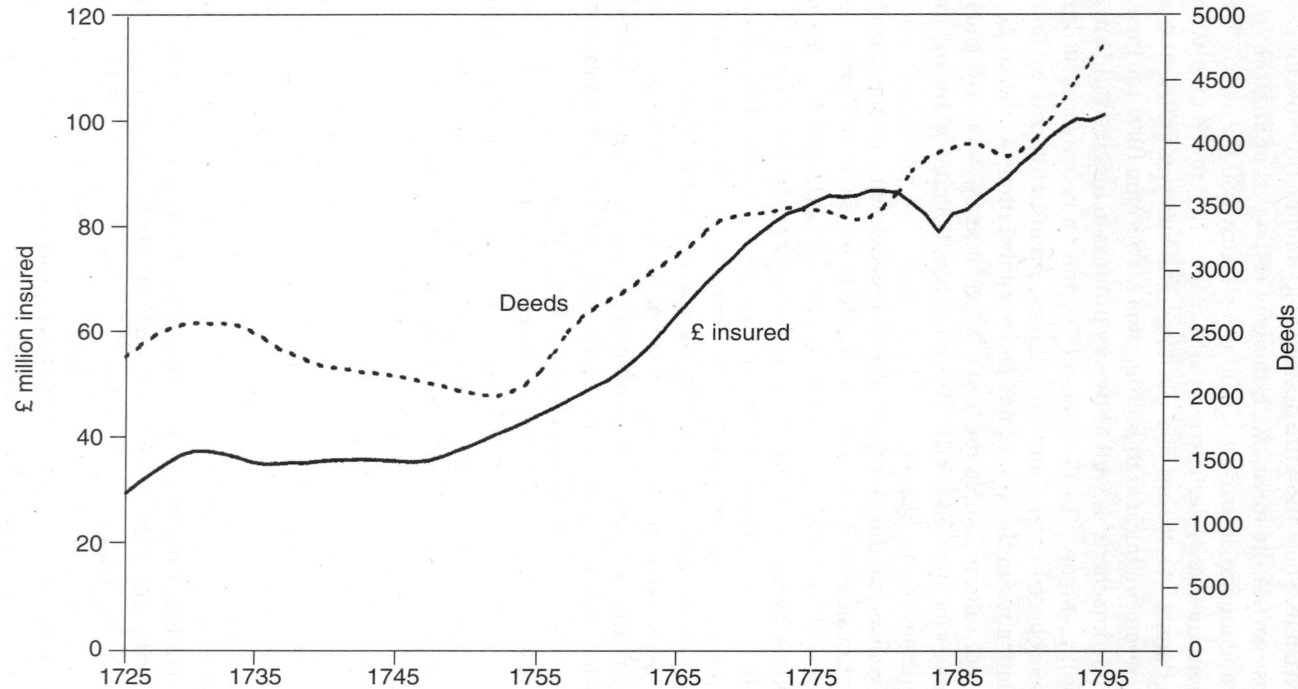


Source: Pearson, *Insuring the Industrial Revolution*, figure 2.1

hazards. Several of the towns generating the greatest volume of premiums per inhabitant for the Sun Fire Office obtained improvement acts, including Canterbury (1727), Salisbury (1737), Exeter (1760), Portsmouth (1768), and Weymouth (1776).

Despite the great diffusion of fire insurance beyond the metropolis, London remained the nation's biggest insurance market, indeed probably the most highly insured place on the planet. Insurances in London rose from £29m in 1725 to £99m by 1795. They expanded most rapidly with the construction boom that peaked around 1730, and again with the huge surge in house-building during the 1760s and early 1770s (see figure 4.1). There were some 95,000 houses in the bills (i.e., the City plus part of Westminster) in 1740, and about 130,000 active insurance policies on London buildings at this time, which suggests that the metropolis was already nearly fully insured by the three mutual and three stock companies operating there. At the end of the century there were some 155,000 policies issued on metropolitan property by these six offices, while there were 141,000 inhabited houses in the whole conurbation. The number of policies, of course, cannot be taken as an equivalent of the number of houses insured; nevertheless these estimates do suggest that no more than a small part of residential London remained uninsured in both 1740 and 1800.

By the middle of the eighteenth century fire insurance in the capital certainly reached well beyond the upper and middling classes. An insurance policy had become an everyday object in many homes, kept carefully by some in a corner cupboard with the best silver and by others, more casually, in a penny pocketbook or a tin box.[78] One illustration of how far fire insurance had penetrated through London society is given by the case of Elizabeth Calloway. Calloway, who kept a noisy and rather disreputable lodging house and brandy shop in Cecil Court, near St Martin's Lane, was able to insure her goods for £150 with the Royal Exchange Assurance in 1735, even though she admitted to her neighbours that 'sometimes she had not the value of twenty shillings in her shop, tho' sometimes she had more.'[79] A fire broke out in her house in the summer of that year, which burnt down two of her neighbours' houses. Suspected of an insurance fraud, Calloway was tried at the Old Bailey for arson, but was acquitted. Upon cross-examination, she appeared to have legitimate grounds for insuring her property. As she testified,

> the cook's shop joining to mine, the wainscot of my closet was often so very hot that I was afraid it would some time or other be set on fire, and for that reason I insured my house in the Exchange Insurance.

Figure 4.2: Average rates of loss (£%) on property insured by English fire insurance offices, 1725–1800

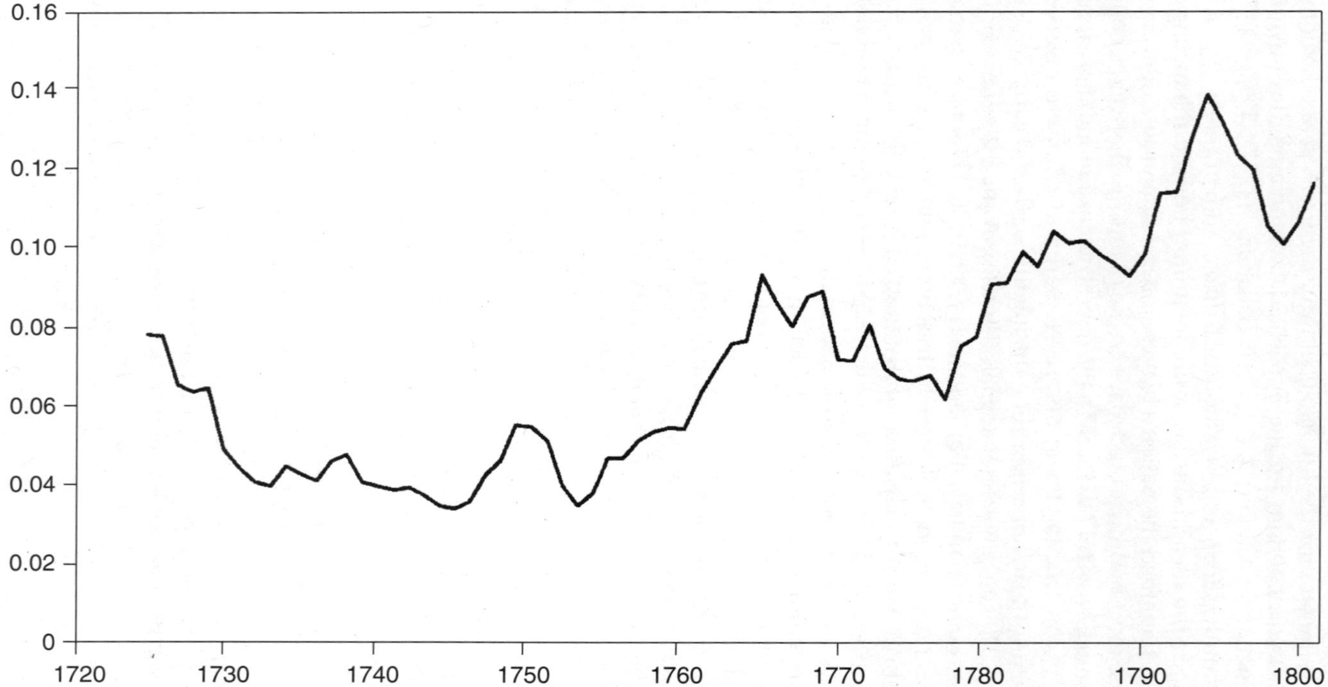


Source: Adapted from Pearson, *Insuring the Industrial Revolution*, figure 1.5

Other witnesses also testified to Calloway's concern about the dangers of candles in the house at night, particularly in the hands of drunken lodgers.

The multiplication of trades, industries, and property types, the survival of timber structures, and the limited impact of building legislation together ensured that fires remained an ever-present hazard in London and made the task of underwriting there increasingly complex. Losses by fire increased from the 1740s in four surges, peaking in 1748, 1764, 1783, and 1793, each peak exceeding the one before (see figure 4.2). Contemporaries were well aware of the problem. One writer, in discussing the best methods to prevent the spread of fires in houses and in shipping, noted in 1775 that fires were less frequent in Paris than in London, though Britain supposedly was the envy of the world for its 'wisdom of council, security of property, and humanity of government.'[80] 'I have heard it confidently asserted by persons well acquainted with London and Amsterdam,' wrote the lawyer Samuel Marshall in 1805, 'that after making all fair allowances, there is, upon average, more property destroyed by fire in the former in one year, than in the latter in seven.' A carpenter's servant at an arson trial in 1788 remarked on the frequency of salvage work generated by fires in the capital: 'I screened the rubbish at the fire; I have been used to that sort of work, these eighteen or nineteen years.'[81]

The intensity and cost of fires were greatest in the south and east of the capital, especially in the densely built riverside districts of Southwark, Rotherhithe, Wapping, Shadwell, and Ratcliffe. The level of fire damage was due to the many timber structures and hazardous materials and the poor fire-fighting facilities in these areas. The rate of destruction, however, as measured by the ratio of houses burnt down to the total housing stock in 1801, was greatest in the crowded central London parishes, covering the area from Holborn to Soho and Covent Garden, as well as in the City itself and the east end.[82] Memories of the Great Fire of 1666 remained acute for Londoners, aided by physical reminders, notably The Monument at the foot of London Bridge. Concerns continued to be raised through to the end of the century. In 1790, for instance, George Stonestreet, the secretary of the new Phoenix Fire Office, argued for the establishment of a night-time fire-watch and a fire jury for London to combat the growing incidence of arsonists trying to defraud the insurance companies.[83]

**Insurance and Risk in a World of Reason**

At one level, fire insurance can be seen as a rational response to the increased awareness of the threat of fire in an urban environment where property values were rising, but where the improvement of fire prevention and fire-fighting methods was limited by technology and by the methods and materials of construction, and where such improvements were usually lagging behind new hazards created by economic and industrial change. Successful fire underwriting, of course, depended on the law of large numbers and the ability to distribute risk in a big enough market. In this sense, eighteenth-century London provided suitable conditions, with a limited number of insurance companies informally cooperating to divide up that market and, through co-insurance, sharing individual risks. In smaller provincial centres, where the dangers of risk concentration were potentially greater, local fire insurance offices survived because of careful risk selection and close monitoring, aided by local and specialist knowledge.[84] Together with supply-side explanations of the growth of insurance, however, there were also a number of general social and cultural factors driving 'rational' responses to the fire hazard, that, arguably, were of equal importance.

Thomas has argued that Protestantism taught men and women to try methods of self-help in the face of calamities, before invoking supernatural aid.[85] From this developed a 'nascent statistical sense,' an awareness of patterns in apparently random behaviour. The search for quantifiable patterns in nature – the basis of insurance economics – was a key feature of the associationism in much eighteenth-century epistemology. Adam Smith, for example, argued that man derived pleasure from observing the similarity of objects and in reducing them 'into proper classes.'[86] For Smith, Hartley, and others, the 'mechanical power' or, more accurately, the neurology of the association of ideas was the means by which the surprise, wonder, uncertainty, or fear in finding novelty in nature could be contained.[87] Novelty could be demystified, and the passions aroused by it could be controlled, when the connection between the novel object or event and the known objects or events that they resemble was established.

> To some class or other of known objects he must refer it, and betwixt it and them he must find out some resemblance or other, before he can get

rid of that wonder, that uncertainty and anxious curiosity excited by its singular appearance.[88]

This idea of the 'domestication' of novelty and risk was reinforced during the eighteenth century by a burgeoning reportage.[89] Bernstein has observed that probability judgments are attached not to events but to descriptions of events. The more vivid and accurate the account, the greater the propensity to assign a probability value to the event described.[90] Eyewitness reports of earthquakes, floods, and fires, given publicity by a growing pamphlet and newspaper press from the late seventeenth century, pushed these events into the popular consciousness, and raised awareness among the educated and propertied classes of the need for preventive or remedial action. The same can be said of the increasing frequency during the third quarter of the century of reports of arson attacks and deliberate fires started by servants and disgruntled employees intent on theft or revenge.[91]

The ideology of private property, whose primacy was acknowledged in the constitutional settlement of 1688, underlined this search for pattern and predictability, by emphasizing the need to reduce uncertainty for the property-owning classes and bolster the social order. It was noted above that there was often a levelling aspect to the street theatre accompanying large urban fires, by which social differences could temporarily disappear as the poor found entertainment in the sufferings of their wealthier neighbours. Fire, therefore, could be viewed as a *social* as well as a physical and economic hazard, and efforts at fire prevention, fire education, and improved fire-fighting could derive from, not just the need to discipline this unruly natural element, but the desire to reduce as far as possible these moments of social levelling. As fire also frequently provided a tool for individual vengeance and a means of collective protest, improved fire prevention could be seen as a prophylactic against social disorder, while fire insurance offered some financial security against the threat to property.

That said, the levelling effect of large fires also offered opportunities to reassert paternalist social relations and the existing divisions of wealth and status. Large conflagrations were often reported as displays of social harmony in the face of a calamity affecting all classes. Municipal leaders commonly led the collective effort to fight fires that threatened their towns, and successive members of the Royal household from Charles II to George III visited the scene of many London fires in person, distributing largesse to encourage fire-fighters from the insurance brigades as well as from the crowd.

Finally, a rational approach to the fire hazard can also be related to the growth of humanitarianism, for efforts at fire prevention can be seen as part of a wider movement that included projects for reviving victims of drowning accidents and suicide attempts, the building of hospitals and dispensaries, and schemes, such as those of Thomas Coram and Jonas Hanway, for rescuing orphaned infants, destitute children, and 'penitent' prostitutes. Such projects, it is true, were justified on a mixture of grounds, including financial and patriotic: saving the poor rates, or arguments about national advantage. Religious compassion, however, also played a role, as it did in humanitarian arguments for the reform of prisons and the law of small debt.[92] Insurance, for its part, offered a privately funded means of rebuilding after fire damage, and thereby of realizing urban reformers' aspirations to greater public safety. This, together with the content of the building laws of the 1760s and 1770s that aimed to enforce a degree of architectural uniformity in townscapes, were influenced by the dominant aesthetic of symmetry and the straight line.[93]

There is some evidence that the insurance industry tried to increase fire awareness among the educated and propertied classes. In 1763 the London insurance offices formed a joint committee to press Parliament for further fire prevention legislation and to reinforce the regulations on party walls. Their lobbying obtained a clause in the London building act of 1764 empowering them, where there was a suspicion of fraud, to rebuild or repair houses damaged by fire rather than pay a claim. This gave insurers direct control over at least some of the building in the capital. Insurance offices also supported the building act of 1772, which encouraged chimney sweeping by imposing fines for occupiers of properties whose chimneys caught fire.[94] Public awareness must also have been raised by the substantial amounts of money and fire-fighting equipment donated to towns throughout England by the Sun and other offices, by their investment in water supplies, and by the expense, time, and effort they invested in prosecuting arsonists from the 1760s.

The reaction of insurance offices to large fires also pressured those looking for insurance into ensuring that their properties complied with insurers' requirements. After the fire at Gravesend in 1727, which cost the Sun Fire Office £9,400, the office resolved that in future it would only insure timber and thatch properties where they did not adjoin a similar building.[95] Measures taken from the end of the eighteenth century to improve the risk assessment of large industrial properties encouraged policyholders to make them safer. These included subdividing risks and hiking up premium rates in response to timber and unsecured combustible materials, unguarded machinery, contiguity to fire hazards, dangerous stoves, pipes projecting through floors and roofs, use of candles instead of oil or gas lights, and dirt, grease, and hazardous waste materials accumulating on floors in candle-lit rooms and around flues and engines. The presence of any of these elements resulted in higher premiums and lower limits on the amount that an insurer was willing to cover, or they could lead to cancellation or a refusal to renew policies.[96] By the 1820s, many of the larger manufacturers had come to accept insurance as an essential part of business management. As one flax mill owner put it, fire insurance was 'a precaution so obviously proper that it is needless to say anything on the propriety of it.'[97]

### Insurance and Risk in a World of Passion and Uncertainty

The purchase of a fire insurance policy, however, cannot just be regarded as a rational response to the perceived dangers of fire and to external legal and financial pressures on manufacturers, builders, and property owners. First, it must be emphasized that policyholders were not buying a scientific product. The fire insurance industry was not entirely rational or optimally efficient in its business practices, nor was it consistently innovative and dynamic in its approach to risk assessment. Pricing for the joint-stock insurance companies was a hit or miss affair, and risk categorization remained crude. For much of this period companies failed to introduce the systematic analysis of their own underwriting data upon which more accurate and differentiated premium rates might have been based, and they failed to design more complex financial structures and systems of accounting that might have offset the increasing volatility of the industry as it expanded and became more competitive. What Daston has called the 'anti-statistical bias' of eighteenth-century insurance was the product of an age that did not yet reject pre-probabilistic practices, or the legal notion of risk as a 'genuine' and unquantifiable uncertainty.

This changed only slowly. As the eighteenth century drew to a close, new sources of combustion hazard appeared and there were novel, larger, and more complex risks in the shape of new machinery, processes, and materials to insure. This increased the pressure on underwriters to discriminate between risks with greater precision, to spread risk across regional and national boundaries, and to put fire insurance on a more scientific and financially sound footing. Yet developments such as the continuous monitoring of the distribution and profitability of insured risks had not progressed very far before 1800. The diffusion of such practices among the major fire insurance offices did not occur until the 1820s when the three major London offices first shared extensive data on underwriting performance in the worst categories of large industrial risks.[98]

Second, customer attitudes towards risk remained ambiguous. Even among the insured, perceptions of hazard events continued to be influenced by a mixture of beliefs in both science and providence. Because of its persistent 'anti-statistical bias,' fire insurance could offer only limited support to the task of domesticating fear. The meaning of insurance, as well as risk, therefore remained profoundly ambivalent. In theory, the purchase of insurance could be seen as a rational management of hazard on the part of the insured, but this was not always the case in practice. Frequently, policyholders took out insurance as a means of alleviating uncertainty about potential losses, but then continued to be careless in and around the sources of fire. This was the case, for example, with Elizabeth Calloway cited above, where her concern to insure against fire was not coupled with any apparent attempt to reduce the drunken behaviour in and around her house, an attitude that naturally raised suspicions about her real motives for taking out the insurance. Prudence was no more an outcome of insurance than it was a product of the science of prediction. Indeed, in references to policies on residential property it is difficult to find evidence of any greater sense of the danger of fire emerging during the eighteenth century that was fostered by the presence of insurance. On the contrary, many contemporaries continued to believe that the security provided by insurance 'naturally' gave rise to 'carelessness and inattention' as well as to more sinister moral hazards, notably arson with intent to defraud insurers.[99]

Moral hazard, however, does not entirely explain the curious coexistence of very extensive insurance against hazards with rather limited attempts to alleviate their physical threat. The principle answer is to be found, much deeper, in the ambivalence towards measurable risk and unquantifiable uncertainty that characterized eighteenth-century Britons. Even some of those advocating a rational approach to fire prevention continued to believe that fires and other disasters were dictated by providence alone. For one such writer in 1775, they were 'unhappy accidents which can never be foreseen by the experience of years, the depth of wisdom, or the aid of learning.'[100]

Insurance, therefore, did not change popular attitudes to physical risk quickly, if at all. The continuing presence of a high proportion of timber in London building at the end of the century suggests that the new regulations of the 1770s, the increasing exhortations to safeguard sources of fire in the home and workshop, and the incentives offered by insurers to those who did, had only a limited impact on behaviour. After major fires in provincial towns, the pressure to rebuild quickly in the face of homelessness and destitution often resulted in a failure to rebuild in brick and tile, realign house-fronts, make streets broader, and reduce the dangers of fire traps. In 1767, the Sun Fire Office reacted to 'heavy losses' in Devon by raising its premium rate on thatched property there by 50 per cent and insisting that insurance on any buildings destroyed by fire would not be renewed if, when rebuilt, they were roofed in thatch. Despite this, thatch fires continued to be frequent, and in 1800 the office even had to extend the higher rate, rather belatedly, to Dorset.[101] Apathetic, negligent, or providential attitudes to fire hazards by property owners, their tenants, and house-builders sat uneasily with the interpretation of insurance as a rational response to measurable risk.

The consequences of such ambivalence were exposed in the most unlikely places. In 1789 Parliament appointed a committee to examine the public and private buildings in and around Westminster Hall. The committee, which included several of Britain's greatest architects – Adam, Holland, Dance, Soane – found that most of the buildings were in 'a decayed and ruinous state, and that a great part of them, from their situation, and the Occupancy thereof, are in great Danger from fire.'[102] The buildings to the east of New Palace Yard, which included the Lottery and Annuity offices,

> are principally constructed with timber, lath and plaistered, or Weather-boarded; in many places propt up, and in others contiguous to low sheds, equally combustible.[103]

The committee examined roofs and cellars, chimneys and flues, the latter running up in 'old decayed piers' and blocked with 'combustible materials,' and came to the unanimous opinion

> that the hazard they have been, and still are, exposed to from fire is so great, that we cannot help being astonished at their having so long and so happily escaped … from the most imminent danger.[104]

The distinguished members of the committee expressed concern that these disturbing conditions, clearly neglected for decades and without any fire engines or supplies of water kept in the immediate vicinity, could be found in the seat of the nation's government. Nothing much came of this alarm, however. The palace of Westminster subsequently burnt to the ground in 1834. This was a nation with the greatest insurance industry in the world, yet also a nation with a persistent and profound ambivalence towards the dangers of fire, which the practice of insurance and the rule of legislators had yet to resolve.

## NOTES

1 Joanna Bourke, *Fear: A Cultural History* (London: Virago, 2005).
2 Keith Thomas, *Religion and the Decline of Magic* (Harmondsworth, UK: Penguin, 1973), 98, 128.
3 Bourke, *Fear*, 56–61. For a similar development in America, see Mark Tebeau, *Eating Smoke: Fire in Urban America 1800–1950* (Baltimore: John Hopkins University Press, 2003), 89–125, 202–43.
4 Ulrich Beck, *Risikogesellschaft: Auf dem Weg in eine andere Moderne* (Frankfurt/Main: Suhrkamp, 1986).
5 Lorraine J. Daston, *Classical Probability in the Enlightenment* (Princeton: Princeton University Press,1988); Ian Hacking, *The Emergence of Probability* (Cambridge: 1975); Geoffrey Clark, *Betting on Lives: The Culture of Life Insurance in England, 1695–1775* (Manchester: Manchester University Press, 1999); Barry Supple, *The Royal Exchange Assurance* (Cambridge: Cambridge University Press,1970), chap. 1.
6 Robin Pearson, *Insuring the Industrial Revolution: Fire Insurance in Great Britain 1700–1850* (Aldershot: Ashgate, 2004).
7 George Griffin Stonestreet, *Reflections occasioned by the frequency of Fires in the Metropolis* (London: J. Walter, 1790), ix.
8 Pearson, *Insuring the Industrial Revolution*, 32–5.
9 E.L. Jones, S. Porter, and M. Turner, *A Gazeteer of English Urban Fire Disasters, 1500–1900*, Historical Geography Research Papers no.13, (Norwich: Institute of Historical Research, 1984), count large fires as those that destroyed ten or more 'houses' (as defined by contemporaries).

10 *Gentleman's Magazine* (hereafter *GM*), 1 (1731), entry for 5 June. The damage estimates are those of Jones et al., *Gazeteer*. The account in the *Gentleman's Magazine* states 200 houses were burnt at a 'computed' loss of £1.5m. The latter figure is undoubtedly a wild exaggeration.

11 *London Magazine* (hereafter *LM*), 12 (1743), 202; *GM* 13 (1743), 217; Jones et al., *Gazeteer*. Shipwash (later Sheepwash) had 74 houses in 1801.

12 As with the figures for Tiverton, Crediton, and Honiton, these estimates express the total number of houses burnt down in recorded fires during the eighteenth century as a percentage of the total numbers of inhabited houses in the 1801 census. This method obviously understates the true relative levels of damage.

13 Jenny Uglow, *Hogarth: A Life and a World* (London: Faber and Faber,1997), 201, 253–4, 277, 309–10, 666–8. For an interpretation of *The Times*, see also Ronald Paulson, *Hogarth: His Life, Art and Times*, 2 vols. (New Haven: Yale University Press, 1971). In 1874, long after his death, fire also devoured Hogarth's painting *Strolling Actresses Dressing in a Barn*, painted in 1738.

14 *The Old Bailey Proceedings Online* (www.oldbaileyonline.org), ref. t17880402-18, David Clary, Elizabeth Gombert, damage to property: arson, 2 April 1788, evidence of Samuel Suddenwood.

15 These details are compiled from a reading of reports of fires in the *London Magazine*, the *Gentleman's Magazine*, and the *Annual Register* 1731–80, as well as the transcripts of arson cases heard between 1735 and 1794, in *The Old Bailey Proceedings Online* (www.oldbaileyonline.org).

16 Donald Gibson, ed., *A Parson in the Vale of White Horse* (Gloucester: Alan Sutton, 1982), 110–11.

17 Henry Fielding, *The History of Tom Jones* (1749, repr. Harmondsworth, UK: Penguin, 1966), 528.

18 *GM* 17 (1747), 342. Another fire in Honiton in 1765 lasted seven hours.

19 *GM* 10 (1740), 91.

20 *GM* 45 (1775), 636.

21 *Annual Register* (hereafter *AR*) (1775), 137.

22 *AR* (1767), 71; *GM* 34 (1764), 395.

23 *LM* 26 (1757), 96.

24 *GM* 1 (1731), 221.

25 *GM* 13 (1743), 494; idem, 1 (1731), 221; *LM*, 38 (1769), 273.

26 *GM* 13 (1743), 494; idem, 32 (1762), 341.

27 For examples of domestic servants setting fire to their employers' houses after a theft, see *GM* 33 (1763), 358, 360.

28 6 Anne c. 31. This stated that servants would face eighteen months hard

labour in jail or else a fine of £100, to be distributed among the victims of the fire. Liverpool Record Office, Liverpool, London & Globe archives, Globe 5, Handbill, 24 June 1803. An extract from this act was attached to the agents' instructions circulated by the Sun in 1807. Sun Fire Office, 'Instructions,' 292–3.

29 Thomas Gray, *The Letters of Thomas Gray*, ed. D.C. Tovey, 3 vols. (London: L. Bell, 1900–12), vol. 2, letter CXVI, 115.

30 *GM* (1758), 551; *AR*, 6 November 1766.

31 Thomas, *Religion and the Decline of Magic*, 93, 98, 128–9.

32 Guildhall Library (hereafter GL), Ms 11932/2, Sun Fire Office, Committee of Management Minutes (hereafter CMM), 13 August 1730, 17 February 1732.

33 Horace Walpole, *The Yale Edition of Horace Walpole's Correspondence*, ed. W.S. Lewis (London: Oxford University Press, 1967), letter to Sir Horace Mann, 28 May 1763; Robert Southey, *Letters from England*, ed. J. Simmons (London: Cresset Press, 1951), 37.

34 Roy Porter, *English Society in the Eighteenth Century* (Harmondsworth, UK: Penguin, 1982).

35 J.T. Smith, *Nollekens and His Times* (1828, repr. London: Turnstile Press, 1949), 196. For London crowds filling the streets at fire alarms, see also Daniel Defoe, *The Fortunes and Misfortunes of the Famous Moll Flanders* (1722, repr. Harmondsworth, UK: Penguin, 1994), 224–6.

36 Tobias Smollett, *The Expedition of Humphrey Clinker* (1771, repr. Oxford: Oxford University Press, 1966), 175–6, 299–300.

37 There is some evidence of the lesser destructiveness of fires, although not of their lesser frequency, outside the capital. There were 551 fires between 1735 and 1800 in which property insured by the Hand in Hand Office was totally destroyed. Fifty-eight of these occurred outside London. The average number of buildings destroyed by each 'country' fire was 1.7, compared to 2.9 in the London fires. Pearson, *Insuring the Industrial Revolution*, 103.

38 L. Stone and J.C.F. Stone, *An Open Elite? England 1540–1880* (Oxford: Clarendon Press, 1984), 368–9.

39 *LM* 20 (1751), 427.

40 All details of fires from *Annual Register*, *Gentleman's Magazine*, and *London Magazine*.

41 *GM* 41 (1771), 469.

42 John Cleland, *Fanny Hill, or Memoirs of a Woman of Pleasure* (1748–9, repr. Harmondsworth, UK: Penguin, 1985), 212.

43 Southey, *Letters from England*, 457.

44 Peter Gay, *The Enlightenment: An Interpretation*, vol. 2: *The Science of Freedom* (New York: W.W. Norton, 1969), 304-6.
45 Edmund Burke, *A Philosophical Enquiry into the Origin of our Ideas of the Sublime and Beautiful*, ed. J.T. Boulton (1759 ed.; repr. London: Routledge & Kegan Paul, 1958), 40, 51, 61–3.
46 'If we are careful to guard ourselves from imaginary sorrows and vain fears, we must also resign many enchanting illusions: for shallow must be the discernment which fails to discover that raptures and ectasies arise from error': Mary Wollstonecroft, *A Vindication of the Rights of Man* (1790), extract reprinted in Andrew Ashfield and Peter de Bolla, eds., *The Sublime: A Reader in British Eighteeenth-Century Aesthetic Theory* (Cambridge: Cambridge University Press,1996), 294–300.
47 Edmund Burke, *Reflections on the Revolution in France* (1790, repr. Harmondsworth, UK: Penguin, 1968).
48 Bourke, *Fear*, 76.
49 Adam Smith, *The Theory of Moral Sentiments*, (Oxford: Clarendon Press, 1976), 28–9, pt. 1, sec. 2, chap. 1.
50 Adam Smith, 'The Principles which lead and direct Philosophical Enquiries; illustrated by the History of Astronomy,' in his *Essays on Philosophical Subjects*, ed. W.P.D. Wightman and J.C. Bryce, *The Glasgow Edition of the Works and Correspondence of Adam Smith*, vol. 3 (Oxford: Clarendon Press, 1980), 33–105.
51 M.P. Tilley, *A Dictionary of the Proverbs in England in the Sixteenth and Seventeenth Centuries* (Ann Arbor: University of Michigan Press, 1950), F135.
52 Samuel Richardson, *Pamela; or Virtue Rewarded* (1740, repr. Harmondsworth, UK: Penguin, 1985), 192.
53 For a similar range of responses to disasters, see Bourke, *Fear*, 276.
54 Defoe, *Moll Flanders*, 300–1.
55 Cleland, *Fanny Hill*, 87.
56 12 Geo. I c. 35. This act was amended in 1739 by 3 Geo. II c. 22, but to no great effect.
57 4 Geo. III c. 14; 6 Geo. III c. 37.
58 14 Geo. III c. 78. John Summerson, *Georgian London* (Harmondsworth, UK: Penguin, 1962), 123-5.
59 Pearson, *Insuring the Industrial Revolution*, 60–1.
60 *LM*, 7 March 1773.
61 M. Dorothy George, *London Life in the Eighteenth Century* (London: Penguin, 1966), 78–82; S. Porter, 'The Great Fire of Gravesend, 1727,' *Southern History* 12 (1990), 19–33; G.V. Blackstone, *A History of the British Fire Service* (London: Routledge, 1957), 15–34.

62 Examples include University of Oxford, *Orders agreed upon by the Heads of Houses for the Preventing and Quenching of Fire*, 23 October 1671; and Edinburgh Town Council, *Fire Ordinance*, 1 May 1674. For similar efforts in early modern French cities, see Penny Roberts, 'Agencies Human and Divine: Fire in French Cities, 1520–1720,' in W.G. Naphy and P. Roberts, eds., *Fear in Early Modern Society* (Manchester: Manchester University Press, 1997), 9–27.

63 Corporation of London, *An Act for Preventing and Suppressing of Fires within the City of London and Liberties thereof* (London: Nath. Brook, 1668); 6 Anne c. 31; 7 Anne c. 17. See Jacob Giles, *The Statute-Law Common-plac'd: or a Second General Table to the Statutes* (2nd ed., London: E. & R. Nutt and R. Gosling, 1730), 113.

64 D.W. Jones, *War and Economy in the Age of William III and Marlborough* (Oxford: Basil Blackwell, 1988), 163.

65 Pearson, *Insuring the Industrial Revolution*, 83–4; Porter, 'Great Fire of Gravesend,' 29.

66 Examples include Commiseratus, *A Proposal to prevent such dreadful Conflagrations as have lately happened in London* (London: Thomas Trye, 1748); Rev Stephen Hales, 'A proposal for checking in some degree the progress of fires,' Royal Society, *Philosophical Transactions*, vol. 45 (1748), 277–9; Anon., *Various methods to prevent fires in houses and shipping and for preserving the lives of people at fires* (London: T. Evans, 1775).

67 Paulson, *Hogarth*, vol. 2, 371; S. West, 'Wilkes's Squint: Synecdochic Physiognomy and Political Identity in Eighteenth-Century Print Culture,' *Eighteenth-Century Studies*, 33 (1999), 65–84.

68 Uglow, *Hogarth*, 642; *GM* (1761), 414.

69 Uglow, *Hogarth*, 477–8. For an 'official' account of the disaster, see Gaetano Ruggieri and Gioseppe Sarti, *A Description of the Machine for the Fireworks, with all its Ornaments: and A Detail of the Manner in which they were exhibited in St James's Park, Thursday April 27, 1749* (London: William Bowyer, 1749). See also the many references to fireworks in Garrick's letters: David Garrick, *The Letters of David Garrick*, ed. David M. Little and George M. Kahrl (London: Oxford University Press, 1963).

70 David Hartley, *Address to the Right Honorable the Lord Mayor and Corporation of the City of London* (London, 1788).

71 L. Angiolini, *Lettere sull' Inghilterra* (1790, repr., Milan: Bompiani, 1944), 24; Christopher F. Lindsey, 'David Hartley (1731–1813),' in *Oxford Dictionary of National Biography* (Oxford: Oxford University Press, 2004). A drawing of the obelisk at Putney can be found on the inside front cover of David Hartley, *An Account of the Invention and Use of Fire Plates for the Security of Ships and Buildings against Fire* (London, 1785).

72 Pearson, *Insuring the Industrial Revolution*, 22.

73 Victoria County History, *Bedfordshire*, vol. 2, 209, 237; GL, Ms 11932/12, Sun Fire Office, CMM, 21 August 1783. Potton and Biggleswade had 237 and 298 inhabited houses, respectively, in 1801, and probably rather fewer in the 1780s.

74 GL, Ms 11932/12, Sun Fire Office, CMM, 9 October 1783.

75 Pearson, *Insuring the Industrial Revolution*, table 3.8.

76 Pearson, *Insuring the Industrial Revolution*, 113.

77 E.L. Jones and M.E. Falkus, 'Urban Improvement and the English Economy in the Seventeenth and Eighteenth Centuries,' *Research in Economic History* 4 (1979), 193–233.

78 *The Old Bailey Proceedings Online* (www.oldbaileyonline.org), ref. t173811011-9, Lucy Brooks, theft, 11 October 1738; ref. t17860222-48, George Lyons, Thomas Hopkins, theft: burglary, 22 February 1786; ref. t17980912-70, William Abell, theft: simple grand larceny, 12 September 1798.

79 *The Old Bailey Proceedings Online*, ref. t17350702-42, Elizabeth Calloway, damage to property: arson, 2 July 1735.

80 Anon., *Various methods to prevent fires in houses*, 64.

81 *The Old Bailey Proceedings Online* (www.oldbaileyonline.org), ref. t17880402-18, David Clary, Elizabeth Gombert, damage to property: arson, 2 April 1788, evidence of Anthony Wray.

82 Pearson, *Insuring the Industrial Revolution*, table 2.2.

83 Stonestreet, *Reflections occasioned by the frequency of Fires in the Metropolis*.

84 Robin Pearson, 'Taking Risks and Containing Competition: Diversification and Oligopoly in the Fire Insurance Markets of the North of England in the Early Nineteenth Century,' *Economic History Review*, 46 (1993), 39–64.

85 Thomas, *Religion and the Decline of Magic*, 784–94.

86 Smith, 'Principles which lead and direct,' 37–8.

87 David Hartley, *Observations on Man, His Frame, his Duty, and His Expectations* (London: James Leake and William Frederick, 1749); James Long, *An Inquiry into the Origin of Human Appetites and Afections, shewing how each arises from Association* (Lincoln, 1747), reprinted in Samuel Parr, ed., *Metaphysical Tracts by English Philosophers of the Eighteenth Century* (London, 1837), 43-170; David Hume, *A Treatise of Human Nature* (1739-40, reprinted Oxford: Clarendon Press, 1978), book I, sections II-IV, 7-13. On the link between the 'physiological dynamics of the imagination' and the passions, see G.S. Rousseau, 'Science and the Discovery of the Imagination in Enlightened England,' *Eighteenth-Century Studies*, 3 no.1 (1969), 108-35.

88 Smith, 'Principles which lead and direct,' 40.

89 Lorraine J. Daston, 'The Domestication of Risk: Mathematical Probability and Insurance 1650–1830,' in L. Krüger, L.J. Daston, and M. Heidelberger, eds., *The Probabilistic Revolution,* Vol. 1: *Ideas in History* (Cambridge, MA: MIT Press, 1987), 237–60.

90 Peter L. Bernstein, *Against the Gods: The Remarkable Story of Risk* (New York: John Wiley & Sons,1996), 279.

91 On the increasing frequency of arson in this period, see Pearson, *Insuring the Industrial Revolution*, 84–5.

92 Paul Langford, *A Polite and Commercial People: England 1727–1783* (Oxford: Clarendon Press,1989), 490; J.S. Taylor, 'Jonas Hanway,' in *Oxford Dictionary of National Biography* (Oxford: Oxford University Press, 2004).

93 Keith Thomas, *Man and the Natural World* (London: Penguin, 1984), 256–7.

94 C.C. Knowles and P.H. Pitt, *The History of Building Regulation in London, 1189–1972* (London: Architecture Press, 1972), 40; *AR* (1772), 178–9.

95 GL, Ms 11932/1, 15, Sun Fire Office, CMM, 31 August 1727; Porter, 'Great Fire of Gravesend,' 28–9.

96 Robin Pearson, 'Fire Insurance and the British Textile Industries during the Industrial Revolution,' *Business History* 34 (1992), 1–19.

97 William Brown, *Early Days in a Dundee Mill 1819–23: Extracts from the Diary of William Brown, an Early Dundee Spinner*, ed. J. Hume (Dundee Abertay Historical Society Publication no. 2) (Dundee: Dundee Abertay Historical Society ,1980), 52–3.

98 Pearson, *Insuring the Industrial Revolution*, 196–7.

99 Samuel Marshall, *A Treatise on the Law of Insurance* (Boston, MA: D. Johnson, 1805), 682; Stonestreet, *Reflections occasioned by the frequency of Fires in the Metropolis*, 4–5.

100 Anon., *Various Methods*, preface.

101 GL, Ms11931/6, Sun Fire Office, General Committee Minutes, 9 April 1767; GL, Ms 11932/16, Sun Fire Office, CMM, 24 April 1800.

102 'Report of the Committee appointed to inspect the several houses ... immediately adjoining to Westminster Hall ... and to report ... in what manner the same may be best secured from the danger of fire ...' (22 July 1789), in Sheila Lambert, ed., *House of Commons Sessional Papers of the Eighteenth Century*, vol. 66 (Wilmington, DE: Scholarly Resources Inc.,1975), 263–9.

103 'Report of the Committee,' 268.

104 'Report of the Committee,' 268.

# 5 A Licence to Bet: Life Insurance and the Gambling Act in the British Courts

TIMOTHY ALBORN

More directly than any other enterprise apart from slavery, life insurance sets a price on human life. As it evolved in Britain during the nineteenth century, the insurance industry introduced a dizzying number of variations on this theme. For the individual purchasing an insurance policy, the value of life was translated into the sum required to care for dependents, loss of access to a wife's inheritance should she die before her father, the sum lost to a creditor in the event of death prior to repayment, and the loss of livelihood suffered by a tenant whose lease ended with the life of a third party. All these reasons for buying insurance established an equivalence between mortality and monetary value – a 'death nexus' that precisely and morbidly expressed the 'cash nexus' derided by Thomas Carlyle as the moral failing of British society. Insurance companies were fond of reminding people that this sort of commodification was often productive of much social and even moral good, and it indisputably met a growing economic demand. But since nobody knew for certain when they would die, a life insurance policy was also, by definition, a wager. And since wagers occupied a quite different category – 'intensely selfish in [their] action, and therefore anti-social and anti-christian,' as one insurance writer called them in 1891 – there was always at least the potential for the life insurance office to take on the darker colours of the gambling den.[1]

Lawmakers first became concerned about the slippery slope between life insurance and gambling during the third quarter of the eighteenth century, when the industry still catered to a relatively small, mostly aristocratic market. Their concern grew out of a rash of cases in which people had taken out policies on the lives of perfect strangers, often celebrities, on the morbid chance that they would die prematurely. As Geoffrey Clark has noted, the Hanoverian gentry preferred this form of gambling over nearly all other varieties; a quarter of all bets in one gentleman's club in the 1770s were on the death of a third party, compared to only 2.5 per cent on horse races. Prior to 1750 gambling on human life was condemned only on account of accompanying criminal acts, such as poisoning a man to collect on his life policy; after that time the wager itself came under increased scrutiny. Clark has plausibly linked this development to growing unease over slavery, since both 'threatened to shatter the emerging free-market ethos that individuals should have the liberty to engage in a commerce of things, but not of each other.'[2] In the event, Parliament intervened much earlier in the former case, with the passage of the Gambling Act of 1774.

The Gambling Act worked by requiring claimants to have a legitimate financial interest in the life of the insured. To prevent the 'mischievous kind of gaming' that had arisen in the previous half-century, it declared all other insurances on human life 'null and void, to all intents and purposes whatsoever.'[3] After 1774 it was only legal to collect on an insurance policy if a person (typically a wife or child) relied on the insured for income or was a creditor who stood to lose if the insured died before repaying the loan. Clark has argued that although the act 'was fairly successful at suppressing outright wagers, it could not uniformly segregate the prudential motives prompting proper, indemnifying insurance from the uninterested passions fueling speculation.'[4] Even so, this statute remained on the books as the official dividing line between life insurance and gambling for the next 135 years, leaving judges, customers, and life offices to make do with its uncertain provisions as best they could.

The Gambling Act's ambiguity recurrently threatened to impede the expansion of life insurance throughout the nineteenth century. As Clark indicates, the chief problem in this case lay in life insurance's dangerous commingling of things and people. The challenge for judges and insurance companies alike was to keep those two categories as separate as possible without overly hindering the growth of the industry. Their efforts were tolerably successful in the case of upper-class life insurance.[5] The increasingly impersonal and standardized nature of these transactions allowed judges to come to terms with the fact that many life policies, though formally instruments of gambling, were largely irrelevant to the moral issues raised by the spectre of betting on human life. The result was that judges followed companies in adopting a set of principles that rendered the act all but a dead letter after mid-century.

The case was far different once life insurance spread from the upper-class market to working-class customers after 1850. For one thing, the primary reason working people bought life insurance – to pay for a relative's funeral costs – did not formally qualify as an 'insurable interest' under the Gambling Act; hence at least half of the tens of millions of such policies issued between 1850 and 1909 were technically illegal. Adding to the problem, judges doubted the companies' ability to restrain their customers' alleged passion for gambling; company directors doubted their ability to prevent salesmen from attracting business by taking bets on neighbourhood fatalities; and customers soon realized that the formal illegality of their policies entitled them to a refund if the person insured failed to die soon enough to 'pay.' The result was that companies sporadically appealed to the Gambling Act to quash what they saw as egregious cases of black-market wagering, while customers increasingly sued for back premiums. In response, late Victorian judges wavered between punishing working-class 'gamblers' for their depravity in treating neighbours like race horses, and punishing the companies for encouraging (through their agents) such allegedly immoral behaviour.

This chapter begins by recounting the relative ease with which companies and judges stabilized the meaning of 'insurable interest' in the case of upper-class insurance, by examining the two leading cases of *Godsall v. Boldero* (1807) and *Dalby v. India and London Life* (1854). It then turns to the more complex case of working-class life insurance, by sampling a succession of trials that exhibited a variety of appeals to the Gambling Act. Finally, it briefly discusses companies' efforts to clarify the act in 1909 by lobbying legislators to revise the meaning of 'insurable interest' for working-class customers, by increasing supervision over agents and customers, and by introducing new forms of marketing that sought to teach customers to associate insurance with financial security rather than gaming. What was at stake in each of these cases was the determination of a boundary between legitimate and illegitimate insurance, in an insurance market that appealed to all social classes because of – not in spite of – the fact that it often shaded imperceptibly into gambling.

## Gambling and Life Insurance, 1807–1854

The branch of upper-class life insurance that did most to expose the Gambling Act's ambiguous language concerned policies taken out by creditors against the contingency of debtors dying before they could repay their loan. To guarantee the legality of such policies, life offices routinely ascertained the fact of the loan; as long as the insurance did not exceed the sum of money that was lent, the lender could not be said to be speculating on the death of the debtor. Once such policies had been in force a few years, however, their legal status became more difficult to determine. What happened if a creditor continued to keep up the insurance policy after the debt had been repaid? Or what if the debt was repaid in installments, but the creditor kept up the original level of coverage? Such questions raised the distinct possibility that many, perhaps the majority, of such policies were technically illegal when the claim was actually paid. And the legality of third-party policies was a major issue in the early nineteenth century when roughly a third of all policies, and probably half of the sums assured, were of this variety.[6]

Lord Ellenborough clarified these legal questions at King's Bench in 1807, although he did so in a way that would create intolerable levels of unpredictability for prospective third-party insurers.[7] The decisive case, *Godsall v. Boldero*, concerned a seven-year term policy for £500 on the life of William Pitt, which was taken out from the Pelican life office as security against a debt. The Pelican had resisted the claim on the grounds that by the time it was ready to pay, the debt had already been cancelled by means of a special parliamentary grant that cleared the former prime minister's outstanding commitments. When Godsall sued for his £500, the company's lawyer invoked the Gambling Act, arguing that 'if this policy may be enforced ... every creditor may gamble upon the life of his debtor by way of insurance, ... and upon his death he would be entitled to double satisfaction of his debt.' He also compared the case to that of a marine policyholder who claimed a total loss even though he had already been indemnified by means of salvage. Godsall's lawyer countered that the Pelican should pay the claim since they had been fairly compensated for the risk, urging that in such contracts 'the premium is not calculated upon the risk of the insolvency of the person whose life is insured, but solely on the probability of the duration of the life.' Ellenborough sided with the Pelican, ruling that the policy was 'in its nature a contract of indemnity, as distinguished from a contract by way of gaming or wagering.'[8]

By restricting third-party life policies to the indemnification of remaining sums owed by insured debtors after they died, Ellenborough endowed life insurers with blanket deniability in the event of such policies falling due. Companies soon discovered that such power was double-edged, since it threatened to dissuade creditors from taking out policies for fear that a company would postpone payment until other means of securing the debt had been exhausted. After the Asylum Life Assurance Company successfully appealed to the Gambling Act to dispute a child endowment policy in 1830, insurers 'received applications for written acknowledgments that the Directors will not avail themselves of any such advantage, in cases which bear a great analogy to that which has just been decided against the public.'[9] A typical company response to this sort of fear was by the Alliance, which spent a decade pondering the proper course to take when 'the Assured has a shifting interest in the Life' after first learning in 1827 that it could challenge any policy that failed Ellenborough's strict standard. Eventually its board decided that it was not worth the trouble to determine the technical legality of the insurance beyond its initial issue.[10] Other offices followed a similar trajectory, first disputing claims in isolated cases, then eventually guaranteeing customers that *Godsall* would have no impact on their decision to meet an initial obligation.

In *Dalby v. India and London Life Assurance Company*, the Court of Common Pleas caught up with the life offices' practice, deciding (in the words of Justice Parke) that a 'much more reasonable construction' of the Gambling Act was 'that, if there is an interest at the time of the policy, it is not a wagering policy, and that the true value of that interest may be recovered, in exact conformity with the words of the contract itself.' The case involved an attempt by the India and London to deny payment on a policy that it had originally accepted as a reinsurance from the Anchor Life Insurance Company, but which had subsequently been taken over by an Anchor director who kept the policy in force. In ordering the India and London to pay, Parke appealed both to the customer's right to know the exact value of his purchase and to the fact that *Godsall* had been 'universally disregarded' by nearly all life offices. The lawyer who argued the Anchor's case, George Bramwell, repeated the earlier claim in Godsall's defence that a life policy was 'a simple and absolute contract to pay a given sum of money on the death of the life,' and hence did not qualify as an indemnity.[11] He added that Ellenborough had bestowed powers on life offices that they had, in practice, been unwilling to exercise: for instance, the right 'to demand the money back, if the debtor's executors, – say, ten years after his death, – become possessed of funds wherewith to pay the debt.'[12]

Parke's decision in *Dalby*, closely following Bramwell's arguments, firmly established that the payment of a life claim was not the same as an indemnification for a loss. To this extent, his reasoning was sound.[13] What his ruling overlooked, however, was the fact that any insurance policy that professed to do more than indemnify against a contingent loss is, by definition, equivalent to a wager. This had been Ellenborough's point when he implied that life insurance was *either* 'a contract of indemnity' *or* 'a contract by way of gaming or wagering.' Judges in the *Dalby* case claimed that their decision left the Gambling Act intact as a secure protection against 'colourable insurances' such as when a 'man might lend another 5*l*., to enable him to insure for 10,000*l*.'[14] But this example was no different from lending a man £10,000 for a few weeks, then keeping all but £5 of that sum in force as a life policy – which is exactly what *Dalby* legalized. Parke's contrary claim notwithstanding, it was illogical to assert that an insurable interest at the outset necessarily meant that it was 'not a wagering policy.'[15]

The fact of the matter was that few people by the mid-nineteenth century were concerned about the possibility that life insurance might qualify as a subset of 'wagering.' Hence the mathematician Augustus De Morgan, in an 1838 critique of *Godsall*, argued that 'the contract of insurance, be it gambling, or be it not, rests entirely upon the permission given by the law to consider a high chance of a small sum as good consideration for a low chance of a large sum.'[16] A half-century later, industry spokesmen were even more brazen in their identification of life insurance and gambling, as when the Law Union's medical officer urged that his line of work was 'a very moral thing, and is very charitable; but there is no doubt it is a form of gambling ... and we all go to the office, and back lives instead of horses.'[17] One reason for this departure from earlier efforts to segregate insurance and gambling into two distinct categories is that late Victorians had started to distinguish between different sorts of gambling, some of which were apparently good for society. Viviana Zelizer's comments regarding American life insurance in the late nineteenth century are just as relevant to British opinion at the time: 'as risk increasingly became an integral part of the ... economic system, certain forms of risk taking and speculation assumed new respectability. Rational speculation that dealt with already existent risks was differentiated from pure gambling which created artificial risk.'[18]

Alongside such shifts in perception had evolved changes in the practice of life insurance, which erased many of its earlier overlaps with 'pure gambling.' One of these was a new willingness by most offices after 1850 to offer standardized 'surrender values' to parties who wanted to drop their policies – a category of people that included many creditors whose debts had been repaid. This practice superseded the previous course taken by customers in such cases, which was to auction off the policy to the highest bidder, who would continue to pay the premiums and then collect the claim when the insured party died.[19] Hence a precisely calculable, private, and wholly impersonal transaction took the place of an unseemly public spectacle, one that the insurance reformer Elizur Wright pointedly compared to slavery.[20] Once such changes were underway, upper-class customers and companies benefited equally from the predictable playing field that was achieved by pretending the Gambling Act did not apply to them, and neither side had an incentive to take the other to court as a means of resolving their grievances.

## The Grey Market in Working-Class Life Insurance

When companies started to extend life insurance to a working-class market after 1860, they opened the way for a whole new crop of technically illegal third-party policies. The main contingency that these 'industrial' offices guarded against, in exchange for weekly premiums of several pence, was the cost associated with providing a 'proper' burial for a family member. Unlike third-party policies involving loans, however, which were at least legal at the outset of the contract, the Gambling Act did not recognize liability to pay funeral expenses as an 'insurable interest' in another person's life. The only exception was when the family member was an adult male who took out the policy in his own name, since the benefit (usually between £10 and £50) could be said to be used to support the man's dependents. No such 'interest' existed in the millions of cases in which husbands wanted to take policies out on their wives, parents on their children, and on through the family tree to grandchildren, cousins, and in-laws.[21] Most of these people could usually find a company willing to sell them a policy on someone else's life, but until 1909 they could not find a statute declaring that it was legal.

Beyond these technically illegal policies, it was certainly the case that many working-class policyholders broke the spirit as well as the letter of the Gambling Act – although the extent to which this happened is difficult to determine. At the very least, reported cases indicate that conditions existed for this sort of street betting to flourish. When a Bradford poor law guardian told of a man suffering from 'cancer in the mouth' who died with twelve policies on his life, he observed that 'the agent insured the man without ever seeing him, but his friends knowing that it was cancer, knew it would be fatal in the end.'[22] Many court cases similarly told of people dying prematurely with several policies on their lives, implying that customers took advantage of their superior knowledge of sickly neighbours to profit at the distant office's expense. The agents who sold such policies were either assumed to be overly lax (as in the Bradford case) or complicit.[23] Companies were usually willing to fight such claims in court, often with a successful outcome, although even here they needed to keep one eye fixed on the tender subject of public relations. Hence when Sophie Haberschitz of the East End was found burned to death in 1909 with ten policies on her life, the implicated offices decided to pay the claims on the grounds that 'it was undesirable lest the world know that such a thing was possible.'[24]

If industrial offices were sometimes reluctant to challenge claims that they assumed to be guilty of criminal intent, they were even less likely to resist 'legitimate' claims on third-party policies just because the Gambling Act said they could. Although any office might, in theory, cart out the act whenever a claim by a nephew or granddaughter involved it in a loss, they did no such thing, for the same reason that upper-class offices ignored *Godsall:* it would have driven away half their business. Unfortunately for the companies, the same reasoning did not work in reverse. The Gambling Act enabled people who held 'legitimate' but illegal policies to exercise an especially brutal form of selection against industrial offices, by suing for a refund when their premiums had exceeded the value of the claim. The associated legal costs were enough to restrict the number of such cases until around 1900, but after this time lawyers started to appear on the scene who were willing to try them on a contingency basis.[25] These lawyers, Edwardian cousins of the ambulance chaser, naturally earned the wrath of industrial insurance managers, as when Alfred Henri of the Liverpool Victoria railed against 'solicitors of a certain type ... who were willing to take up these cases for what they might get out of them.'[26] Their reputation was substantially higher among the large number of working-class policyholders who were stuck in what had become an unprofitable contract. Yet even those customers who won their suits soon learned that the economics of illegal insurance came with some troubling fine print: legal fees could run nearly as high as the claim, once lawyers averaged in all their time from cases they had lost.[27]

As *Dalby* demonstrates, the prevalence of business-friendly judge-made law often allowed Victorian markets to operate quite efficiently despite such statutory obstacles. Yet no judge delivered a *Dalby*-style ruling in the late-nineteenth century clearly stating that working-class 'life-of-another' policies were not equivalent to wagers. There are several reasons for this, relating to distinctive traits of industrial insurance, popular assumptions about working-class gambling, and conflicting views held by different judges. On the first of these points, the large-scale and unpopular reputation of industrial insurance companies affected both sides of the blurry line separating 'pure gambling' from 'rational speculation.' The three largest industrial offices (the Prudential, Refuge, and Pearl) dominated their dozen or so competitors and were each writing millions of new policies a year by 1910. The companies' larger size and centralized organization rendered them more vulnerable to losses at the hands of parties whose local knowledge was an advantage in insurance wagers, but also made them more capable of surviving an expensive court battle if they chose to resist payment. The companies' unpopular reputation, and especially that of their salesmen, gave customers a fighting chance of convincing a judge that they had been hoodwinked into buying an illegal policy and hence deserved to get a refund of their premiums. Part of this reputation derived from the assumption that burial insurance qualified as illicit 'gambling' on the deaths of neighbours and relatives; but much of it also stemmed from the assumption that even the 'bona fide' service offered by the companies – financial security against the cost of burial – encouraged needlessly lavish funerals among the poor.[28]

Assuming that burial insurance did qualify as gambling, it was also the case that people who bought it and companies that sold it were far more likely than upper-class insurance customers to be viewed by the rest of society to be practicing 'pure gambling' instead of 'rational speculation.' Gambling of any variety appeared darker to Victorians whenever the gamblers were poor people.[29] The Gaming Act of 1845 (as distinct from the Gambling Act, which only applied to insurance) was mainly enforced among the poor: hence private clubs and race-tracks remained effectively legal, while off-course betting was not. As Roger Munting has argued, this double standard reflected the middle classes' 'paternalistic care for the poor who might be led astray by the machinations of bookmakers'; yet that sentiment stood in clear tension with the contrary middle-class 'drive to cash in on the demand for gambling.' The result was that working-class gambling 'inhabited a twilight world' in late Victorian legal and moral discourse, not unlike that which enveloped industrial insurance at the same time.[30]

The scale and reputation of industrial insurance help to explain why companies and their customers took so many cases to court between 1880 and 1909. They do not explain why, once the cases got there, judges had so much trouble discovering a 'reasonable construction' of the Gambling Act that would settle the matter. The problem was not that judges had no opinions where industrial insurance was concerned; what P.S. Atiyah has called 'the hortatory aspect ... of the law of contract' was as much on display in this realm of insurance law as in any other.[31] The problem was that judges could not decide exactly what or whom they should be exhorting. To add to the confusion, a clear split developed after 1900 between higher courts, which became increasingly concerned to establish 'principles' that would allow the companies to get on with their business; and county courts, where judges tended to ignore higher court rulings in order to 'get at the agents' by forcing companies to pay.[32] The result was a patently uncertain legal framework, which industrial life offices ultimately found to be intolerable.

## The Gambling Act on Trial

In their respective battles to stack the deck in their favour, working-class customers and companies told stories at trial in order to convince judges that the Gambling Act entitled them to gain at the other's expense. When policyholders sued for a return of premiums, they presented themselves as victims of the insurance agent's misleading claim that such policies were legal. In their defense, life offices tried to shift blame back onto the policyholder or the agent, depending on the circumstances of the case. The insurance agent, who received so much of the blame in these trials, was the least likely to be asked to testify, lest he refute the other parties' professions of innocence.

When a Liverpool woman sued the Refuge in 1903 after paying £82 on two policies worth £72, she argued that the agent had told her 'it would be all right – she could draw the money.' The judge agreed that this was tantamount to fraud on the company's part, and awarded her £34 – ruling that the rest of the payment lay outside the statute of limitations.[33] Alice Crosty used the same argument to win £53 back from the Scottish Temperance life office in 1909, on a policy she had taken out on her aunt's life. With less success, Johanna Butt of Swansea tried to claim that 'people came and asked her to pay premiums' in a case where she was accused of taking out fifteen policies on the same man's life. [34] For the most part, the fact that all these allegations of misrepresentation were made by women simply reflects the economic reality that buying insurance – like pawning, food shopping, and rent payment – qualified as 'women's work' in the working-class division of household labour.[35] Yet probably it also indicated a conscious strategy by such women and their lawyers to capitalize on the middle-class assumption, shared by many working men, that insurance salesmen habitually took advantage of their female customers' naivety as they made their way from the doorstep into the front room.[36]

Life insurance offices tried to counter such claims by insisting that their customers, far from being innocent victims, were seasoned veterans at the 'game' of demanding back premiums when the person whose life they had 'gambled' on refused to die in a timely fashion. When two Walworth women sued the Liverpool Victoria in 1909 for £26 in back premiums after their father died, citing 'misrepresentation of one of their agents,' the society's lawyer countered that it had offered the women the £10 due at the death, 'but it had been refused by them because their father lived longer than they expected, and the transaction had been unprofitable to them.'[37] Although successful in this case, such reasoning was a risky legal strategy, since companies could all too easily incriminate themselves along with their customers. Hence a judge found against the Royal Liver in 1903 when it refused to refund Mary Wilson of Padiham £36 in premiums paid on a policy on her father-in-law's life, despite its lawyer's argument that she 'had been speculating in insurance for a considerable time, and ... was prepared to take the risk.' The judge was not impressed by the society's efforts to counter Wilson's charge of misrepresentation with the claim that 'many insurance companies took and honoured those wagering policies, as the Royal Liver was prepared to do in the case.'[38]

In responding to these stories, late Victorian judges sent a decidedly mixed set of messages to customers and companies alike. Some, especially at the county level, blamed the companies for making a mockery of the Gambling Act and punished them by requiring them to return the premiums paid for illegal policies.[39] Others did not accuse the directors of encouraging gambling, but did fault their agents, as when a Swansea judge forced the Royal Counties Friendly Society to refund a collier's premiums with costs in 1902. Although the judge claimed that he 'would not think of blaming the directors,' he did feel the need to 'warn people about this, so that they will not enter into these contracts,' and he concluded: 'These agents behave so badly. I should like to hit some of these societies through their agents.'[40] Another judge allowed the Liverpool Victoria to deny five claims on the short life of a girl who died of tuberculosis in 1906, but required it to pay £20 in costs – arguing that 'so long as there are agents who lend themselves to this trafficking ... there will always be found people weak enough or greedy enough to listen to the tempters.'[41] A third set of judges similarly blamed the agents, but had ample suspicion left over for the policyholders as well. Hence the judge in the Walworth case admitted that 'canvassers for insurance companies were apt to misstate things' but also offered this taunt to the allegedly victimized sisters: 'The whole mischief is that your father lived too long. Is that not it?' A Bristol judge similarly denied £25 in back premiums for a £19 policy against the death of 'an elderly man called Mark Barnes,' appending to his ruling the wry observation that 'owing to Mr. Barnes's perversity in continuing to live, poor Mr. Tilley had overpaid.'[42]

In *Harse v. Pearl* (1904), which held that policyholders should be assumed to be parties to illegal insurances unless fraud on the part of the agent could be proven, the Court of Appeal did make some strides towards stabilizing the meaning of the Gambling Act in application to working-class insurance.[43] One of the judges in this case, Lord Mathew, expressly grounded his ruling on the principle that life offices were 'entitled to the administration of the law on fixed principles.' The way the court arrived at these 'fixed principles' in *Harse* was by invoking the legal fiction that insurance salesmen could not be expected to understand how the Gambling Act had defined insurable interest, and hence could not be guilty of misrepresentation. The case was a typical one: Harse had taken out policies on his parents' lives, then demanded back premiums from the Pearl once his payments had exceeded his claim. The trial jury had found for the Pearl on the grounds that 'the Agent represented that the Policy would be valid ... [and] did not know that what he was saying was untrue.' The Court of Appeal confirmed this verdict, on the assumption that salesmen's claims regarding the validity of third-party policies were statements of 'the general law of the land in relation to insurance,' which were 'made innocently to a person who was most desirous of entering into an illegal Contract.'[44]

In reaching its verdict, the judges offered a unique twist on the usual brand of moralizing about dodgy agents preying on innocent (or even not-so-innocent) working-class victims. Most industrial insurance salesmen, they argued, were cut from the same cloth as their customers, and hence were unlikely to be in a position to lead their customers too far astray. This corresponded with the socioconomic reality of most insurance salesmen at the time, and it certainly corresponded with the agents' self-ascribed mission to put themselves 'on a level with all the policy-holders, no matter how humble their position in life may be.'[45] From this premise, the judges concluded that customers and agents were equally ignorant of the Gambling Act – hence relieving insurance salesmen of any 'greater obligation to know the law than the persons they approach for the purpose of effecting policies.' Since the Pearl was not 'in any way bound to appoint Agents with some special knowledge of law,' it stood to reason that *caveat emptor*, not the Gambling Act, was the relevant 'general principle' in such cases.[46]

Unfortunately for the life offices, *Harse* was only partially successful at putting an end to the rising tide of litigation that had been such a problem since 1900. This was especially the case in county courts, where judges were often determined to punish the industrial offices by assuming fraud on the part of their agents. Hence when Hannah Brown sued the Britannic life office in 1907 in the Preston County Court to recover premiums for a policy on her mother's life, the office failed in its attempt 'to prove that both the Company and the assured were in pari delicto, as in the Harse case.' Instead, the judge sternly insisted that the Britannic was responsible for its agents' actions: 'The policy was signed by five officials, including two directors, yet not a single one thought it incumbent upon him to consider whether the insurable interest was valid under an Act 125 years old.'[47] Although *Brown* was subsequently reversed on appeal, as were a number of similar lower court rulings, the trickle of such rulings grew to a flood in 1909. A November 1909 editorial in the *Insurance Record* entitled 'Trouble in the Industrial Assurance World' cited the case of a Welsh district in which 'one company alone has had no fewer than one hundred and forty County Court actions brought against it in about two months, for the return of premiums on alleged illegal assurances.' It was the Edwardian equivalent of a class-action suit: 'In several districts during the past six weeks circulars confidently believed to emanate from a firm of solicitors, have been distributed, inviting policyholders to take proceedings for the recovery of premiums; and in Lancashire certain solicitors, have called and addressed public meetings with the same object.'[48] As with many modern class-action suits, new legislation soon followed to prevent the recurrence of such alarming disruptions to business as usual.

## After 1909: From Judgment to Surveillance

The new law in question was the Assurance Companies Act of 1909, most of which had to do with upper-class life business. As the act was making its way through Parliament, the industrial offices lobbied strenuously to include a provision that would prevent customers from being able to cite 'the old Act of George III' in order to recover their premiums. Their preferred solution, endorsed in section 37 of the act, was to legalize retroactively all existing 'bona fide' third-party policies, 'having regard to the change in the social condition of the people, and to the obligation which the law has placed upon the children and grandchildren since 1774.'[49] A different clause dealt with future insurances by legalizing 'life of another' policies on parents, grandparents, grandchildren, brothers, and sisters. These modifications left some legal uncertainty intact, mainly because they defined the amount of a 'bona fide' policy (whether issued before or after 1909) as the sum that 'the relative reasonably might expect' to pay for a funeral. 'Reasonable' funeral expenses remained a bone of contention, with some trial judges setting the bar as low as £10 and companies issuing policies up to £25, and nobody was too sure what to do about people who took out several policies from different offices.[50] Furthermore, the new law's extended definition of legitimate kinship still excluded thousands of stepchildren, half-siblings, and cousins who continued to buy third-party policies after 1909, and hence continued to provide fodder that enterprising attorneys could use to initiate new litigation.

To prevent these remaining issues from becoming a commercial liability, life insurers began to pay more attention to their agents' methods of attracting business. Sidney Webb reported in 1915 that they had started to 'scrutinise closely all policies purporting to be on the "life of another,"' to require signatures from lives insured, and to fine agents who exceeded the cap on policy size, although he doubted that this was enough to rein in agents' bad behaviour.[51] More significant than these partial concessions to the spirit of the 1909 act was the offices' increasing tendency after 1918 to extend middle-class marketing devices to their customers. Although surrender values for such policies continued to be rare, owing to the fees involved, companies like the Prudential began awarding 'free policies' and bonuses to customers after several years.[52] They also started to offer endowment insurances, which by 1900 had already replaced whole-life coverage as the most popular middle-class policy; these provided term coverage for ten to twenty years, then converted to an annuity if the policyholder was still alive to collect. Industrial offices went from issuing 3.5 million such policies in 1912 to 13 million in 1931, by which time they comprised a quarter of their sales.[53] By offering free policies, and by combining life insurance with an old age pension, the companies gave customers a reason to hold onto their policies even after the insured survived their predicted time of death.

Legislative and administrative reforms solved most of the strictly economic problems that the Gambling Act had once put in the way of industrial insurance. The 1909 revisions greatly reduced the number of people who could claim that their policy was illegal, and the companies' new marketing methods greatly reduced their customers' incentive to sue. Hence from the industrial insurance industry's perspective, it made sense to pretend, as their upper-class counterparts had been doing for a century, that 'gambling' no longer had anything to do with their business. As J.A. Jefferson of the Britannic office confidently assured Sir Benjamin Cohen's parliamentary committee on industrial insurance, 'the British working classes of to-day are not gambling and thinking only of having a bit on the old man'; the fact that nearly 80 per cent of his company's business was comprised of 'life of another' policies – all of which would have been technically illegal under the Gambling Act – was 'all part and parcel of the assurance.'[54]

Many social critics were not as willing to let the matter rest. In his 1915 Fabian Society report on industrial insurance, Webb scolded the companies for having gotten section 37 'smuggled into the Life Assurance Companies Act almost without discussion,' and called the companies' high caps on funeral expenses 'an abuse which calls for a remedy.' Cohen accused the 1909 Act of giving 'a right ... to the poor man and not to the rich' and berated the companies for encouraging, if not gambling *per se*, 'economic waste on expenses of every kind in connection with death in working-class homes.'[55] Once they had solved the 'gambling' problem to their own satisfaction, however, the industrial offices were just as successful at keeping these continuing 'collectivist' criticisms at bay. Two interwar inquiries produced no significant new laws, and a further attempt to nationalize industrial insurance in 1950 came to nothing.[56] One reason why companies were able to resist such reforms for as long as they did was because they had figured out when to move their problem out of the courts and back into the market, where 'collectivist' judges could rarely touch them.

## NOTES

The author thanks Tom Baker, Peter Buck, Josh Getzler, the CUNY Victorian Studies Group, and the New England Insurance and Society Study Group for feedback on earlier drafts. A version of this essay previously appeared in the *Connecticut Insurance Law Journal*.

1 C. Little, 'Fire Insurance: Is It a Species of Gambling?' *Norwich Union Magazine*, no. 1 (1891), 2–3.
2 Geoffrey Clark, *Betting on Lives: The Culture of Life Insurance in England 1695–1775* (Manchester: Manchester University Press, 1999), 50, 52–3, 63.
3 Cited in Dermot Morrah, *A History of Industrial Life Assurance* (London: George Allen and Unwin, 1955), 74.
4 Clark, *Betting on Lives*, 26.
5 I use the term 'upper-class' in this chapter to denote the aristocrats, professionals, and merchants who comprised the primary market for life insurance up to the 1850s, as distinct from the working-class or 'industrial' customers discussed below.
6 Thirty-nine per cent of policies issued by the Clerical, Medical and General Life Assurance Society between 1824 and 1845 were on third

parties (Renewal ledgers, Acc. 2006/063, HBOS plc archives, Edinburgh); as were 34 per cent of policies in force in 1870 at the Legal and General Life Assurance Society (Life policy registers, Ms. 18,473/1-7, Guildhall Library, London).

7 This was in keeping with Ellenborough's wider pattern of decisions that 'barred the way repeatedly to attempts to modernize the law': P.S. Atiyah, *The Rise and Fall of Freedom of Contract* (Oxford: Clarendon Press, 1979), 422.

8 *English Reports* (Edinburgh: W. Green, 1900–1911), 103, 502–4.

9 *Circular of Bankers,* 7 May 1830.

10 Alliance Assurance Company Board Minutes, Ms. 12,162/1 (23 May 1827) and 3 (22 February 1837, 10 July 1839), Guildhall Library, London.

11 *English Reports* 139, 476, 469. Bramwell went on to be a leading architect of 'freedom of contract' doctrine in English law: Atiyah, *Rise and Fall,* 374–80.

12 *English Reports* 139, 470.

13 See Viviana A. Rotman Zelizer, *Morals and Markets: The Development of Life Insurance in the United States* (New Brunswick, NJ: Transaction Books, 1983), 45: 'When a house burns down ... it is possible to reach some objective measurement of the losses involved. When a man dies, however, no accurate measure of value is possible. Therefore, the principle of indemnity cannot be fully applied to life insurance and a life contract assigns the risk a fixed value.'

14 *English Reports* 139, 473.

15 On the *Godsall* and *Dalby* cases, and their impact on American life insurance practice, see Murphy Sharon Ann Murphy, 'Security in an Uncertain World: Life Insurance and the Emergence of Modern America' (PhD diss., University of Virginia, 2005), 145–59.

16 Augustus De Morgan, *An Essay on Probabilities, and on their Application to Life Contingencies and Insurance Offices* (London: Longman, Orme, Brown, Green, and Longmans, 1838), 247.

17 R. Hingston Fox, 'The Assurance of Impaired Lives, Chiefly with Reference to Special Forms of Assurance,' *Clinical Journal* 6 (1895), 258.

18 Zelizer, *Morals and Markets,* 86; see also G.R. Searle, *Morality and the Market in Victorian Britain* (New York: Oxford University Press, 1998), 78–86.

19 Until the Insurance Policies Act of 1867 officially legalized such purchases (assuming the title to the policy was properly assigned to the pur-

chaser), such auctions were technically illegal under the Gambling Act – but, as in the case of creditors collecting claims despite the cancellation of the debt, the act was seldom applied to them.

20 L. Clendenin, *A Brief Sketch of the Life and Works of Elizur Wright* (Chicago: American Conservation Co., 1932), 66–7.

21 Morrah, *History of Industrial Life Assurance*, 75. Partial legal recognition of the widespread practice of insuring children's lives was achieved in the 1875 Friendly Society Act, which allowed families to insure up to £6 per child; although this formally extended only to mutual 'collecting societies,' the courts soon extended this provision to joint-stock companies under common law. See Sidney Webb, 'The Working of the Insurance Act,' *New Statesman* 2 (1914), special supplement, 27.

22 *Report from the Select Committee of the House of Lords on Children's Life Insurance Bill* (London: Herbert Hansard and Son, 1890), 70.

23 *Assurance Agents' Review* 19 (1906), 42–3.

24 Industrial Life Offices Association Minutes, Ms. 29,802/3 (13 July 1909), Guildhall Library, London.

25 Officially, Edwardian lawyers were barred from charging contingency fees. The legal challenges described below, however, would only have been feasible on such a basis; hence it seems likely that lawyers informally accomplished this, for instance by voluntarily foregoing their fee in the event of a negative verdict. I am grateful to Joshua Getzler for this suggestion.

26 Industrial Life Offices Association Minutes, Ms. 29,802/2 (19 January 1909), Guildhall Library, London.

27 Laurie Dennett, *A Sense of Security: 150 Years of Prudential* (Cambridge: Granta Editions, 1998), 403.

28 Timothy Alborn, 'Senses of Belonging: The Politics of Working-Class Insurance in Britain, 1880–1914,' *Journal of Modern History* 73 (2001), 576–9.

29 This may very well be due to the fact that 'already existent risks' – for instance, a joint-stock company's financial future – were off limits to working-class gamblers, who lacked the requisite capital to become shareholders. They did, in contrast, have access to 'artificial risks' such as the outcome of card games, lotteries, or horse races.

30 Munting, 'Betting and Business: The Commercialisation of Gambling in Britain,' *Business History* 31 (1989), 68; Searle, *Morality and the Market*, 232.

31 Atiyah, *Rise and Fall*, 395.

32 On the relationship between county courts and high courts in the late

nineteenth century see Patrick Polden, *A History of the County Courts, 1846–1981* (Cambridge: Cambridge University Press, 1999).

33 Industrial Life Offices Association Minutes, Ms. 29,802/2 (report on *Welsh v. Refuge*, 11 August 1903), Guildhall Library, London. In this and subsequent cases, monetary sums are rounded to the nearest pound.

34 *Insurance Record* 47 (1909), 529, 336.

35 Ellen Ross, *Love and Toil: Motherhood in Outcast London, 1870–1918* (Oxford: Oxford University Press, 1993).

36 See, for instance, the Trades Union Congress resolution from 1909 that 'unfair advantage is often taken [by insurance salesmen] of the womankind when the husband is away': repr. Industrial Life Offices Association Minutes, Ms. 29,802/3, Guildhall Library, London.

37 *Insurance Record* 47 (1909), 25.

38 *Insurance Record* 41 (1903), 509.

39 *Assurance Agents' Review* 8 (1895), 147; 9 (1896), 62.

40 *Insurance Record* 40 (1902), 174.

41 *Assurance Agents' Review* 19 (1906), 42–3

42 *Insurance Record* 47 (1909), 25, 593; *Post Magazine* 70 (1909), 53.

43 A second ruling, *Griffiths v. Fleming*, accomplished even greater levels of certainty for the narrower category of wives taking out policies on their husbands: see *Post Magazine* 70 (1908): 207.

44 Industrial Life Offices Association Minutes, Ms. 29,802/2 (report on *Harse v. Pearl*, 19 February 1904), Guildhall Library, London.

45 Frederick H. Gisbourne, *How to Conduct an Agency* (London: n.p., 1895), 5.

46 Industrial Life Offices Association Minutes, Ms. 29,802/2 (report on *Harse v. Pearl*, 19 February 1904), Guildhall Library, London.

47 Industrial Life Offices Association Minutes, Ms. 29,802/2 (28 April 1908), Guildhall Library, London; *Insurance Record* 45 (1907), 564.

48 *Insurance Record* 47 (1909), 567.

49 Industrial Life Offices Association Minutes, Ms. 29,802/3 (21 September 1909), Guildhall Library, London.

50 Webb, 'Working of the Insurance Act,' 28. See, e.g., *Tofts v. Pearl Life Assurance Company* (1913), in which the Wymondham County Court rejected the Pearl's claim that £40 (covering Tofts's mother and father) constituted 'an unreasonable amount for mourning'; this decision was upheld on appeal: *Times* 18 December 1913, 22 October 1914.

51 Webb, 'Working of the Insurance Act,' 28.

52 Arnold Wilson and Hermann Levy, *Industrial Assurance: An Historical and Critical Study* (London: Oxford University Press, 1937), 193.

53 Paul Johnson, *Saving and Spending: The Working-Class Economy in Britain 1870–1939* (Oxford: Clarendon Press, 1985), 41.
54 Departmental Committee on the Law and Practice relating to Industrial Insurance, *Minutes of Evidence* (London: HMSO, 1931), 233, 249.
55 Webb, 'Working of the Insurance Act,' 27–8; Wilson and Levy, *Industrial Assurance*, 141–2.
56 Dennett, *Sense of Security*, 260–2, 294–9.

# 6 'The Rules of Prudence': Political Liberalism and Life Assurance in the Nineteenth Century

LIZ MCFALL

Considering nineteenth-century British life assurance from the perspective of its appeal opens up a variety of questions. Most obviously, it calls attention to how the life assurance industry[1] sought to attract customers through its promotional work. This was no easy matter; life assurance was never going to sell itself. It was (and still is) a technically complex product, it sought to gain a foothold in a market saturated with competing savings and investment products, there were doubts about the financial safety and probity of a number of the companies trading in it, and if this were not enough, it provoked disquiet in some quarters on moral and religious grounds. The promotional strategies life assurance companies developed to overcome such objections, and form an enduring appeal to the public, are fascinating in their own right. They make more historical sense, however, when the question of appeal is considered more broadly. Insurance's appeal, in short, is about more than how it attracts customers; it is also about how it demands attention, appraisal, and reappraisal more generally.

Life assurance demands this broader appraisal in part because of its role in ushering forth a new social world, one that turned on the apparent triumph of calculative rule over nature. The role of life assurance in harnessing the emerging knowledges of statistical and actuarial science to tame the effects of chance has been relatively well documented.[2] The appeal life assurance companies marshalled through the promotional assemblage of advertising, publicity, sales promotion, and agents' training manuals made loud proclamations about how firmly rooted their product was in the regularities, rules, and laws of actuarial science. Through trumpeting the use of technical, actuarial procedures to uncover the hidden 'laws' of mortality and sickness, life assurance companies helped promote insurance as an exemplary product for an emerging social world.

As powerful as such a claim was, it did not stand alone. It was tied to and in fact underwrote a broader claim that sought to translate life assurance into a form that would harmonise with existing ideals of conduct.[3] The technical certainties claimed of insurance per se and the particular features of commercial life assurance products were to this end offered in the promotional literature as a sort of guarantee of its capacity to shape desirable forms of conduct. While the whole sum assured in a life assurance contract was realizable even if only one premium had been paid, individuals were strictly separated from those funds through the punitive financial penalties attached to early surrender. This, together with a grounding in the principles of actuarial science, allowed assurance companies to claim an unrivalled capacity to foster prudent behaviour. Claims about insurance's capacity to cultivate prudence lay at the very heart of the promotional enterprise. They were articulated in reference not only to individual conduct but to the capacity of life assurance to counter a whole raft of social evils resulting from poverty. In promising a solution that could combine the collectivized management of risk with the promotion of individual market-based freedoms, life assurance was not only a calculative technology but one that fit neatly with the emerging principles of political liberalism.

While liberalism took shape as a relatively coherent political ideology in the nineteenth century, historically it has nevertheless encompassed a variety of sometimes competing, ideas, values, and principles. Life assurance, while in accord with the market-based freedoms championed in all versions of liberalism, arguably has tighter connections to particular Victorian variants of liberal thought. In casting the responsibility for managing risk on the shoulders of private individuals free to choose marketed products, nineteenth-century life assurance was in accord with what Pat O'Malley has termed 'prudentialism.'[4] But in some strands of Victorian liberalism, freedom was about more than the negative freedom to choose. Effective individual freedom for some Victorian thinkers could only be achieved through education designed both to enlighten and to instil virtuous and responsible conduct. This positive concept of freedom resonates through the literature surrounding the nineteenth-century life assurance project, which repeated *ad nauseum* reasons, arguments, and rules about insurance, prudence, and responsibility. This chapter argues that the appeal of life assurance can best be understood by tracing the history, not only of the enterprise itself, but also of its connections to the philosophical and intellectual heritage upon which Victorian liberalism drew.

The figure of prudence lies at the very centre of this intellectual heritage. The chapter begins by exploring moral philosophical formulations of prudence in an effort to mark their influence on nineteenth-century liberal thought. It moves on to consider how closely the key principles of Victorian liberalism were mirrored in the promotion of life assurance before concluding with a discussion of the place of insurance as an emblematic technology of liberal political rationality. The overarching aim is to show how closely related the life assurance project was to a prudentialist Victorian liberalism that simultaneously championed individual market-based freedom and moral regulation.

## Prudence and Liberalism

In *The Civilising Process* Norbert Elias argued that the lengthy and complex networks of interdependent relations in 'Western' societies after the Middle Ages created a demand for more highly regulated, stable, predictable, and habitually restrained forms of conduct. Elias's characterization of the civilizing process has provoked criticism on a number of grounds, but his account of the ways in which manners, rules, and the various norms of civilized conduct were deployed to stabilize and regulate diverse forms of behaviour is a necessary element in the history of contemporary forms of commerce. Nevertheless the drive to contain the worst excesses of human desires and passion is perhaps an older one than Elias suggests. Tracing the notion of prudence reveals a diverse and sometimes contradictory history of efforts to cultivate certain forms or ideals of conduct by different means and towards different ends. For Thomas Aquinas:

> Prudence is a virtue most necessary for human life. For a good life consists in good deeds. Now in order to do good deeds, it matters not only what a man does but also how he does it; to wit that he do it from right choice and not merely from impulse or passion. And, since choice is about things in reference to the end, rectitude of choice requires two things; namely, the due end, and something suitably ordained to that due end. ... Consequently an intellectual virtue is needed in the reason, to perfect the reason, and make it suitably affected towards things ordained

> to the end; and this virtue is prudence. Consequently prudence is a virtue necessary to lead a good life.[5]

The word prudence derives from the Latin *providere,* meaning to foresee, to take precaution, to provide for, and it is this sense that informs Aquinas's early Christian understanding of prudence as one of the four cardinal virtues alongside justice, fortitude, and temperance. Prudence, in Christian thought, is about the capacity to discriminate between good and evil courses of action and to choose the good. For Aquinas, a properly developed, reasoned capacity for prudence will hold passions and appetites in check. Prudence is championed as a form of intellectual reason that can be developed specifically to help attain the kind of control over the impulses, appetites, passions, and emotions that Elias describes as a necessary element of the civilizing process. With ongoing, subtle reinvention, prudence retains this centrality as an ideal, and as a virtue, into the seventeenth and eighteenth centuries. In Thomas Hobbes's definition of prudence, the key lies in experience, which, properly applied, can aid discrimination and foresight. This foresight can only ever be partial, as 'though it be called prudence, when the event answereth our expectation; yet in its nature it is but presumption': only Providence can 'see' with any certainty the things that are to come.[6]

Hobbes's prudence places particular emphasis on the capacity to put off short-term satisfaction for the longer-term good. This capacity did not, in Hobbes's view, arise naturally, as 'men cannot put off this same irrational appetite whereby they generally prefer the present good (to which by strict consequence, many unforeseen evils do adhere) before the future.'[7] Individuals may not 'naturally' possess the capacity for prudence, but prudence nevertheless *should* be cultivated as a tame and methodical route to the optimum gratification over the longest term. Prudence here is the proper pursuit of our own final interests and happiness. This studied pursuit of self-interested prudence was championed by Hobbes over the alternative he perceived of passion fuelled, protracted and bloody civil wars.

A not entirely dissimilar sense of prudence can be traced in the eighteenth century in the work of Adam Smith. In Smith's schema prudence is an aspect of *amour de soi* or self-love, a form of moral caring for the self entirely free from the contemporary pejorative associations of the term.[8] Prudence concerns 'care of the health, of the fortune, of the rank and reputation of the individual, the objects upon which his comfort and happiness in this life are supposed principally to depend.'[9] Prudent individuals are frugal, steady, and industrious and crucially, in the context of the imminent appeal of life assurance, have an ability to sacrifice 'the ease and enjoyment of the present moment for the probable expectation of the still greater ease and enjoyment of a more distant but more lasting period of time.'[10] This emphasis on the deferral of gratification in the service of future ease accords with a formulation that places security as the first and main objective of prudence. Prudence

> is rather cautious than enterprising, and more anxious to preserve the advantages which we already possess, than forward to prompt us to the acquisition of still greater advantages. The methods of improving our fortune which it principally recommends to us, are those which expose to no loss or hazard; real knowledge or skill in our trade or profession, assiduity and industry in the exercise of it, frugality, and even some degree of parsimony, in all our expenses.[11]

Smith's discussion draws upon the long ruminations about the character of prudence as a virtue in the philosophies of Plato, Aristotle, and Epictetus among others. In Smith's work, however, prudence takes on a more robust character as an ideal upon which new forms of financial and economic conduct could draw. Smith regards the 'desire to better our condition' as the foremost motive of behaviour in commercial society, but not because human beings are essentially prudent, self-interested, or materialist. Rather, the desire for material improvement is really, as in neo-Stoic moral philosophy, all about the desire for sympathy. Ultimately, economic activity is fuelled by 'something symbolic and intangible: approbation from others.' By themselves, material things afford only 'contemptible and trifling' satisfaction; it is 'the regular and harmonious movement of the system, the machine or oeconomy' that inspires individuals to toil and strive.[12]

The crucial point for present purposes is the influence of these moral philosophical debates about prudence on the key systems of thought upon which the emerging mode of liberal government was founded. While, as Stefan Collini has pointed out, the differences between eighteenth-century political discourses of 'virtue' and nineteenth-century discourses of 'character' are profound, the 'survivals and mutations' from moral philosophy manifest in nineteenth-century liberalism are crucial to understanding its logic and rationality.[13] Liberal government prioritized a market-based form of individual self-rule that was targeted to manipulate the human drive to better conditions by drawing upon the mechanisms of fashion and taste. For theorists like Hobbes and later Adam Smith, a system of government that fostered economic activity driven by a cultivated form of self-interested prudence could act as a necessary corrective to the rule of passions in the service of aristocratic or religious ideals.[14] Liberal (self-) government relied upon voluntary compliance with a market-based system of organization that could manipulate the drive to 'better our conditions' in part by drawing upon the mechanisms of fashion and taste.

> Administering self-rule in a market society involved understanding human motivations, including the desire to consume, rather than simply measuring productivity or overseeing obedience. As a consequence, the knowledge that increasingly seemed essential to liberal governmentality was the kind cultivated by moral philosophers: an account of subjectivity that helped explain desire, propensities, and aversions as being universal to humans as a group.[15]

Questions about human motivation were a central preoccupation of moral philosophy, and for this reason it offered an ideal intellectual platform for emerging liberal rationalities of government. These questions concerned moral philosophers more for their social implications than their spiritual or psychological ones. They were addressed towards achieving a better understanding of the regularities of the moral universe and the principles underpinning the human willingness to submit to government. As individuals were assumed by eighteenth-century moral philosophers to be instances of a universal human nature, so knowledge about that nature could offer the grounds for a theory of government based on individual self-rule structured by the market.[16] It is for this reason that ideas about prudence and self-interest occupy such a prominent position in the liberal political rationalities of the nineteenth century. Fundamentally these were rationalities grounded on a set of knowledges and ideas about the character of human motivation, the drives to acquire, to consume, and to emulate. An appreciation of how ideas about prudence and self-interest were remodelled in the political discourses of nineteenth-century liberalism, as will be suggested below, offers valuable insight into the shape taken by the life assurance project.

The intellectual debt liberalist political rational*ities* owe to the varied, contradictory, and competing discourses of eighteenth-century moral philosophies helps explain why it is more accurate, if more cumbersome, to insist upon the plural. As a number of writers exploring the history of liberal ideas have observed, there is some debate about how core concepts like freedom and self-interest were adopted and understood by key nineteenth- and twentieth-century liberal thinkers. Following John Stuart Mill's *On Liberty,* liberalism is widely characterized as promoting a negative concept of freedom, but this is not in any straightforward sense the type of freedom envisioned by all Victorian liberal thinkers.[17] Samuel Smiles's populist philosophy of self-help, enterprise, and thrift was 'negatively' liberalist in its disdain for state interference, but the provident and temperate spirit he endorsed depended on self-denial, a virtue that had to be acquired 'positively' through education. Citing the words of John Sterling, Smiles agrees that the 'worst education which teaches self-denial is better than the best which teaches everything else and not that.'[18] This positively inculcated form of self-governing freedom is also present in T.H. Green's entanglement of liberty with responsibility in the manner favoured by evangelicals and nonconformists. Here liberty involves 'the liberation of the powers of all men equally for contributions to a common good.'[19] For citizens to be able to exercise this form of liberty they required virtue, and virtue could best be instilled by education and legislation. Thus, in Green's schema, state coercion should be applied to create the conditions in which men can develop a character disposed to do good. It comes as little surprise then that Green was a supporter of prohibitionism. Prohibitionism, he maintained, fostered virtue, so it followed that it must also foster true freedom. This was not the freedom to do as one pleased but the freedom to 'turn to the best account all the talents and capabilities God had given.'[20]

The combination of liberalism with prohibitionism strikes an odd note from a contemporary perspective where 'social' liberals on the left and the right regard issues of drug and alcohol use, as with sexual conduct, as matters of private conscience. But Green's prohibitionism was no idiosyncrasy; the temperance movement was in close sympathy with key strands of Victorian liberalism. The tenets of sacrifice, education, restraint, and religious feeling were common to both and both were preoccupied with self-help and the cultivation of character.[21] This concern with self-cultivation is akin to self-command, which, understood as a 'second-order' virtue, Alisdair Macintyre argues, is necessary in Adam Smith's philosophy for the achievement of 'first-order' virtues like prudence.

> On Smith's view Knowledge of what the rules are, whether the rules of justice or of prudence or of benevolence, is not sufficient to enable us to follow them; to do so we need another virtue of a very different kind, the Stoic virtue of self-command which enables us to control our passions when they distract us from what virtue requires.[22]

What this amounts to is a view that, to be effective, prudence has almost to be made practical through techniques of self-command. Whether Smith imagined the preoccupation with the cultivation of character in Victorian liberal movements as necessary to support market-based self-rule is a moot point. What is clear is that throughout the nineteenth century, for many pro-free-market liberals, economic activity had to be underpinned by a morally 'cultivated' character distinguished by the habits of thrift and restraint that understood the moral significance of wealth-'getting' rather than -'having.'[23] A liberal vision in this mould, which brought together science, religious feeling, and active self-sacrificing philanthropy in a missionary approach to the social problems of industrial society, and combined a rule-bound formalism with an emphasis on individual responsibility for future financial planning, was instantiated in a range of different movements. One of the most significant of these was the nineteenth-century British life assurance project.

## The Missionaries of Life Assurance

The history of life assurance – even in Britain where it met less resistance than in most other European countries and the United States, as has been demonstrated elsewhere – was one of numerous failures and false starts.[24] That this difficult history can be attributed, as Vivianna Zelizer argues, to an entrenched public resistance on the grounds that life assurance blasphemously defied a normative division between the marketable/profane and non-marketable/sacred seems increasingly unlikely.[25] In Britain, the close relations between the religious establishment, the life assurance industry, and the ascending political rationalities of the eighteenth and nineteenth centuries make such an explanation of the industry's difficulties untenable. Resistance to life assurance on theological grounds certainly existed in Britain, but it was too patchy to have accounted for the industry's many troubles. It is clear, moreover, that life assurance institutions cast themselves as engaged in something of a moral enterprise. References in company documentation are repeatedly made to insurance on lives as a project, a mission, pitched to rid the world of so many 'social evils.' It is how this 'missionary' ethos in life assurance promotion links to Victorian liberalism that forms the main topic of this section.

Throughout the nineteenth century, the burgeoning enterprise of life assurance was supported by a vast printed literature that came in a bewildering array of forms. There were explicitly promotional materials including advertisements, pamphlets, prospectuses, and handbooks issued directly by the companies themselves. By the end of the century a whole subset of trade press, often commercially linked to larger firms, existed, aimed at agents, potential customers, and other interest groups, with titles including *The Insurance Post, The Policy Holder Journal, The Insurance Spectator of London, The Insurance Agent, The Insurance Review, The Insurance Sun, The Insurance Guardian, Insurance and Banking Review, The Insurance Journal,* and *The Insurance Gazette*. In addition, there were a range of publications with no direct connection to the industry in which the topic was regularly featured. Life assurance provoked comment from political economists, mathematicians, and statisticians in the pages of outlets like the *Edinburgh Review*, it prompted advice in household management journals, it was regularly satirized in magazines like Punch and popped up surprisingly often in the novels of the period.[26]

One of the most striking features of much of this printed material, especially the promotional matter, is the extent to which it relied upon the repetition, regurgitation, and repackaging of a relatively small number of themes. Prominent among these were claims about the inherent propriety, piety, and prudence of the practice of life assurance. No company prospectus was complete without some reference to the intrinsic benevolence of the institution, albeit simply to the superfluity of mentioning again this manifest and incontrovertible characteristic. This printed matter reveals how extensive the promotional assemblage – comprising advertising, publicity, sales promotion, and personal selling – deployed by nineteenth-century life assurance companies was.[27] The industry drew upon a range of devices including the commodity spectacle of the bonus declaration system, corporate architecture and design, and iconic visual imagery[28] as part of a steady and relentless effort to persuade the public that insurance was not only safe but a duty of all rational and responsible individuals.

Companies put a huge amount of effort into translating the practice of insurance into a form that would chime with existing ideals of conduct. Promotional matter, especially prospectuses, spelt out the technical rules of insurance, as premium tables, policy exceptions, and the various different schemes available required lengthy explanation. But this material also conveyed rules of a different form in an apparent bid to promote a sense of insuring as part of a broader repertoire of prudent conduct. Life assurance was not the only method of financial planning available, and special attention was given to establishing the differences between life assurance and saving not only in technical but also in moral terms. The great, unique selling point of life assurance was, of course, that the sum assured became realizable as capital in the event of death from the moment the policy was taken. Thus, where it might take many years to set aside a given sum by saving, the whole sum assured would be realizable even if only one premium had been paid. Life assurance companies of course made much of the financial appeal of this feature, but they were also keen to describe its moral advantages. Individuals who set aside funds for the future well-being of their dependents via insurance were strictly separated from those funds. Then, as now, the early surrender of insurance polices would result in punitive financial penalties. This countered the temptation to dip in, but assuring also claimed finer benefits. Life assurance, the Scottish Widows Fund asserted,

> completely obviates all those baneful evils into which a habit of saving is apt to degenerate, for such a habit although originally springing from most proper and legitimate motives, not infrequently ends in debasing the mind to a disposition of avaricious hoarding.[29]

Avaricious hoarding, or 'having' rather than 'getting,' was to be avoided but securing adequate means for the future well-being of dependents through a little self-denial was not. Life assurance companies aimed to ensure that their agents knew how to explain to prospects the means by which the price of a premium might be secured even by those of limited means. The following extract from an agents' manual offers particularly explicit advice.

> To the industrial classes, the mechanic, the artisan, and the labourer, agricultural or otherwise – show that by the saving of a few pence weekly or

> by abstinence from the alehouse, and the gin-shop, or even the mere abridgment of half-a pint of his daily modicum of beer, he may secure a provision for his wife and family when he is in the grave … To the middle classes of society, show by what small increments the means of saving may be obtained by self-denial … a few tavern visits less, an occasional mislaying of the key of the wine cellar, a tight stopper in the spirit bottle, a few less cigars smoked, a waterside visit put off till next year, a party omitted to be given, a slight forgetfulness of the length of time a coat or a silk gown has been worn, a few less fly or cab fares to parties or scenes of amusement, Sunday trips in steamboats or on railroads, omnibus fares, and a thousand other matters of the kind, present an ample variety of sources for furnishing the small annual sum requisite to insure an ample provision for a family.[30]

In this manner, rules designed to enable 'all classes' to insure as an element of responsible, prudent conduct were outlined. Such injunctions were echoed across the industry: purchasing life assurance was 'not spending, but saving'; it was 'not a private but a public benefit'; it was, in fact, 'a moral, social and religious duty.'[31]

This 'character-ful' interpretation of life assurance as having all the Victorian liberal hallmarks of temperance, sacrifice, and restraint was carefully transmitted to consumers, notably through the medium of the sales force or 'agents.' Agents were absolutely central to the promotional enterprise and were subject to companies' continual exhortations to apply themselves to the business of selling insurance with 'missionary' zeal. Manuals and handbooks featured elaborate claims about the social, religious, and moral value of insuring in an effort to induce agents to devote the proper energy to overcoming the obstacles they faced in selling the product.

This was clearly an uphill struggle. As the author of one manual noted, despite life insurance's capacity to promote 'economy, forethought, prudence, industry, perseverance, self-sacrifice and all the qualities which most distinguish and ennoble the human character,' few had yet availed themselves of its many advantages. The language used here was echoed in other insurance manuals, and it paraphrases too closely to be accidental that of an open letter penned by the Bishop of Durham regarding how the Society for Bettering the Condition of the Poor[32] might best alleviate poverty. The coincidence of language and rhetoric is highly suggestive of an effort to situate life assurance as a self-cultivating technique equipped to promote character. Despite such advantages, 'out of a population of some 30,000,000 it is questionable if more than 250,000 are insured by all the insurance offices,'[33] while in the 'unbiased' words of another writer:

> the truth is that, whist all conditions of men, rich and poor, old and young, married and unmarried, are constantly exhorted to assure their lives by means of pamphlets, hints, suggestions, and even the threats of agents, the public as a matter of fact do not assure, generally speaking. They are reminded that a man who does not provide for his household is worse than a heathen. They admit the fact, but are too puzzled to know what to do. In the endless labyrinth of reports and prospectuses (issued, by the way, at the expense of assurers), how are the uninitiated to discern the sound office from the rotten, the cheap from the dear or the liberal from the illiberal?[34]

Agents were widely regarded as the key to expansion. But if agents were to succeed, huge improvement in their performance was necessary. According to Phillip's estimate, there were around forty thousand agents operating out of two hundred life offices, but these were not in the main the 'efficient, active, zealous, intelligent and persevering Agents' he felt were necessary. Agents should be doing their duty actively 'on public grounds,' as 'to be an agent in *name* and not in *reality* is a public evil.'[35] The importance of diligence and perseverance against all setbacks was a sentiment echoed across the trade press and agents' manuals.

> It is quite clear that the only method to be depended on for obtaining business is personal application to the parties; and that where that plan of bringing the matter before the public is adopted, and conversation on the subject had on every convenient opportunity, the expensive and useless plan of advertising may be completely superseded. Whilst one agent may be puffing his office in every newspaper in his neighbourhood from year to year, the *working* agent is steadily, noiselessly, and successfully accumulating a large and extensive business, and securing for the families around him the means of independence and comfort.[36]

This insistence that the key to success lay in 'a perseverance nowise daunted by a refusal, but rather stimulated to increased exertion' betrays a consciousness of the difficult conditions in which agents operated. The 'steady rhythm of failure' encountered even by successful agents in the United States later in the century might equally be applied in this context.[37] Insurance archives bear witness to this in files of standard letters exhorting agents, with varying degrees of severity, to improve their performance.

> The Directors regret to observe that for some time your Agency has not contributed to the business of the Society. In an old Institution like this, it is of the utmost importance to have a constant influx of new Members, so as to keep up or increase its Bonus-giving power. Pray do your utmost, and every assistance which we can render you will be cheerfully given.
>
> I regret to observe that notwithstanding the advantages this society offers to the public your agency has not been more successful ... The managers trust you will not only use your personal influence to obtain life proposals, but will also adopt such means as you may think expedient, for placing the agency in a better position than it is at present.[38]

A range of tactics were deployed to persuade agents to try harder. Companies educated, cajoled, threatened, inspired, and sweetened agents with technical handbooks, ethical pleas, admonishing letters, tales of triumph against the odds, and offers of improved commission. This amounted to a sustained pressure upon agents akin to that which the agents were expected to exert upon their prospects. Central to all this was a sociotechnical project to equip or, in Michel Callon's terms, to 'format' agents[39] – and consumers by proxy – with technical, practical, and moral knowledges about insurance. Publications and tracts with titles like *Life Assurance: Objections Answered; Why Should I Insure My Life? A Dozen Sound Reasons;* and *A Gift to the Uninsured: 30 Short Replies to 30 Common Objections* were legion.[40] These publications were not directly promotional matter but a form of indirect promotional publicity – they seldom bore company marks but they were often authored and distributed by company personnel.[41] Through such means companies sought, *ad nauseum*, to explain the technical, actuarial principles of insurance, the social and moral reasoning behind it, and the practical means by which consumers could learn the 'rules' of prudence.

Attempting to communicate so many different things may seem somewhat unwieldy, but it was nevertheless a highly integrated promotional strategy. Life assurance companies did not rely exclusively on cultivating morally charged messages about the quasi-sacred, benevolent character of their enterprise, but astutely combined this with claims about the regularity and certainty offered by the actuarial knowledges upon which insurance was based. Thus the industry's claim to offer a financial service to the orderly, pious, and prudent was underwritten by its apparent basis in objective, scientific laws. In pitching the enterprise in this way life assurance companies mirrored the emphases in Victorian liberalism on combining an economic liberalism that endorsed individual financial responsibility within the context of a 'free' market with a political liberalism that understood freedom and prudence as virtues that had to be technically *cultivated* for particular purposes.

These sorts of messages can be read as a practical exercise in the principles of liberal government. It was, in part, through such messages that life assurance companies modelled themselves as a benevolent, moral enterprise which drew upon liberal values to promote very specific ideals of good conduct. These were ideals, moreover, that could take practical form in the thrifty habits of household accounting and saving. Through 'simple industry and thrift,' through 'putting some [pennies] weekly into a benefit society or an insurance fund' as Smiles's liberal bible insisted, ordinary working people could achieve character and independence.[42] The life assurance project sought to induce participation on the grounds that it was both economically rational and morally responsible. In particular, the life assurance project relied heavily on the assumption that individuals would be destined to participate in a market project that appeared – through the much-trumpeted twin mechanisms of a basis in actuarial mathematics and a commitment to benevolent morality – to act in their prudent self-interest.

This assumption was a little optimistic. By the middle of the century, despite significant advances, life assurance had not achieved quite the level of general adoption that had been hoped for. Notwithstanding the mountains of paper devoted to reassuring the public of the soundness of the principle and practice of 'respectable' insurance companies, there was by the 1850s mounting evidence that not all companies were as 'safe' or as 'prudent' as they claimed. The collapse of companies like the Great Middlesex in the 1830s and the difficulties rumoured by the 1850s to be facing companies like the Albert and European helped fuel lobbying for tighter regulation of the industry. In response to public concern Parliament appointed a Select Committee of Inquiry into Assurance Associations in 1853. The committee sought reassurance from the industry that the threat of unsafe or bogus companies could be managed through a tighter regulatory framework that demanded greater transparency and more precise, objective measurement of companies' assets and liabilities. This, as Theodore Porter has argued, reflected a broader governmental clamour for objectivity that was obstinately resisted by company actuaries.[43] Strict adherence to actuarial methods alone, actuaries giving evidence insisted, could not make companies safe – that depended on prudence, judgement, discretion, and, most especially, an understanding of local risks. Even a light-touch regulatory framework levelled at standardizing calculations was resisted on the grounds that the true solvency of companies could not be adduced from summary figures of assets and liabilities. These figures would have limited value without a robust actuarial assessment of the companies' contingent risks, and that depended on the quality of lives companies had underwritten.

This feature was generally referred to in promotional matter under the heading of 'select lives,' which stood as shorthand for rigorous screening of proposed lives on medical, personal, and social grounds. In order to secure admission to a life assurance company, the life of the 'proposed' had to be deemed of sufficient quality to merit insuring, 'the door of an insurance office being shut against a whitened tongue or a quickened pulse.'[44] The method of selection took a variety of forms, from an appearance before the board to medical and character references and eventually a detailed medical examination. Whatever method used, the procedures for selection were outlined formally in considerable detail by the major companies, and understood in actuarial terms as key to sound economic management.

What this is pointing to is the dependence of the life assurance project on an elaborate assemblage of technical as well as moral rules. These rules both governed the internal management of the 'respectable' companies and dominated the appeal they made to recruit individuals through articulating and disseminating, principles, rules, and techniques of prudence. The prevalence of rules may seem a little out of synch with life assurance construed as an emblematic technology of liberal economic governance structured around market-based 'freedoms.' As I'll argue below, that apparent disjuncture has much to do with the character and historical plurality of liberalist political rationalities, and with the plasticity of insurance as a governmental technique.

## Concluding Comments: Insurance, Actuarialism, and Liberalism

> Insurance, then is the practice of a certain type of rationality. It has no special field of operations; rather than being defined in terms of its objects; it is a kind of ubiquitous form. It provides a general principle for the objectification of things, people and their relations.[45]

A baseline definition of insurance would describe it as a technology that compensates the effects of chance or 'risk' through the mechanism of mutuality organized according to the laws of large numbers.[46] Individual losses caused by death and accident are offset by spreading them across a community, diverting the effects from the individual to the community, definitively, in Francois Ewald's analysis, in accordance with principles of justice. Via the insurance technique, Ewald argued, a distinctive idea of justice emerges in which establishing cause, blame, or fault is set aside in favour of distributing a collective burden across a community of members whose contributions can be fixed according to explicit rules. In his genealogy of the welfare state, Donzelot explains that as cause is so difficult to ascertain juridically, defining accidents as the 'effects of an unwilled collective reality' has a powerful appeal.[47] Where social problems are viewed from the angle of collective interdependence, rather than in terms of individual duties and failings, the insurance technique, he argued, offers a considerably *more effective* and *more moral* solution. It was this potential to provide an effective, moral solution that made insurance techniques central to the international debate on how social problems might best be managed in the years running up to the First World War.[48]

This vision of insurance as a technique that can transform the social milieu through operationalizing solidarity is of course not quite in line with the liberal model outlined above. Indeed, the 'new school' discourse of solidarity Donzelot was concerned with was articulated in opposition to classical liberal ideas. Despite its fit with the solidarity project and the emerging principles that would inform the formation throughout some European countries of 'welfare states,' the insurance technique has since the eighteenth century lent itself without prejudice to a variety of political projects.[49] Insurance has a generality of principle and technique that has allowed it to bend to quite different governmental modes.

For O'Malley, writers like Ewald and Donzelot cast the insurance technique as dominating throughout the twentieth century because of its superior efficiency in regulating populations.[50] This evolutionary-inflected argument, O'Malley argues, underplays the fragmentary and dynamic nature of social relations across time against which insurance has assumed a variety of forms and intersections with distinct political programs. Technologies, he insists, come to prominence as a consequence of the ascendant political rationalities in any given context. To support his case he describes how the socialized insurances of actuarialism, described by Ewald and others, began to give way from the late 1980s to a reactivated 'prudentialist,' Victorian-style liberalism. While the guiding philosophy behind socialized actuarial techniques like unemployment and sickness benefits had been to improve labour productivity and national efficiency by reducing the effects of social problems, by the 1980s, such techniques had come to be seen by neo-liberals as in need of stripping back if the proper efficiency and enterprise of populations was to be restored.

> This should not be taken to imply that neo-liberalism opposes actuarialism, for it accepts that individuals should manage risks. Rather, it implies that they should be prudent instead of relying upon socialized securities. They should cover themselves against the vicissitudes of sickness, unemployment, old age, accidental loss or injury by making such privatised insurances as they see fit – including taking out the private insurances they can afford. In this fashion, risk-management techniques certainly play a vital role, but this is not the socialized actuarialism of Donzelot, Simon, Ewald and others. Better understood as *prudentialism,* it is a technology of governance that removes the key conception of regulating individuals by collectivist risk management, and throws back upon the individual the responsibility for managing risk.[51]

Prudentialism, then, is used by O'Malley to describe a form of privatized actuarialism that came to the fore by the mid 1990s as a result of a series of political interventions designed to promote the play of market forces across a range of different areas of government, from crime control to health and personal financial planning. A quite particular conception of the individual as responsible/moral and rational/calculating was, O'Malley notes, a recurrent theme in these interventions. Informed by data about risks, the rational, responsible individual combines calculative self-interest with actuarialism as part of a prudent strategy for the everyday management of risk. Understood in this way, prudentialism involves not merely the privatization of actuarial risk management but a recasting of the individual as rational, responsible, knowledgeable, and calculative.

O'Malley's characterization of prudentialism is underpinned by an astute assessment of how the fit between given technologies and specific political programs shifts over time. In flagging the partial transformation to a privatized form of actuarialism in the last decades of the twentieth century, O'Malley resists the temptation to see in insurance technologies an irresistible direction to the governing of populations. Ewald, for instance, may have defined insurance as the practice of a certain type of rationality, a ubiquitous kind of form with no special field of operations, but it is clear nevertheless that in his schema insurance has particular valency as a political technology that can institute judgments about justice, and social justice in particular. There is something of a slippage in the work of authors like Ewald and Donzelot, which identifies on the one hand the malleability of insurance as a technology that can lend itself to many objects whilst on the other privileging a sort of sovereign historical association with the political rationality of socialized actuarialism.

This raises some difficult questions about how the relationship between distinct modes of government and technologies that lend themselves to government is to be understood. In highlighting neoliberalism as promoting a new form of *privatized* actuarialism or prudentialism, O'Malley persuasively demonstrates that ascendant political rationalities utilize those technologies best suited to their purposes. The problem that arises is how best to account for the partial, fragmentary, and contradictory character of this relationship. At any one time an ascendant political rationality may utilize ideas drawn from a range of political philosophies. Crudely speaking, this might involve the peculiar blend of moral conservatism with free-market liberalism associated with the New Right in the 1980s. In the context of the nineteenth century, liberalism was an emerging philosophy of government that drew upon a long and diverse philosophical heritage to formulate an approach to governing what was only beginning to be defined as 'the social.' So the strands within Victorian liberalism described above may be characterized as prudentialist in their emphasis upon individual responsibility exercised within a free market, but the emphasis on a rule-governed prudence (found in life assurance promotion as much as in political, nonconformist and evangelical tracts) targeted towards moral, spiritual, and earthly enlightenment evades easy description. Moreover, the emphasis on market-based freedoms that mark liberal modes means, by definition, that liberalist governments have a thinly articulated relationship with the institutions managing the technologies they may want to use.

This is the nub of the dilemma raised by O'Malley's model of prudentialism. The relationship between liberalism as a modelled political philosophy and the mechanics of the technologies, institutions, and practices that enact it is necessarily loose. As Graham Burchell remarks of early liberal governmental reason, it does not so much set out what government policy should be as define its essential problem-space as a real, open-ended space for politico-technical invention.[52] Thus arises the gap between what liberal political rationalities may define as governable and the mechanics of how that governing should be carried out. More concretely, where a political program of socialized actuarialism may have the institutions and technologies for administering the appropriate social insurances under its more or less direct management, this, by definition, cannot apply under the model of privatized actuarialism. Prudentialism strips back social insurances and relocates the responsibility for managing risk to the rational, calculating individual. In practice this means that the relevant information and technologies for risk management are under the control of market or quasi-market institutions. The government's role then becomes one, not of controlling the policies of relevant institutions, but of manipulating the environment such that taking individual responsibility becomes the most palatable, profitable, and effective mode of provision for security against risk.

Nineteenth-century life assurance institutions traded their product in a manner that closely mirrored mainstream currents within Victorian liberalism. In promoting a product that so neatly captured the spirit of market-based self-government and that so insistently trumpeted the rules of prudent conduct, life assurance companies may seem to be in uncanny sympathy with liberalism in general, and with a 'prudentialist' Victorian liberalism in particular. But while this may be a fair assessment in the round, in practice matters are not quite so straightforward.

Liberal theories of government were informed by debates about the character of prudence, self-interest, and human motivation that had preoccupied moral philosophers for centuries. These debates provided an intellectual heritage upon which liberal theories of government drew to provide a framework for an economically structured form of government at a distance. Life assurance was one of those techniques that seemed to spring up to fill the gap between liberal governmental theory in the abstract and the management of concrete social problems. It would, however, be a mistake to read life assurance as an inevitability of liberal government. Rather, life assurance should be understood as a privatized version of actuarial technology that has at its core the generality of principle that allows it to commend itself to a variety of distinct political rationalities. Thus when Cheysson refers to insurance as the only science to have mathematics at its base and morality for its crown, he refers to its role within a model of socialized actuarialism.[53] That the same claim could equally be applied to life assurance within a prudentialist mode of government illustrates something of its breadth of appeal. The appeal of insurance stems from its immersion in a number of intersecting universes connecting commerce, religion, government, and science. Promotional material directs attention to how the industry sought to attract customers, but at the same time it offers a source for exploring much broader questions about how life assurance 'fitted' in the world.

## NOTES

1 In general usage, the term 'life assurance' has no specific meaning distinct from that of 'life insurance'; its use tends only to denote the specific, predominantly commercial and private, form taken by life as opposed to other forms of insurance in Britain from the late eighteenth century.

2 See for example Ian Hacking, *The Taming of Chance* (Cambridge: Cambridge University Press, 1990); Theodore Porter, *Trust in Numbers: The Pursuit of Objectivity in Pubic Life* (Princeton: Princeton University Press, 1996).

3 See Liz McFall, 'The Disinterested Self: The Idealized Subject of Life Assurance,' *Cultural Studies* 21, nos. 4–5, (2007), 591–609.

4 See Pat O'Malley, 'Risk and Responsibility,' in Andrew Barry, Thomas Osborne, and Nikolas Rose, eds., *Foucault and Political Reason* (Chicago: University of Chicago Press, 1996).

5 Thomas Aquinas, *Summae Theologica* (New York: English Dominican Province, 1947), 3 vols., pts. 1–2, q. 57, art. 5.

6 Thomas Hobbes, *Leviathan*, in *The English Works of Thomas Hobbes of Malmesbury*, vol. 3 (London: John Bohn, 1838/1966), 15.

7 Hobbes, quoted in Art Vanden Houten, 'Prudence in Hobbes's Political Philosophy,' *History of Political Thought*, XXIII, 2 (2002), 266-287.

8 See Vivienne Brown, *Adam Smith's Discourse: Canonicity, Commerce and Conscience* London: Routledge, 1994).

9 Adam Smith, *The Theory of Moral Sentiments*, edited by Raphael and Macfie (Oxford: Oxford University Press, 1976), 215.

10 Smith, *Theory of Moral Sentiments*, 213.

11 Smith, *Theory of Moral Sentiments*, 213.

12 Pierre Force, *Self-Interest before Adam Smith: A genealogy of economic science* (Cambridge: Cambridge University Press 2003), 47; Smith quoted in ibid., 160.

13 Stefan Collini, 'The Idea of "Character" in Victorian Political Thought,' *Transactions of the Royal Historical Society*, 5th ser., vol. 35 (1985), 29–50. Although Collini's purpose is to stress the distinctiveness of 'character' against eighteenth century ideas of 'virtue,' he nevertheless makes the lineage clear.

14 As Force, *Self-Interest*, explains, while Hobbes and Smith drew their definitions of prudence and human motivation from the distinct and sometimes opposing moral philosophical traditions of Epicureanism and Stoicism, respectively, their advocated systems of government both regarded the pursuit of commercial self-interest as a route to civil peace and stability. For more on the governmental role of self-interest, see Paul du Gay 'Which Is the Self in Self-Interest?,' *The Sociological Review* 53, no.3 (2005), 391–411; and Albert O. Hirschman, *The Passions and the Interests: Political Arguments for Capitalism before Its Triumph* (Princeton: Princeton University Press, 1977).

15 Mary Poovey, *A History of the Modern Fact* (Chicago: University of Chicago Press, 1998), 147.

16 Poovey, *History of the Modern Fact*.

17 See Quentin Skinner, *Liberty before Liberalism* (Cambridge: Cambridge University Press, 1997). For a discussion of more positive concepts of freedom, see Eugene Biagini, 'Neo-roman Liberalism: "Republican" Values and British Liberalism, ca. 1860–1875,' *History of European Ideas*, 29 (2003), 55–72; and Boyd Hilton, *The Age of Atonement: The Influence of Evangelicalism on Social and Economic Thought, 1795–1865* (Oxford: Clarendon, 1988).

18 Sterling in Samuel Smiles, *Self-Help with Illustrations of Character and Conduct* (Boston: Ticknor and Fields, 1866), 280.

19 Green in Biagini, 'Neo-roman Liberalism,' 60.

20 Green in Biagini, 'Neo-roman Liberalism,' 61.

21 See Collini, 'The Idea of "Character,"' and Smiles, *Self-Help with Illustrations.*

22 Alisdair Macintyre, *After Virtue: A Study in Moral Theory* (Notre Dame, IN: Notre Dame University Press, 1981), 218.
23 Hilton, *The Age of Atonement*.
24 See Geoffrey Clark, *Betting on Lives: The Culture of Life Insurance in England 1695–1775* (Manchester: Manchester University Press, 1999).
25 Viviana Zelizer, *Morals and Markets: The Development of Life Insurance in the United States* (New York: Columbia University Press, 1979).
26 The fate of the rotten Anglo-Bengalee company is a subplot in Dickens's *Martin Chuzzlewit*, but life assurance is also referred to in such novels as George Eliot's *Middlemarch* and Wilkie Collins's *The Woman in White*. Eric Wertheimer in *Underwriting: The Poetics of Insurance in America, 1722–1872* (Stanford: Stanford University Press, 2006) makes an inventive case for how insurance colonized economic life, using American literary references to Benjamin Franklin, Herman Melville, R.W. Emerson, and others.
27 The emphasis in many studies of consumption underrates the significance of advertising and promotional activity in nineteenth-century service industries, especially railways and financial services. These industries deployed much more sophisticated promotional tactics than has been widely acknowledged in the social and cultural study of consumption. Cf. Liz McFall, *Advertising: A Cultural Economy* (London: Sage, 2004).
28 See Timothy Alborn, 'The First Fund Managers,' *Victorian Studies* (Autumn 2002), 65–92, on the bonus declaration system. See also Liz Mcfall and Francis Dodsworth, 'Fabricating the Market: The Promotion of Life Assurance in the Nineteenth Century,' *Journal of Historical Sociology* 22, no. 1 (2009) on the promotional use of corporate architecture and design.
29 Pamphlet, 1837, Box 7, Insurance Series, John Johnson Collection of Printed Ephemera, Bodleian Library, Oxford (hereafter JJ.)
30 Anon., *Elements of Success of a Life Assurance Agency*, n.d., c.1850? 16. GD294/29, National Archives of Scotland, Register House, Edinburgh (hereafter NAS.)
31 United Kingdom Temperance and General Provident Institution, 1887; Box 8, JJ; Mentor Life Assurance prospectus, Box 4, JJ; Risborough-Sarman, Insurance Guardian, Life Assurance Leaflets, new series, no. 4, 1868.
32 The Bishop of Durham's letter, quoted in Hilton, *The Age of Atonement*, 99, read, 'Whatever encourages and promotes habits of INDUSTRY, PRUDENCE, FORESIGHT, VIRTUE, and CLEANLINESS among the poor, is beneficial to them and to the country; whatever removes, or diminishes, the incitement to any of these qualities, is detrimental to the state and

pernicious to the individual.' The wording 'Whatever tends to promote the habits of forethought, industry and economy (without hoarding) in the community, whatever tends to give a larger number "a stake in the state," and to increase the stake of those who already hold one – whatever tends to promote prosperity, to diminish pauperism, to alleviate and largely to prevent destitution, to keep those who might become criminals out of the way of temptation – whatever does all this (as we contend life assurance does) it is the obvious duty of the consistent politician to watch over and promote by every means within his reach,' appears in Risborough Sarman, Insurance Guardian, Life Assurance Leaflets, new series, no. 4, 1868.

33 J.H. Phillips, *The Life Assurance Agent's Manual* (London, 1857), 5.

34 Francis Guy, *Unbiased Notes on Life Assurance* (1871), 11. BOD200h81 4, Bodleian Library, Oxford (hereafter BOD).

35 Phillips, *Life Assurance Agent's Manual*, 6.

36 Anonymous, *Elements*, 7.

37 Anonymous, *Elements*, 7; Vande Creek, 'Solomon Huebner and the Development of Life Insurance Sales Professionalism, 1905–1927,' *Enterprise and Society* 6, no. 4 (2005), 657.

38 NU173, Letter Norwich Union to Agents, c.1880, Aviva Companies Archive, Norwich, MS18262 (hereafter Aviva); Letter Sun Life to Agent, 1878, Guildhall Library, London (hereafter GH).

39 Michel Callon, ed., 'Introduction: The Embeddedness of Economic Markets in Economics,' *The Laws of the Market* (Oxford: Blackwell, 1998).

40 Pamphlets by Sim (1889); Risborough-Sarman, Insurance Guardian, Life Assurance Leaflets, new series, no. 4, 1868; W. Hannam (1857), BOD.

41 Indirect or 'below-the-line' promotional publicity is still often perceived by consumers to offer a more objective source of information and is often preferred by companies as a means for communicating complex information.

42 Smiles, *Self-Help with Illustrations.*

43 Porter, *Trust in Numbers.*

44 Anonymous, *Elements*, 16.

45 Francois Ewald, 'Insurance and Risk,' in Graham Burchell, Colin Gordon, and Peter Miller, eds., *The Foucault Effect: Studies in Governmentality* (London: Harvester Wheatsheaf, 1991).

46 See Ewald, 'Insurance and Risk.' Both Ewald and Ian Hacking, *The Taming of Chance*, emphasize the epochal break signified by statistically informed insurance techniques, but as Clark, *Betting on Lives*, documents,

the insurance industry flourished in England prior to the widespread acceptance and articulation of statistical knowledges in the nineteenth century.

47 Jacques Donzelot, 'The Promotion of the Social,' *Economy and Society* 17, no. 3 (1988), 395–427.

48 See Liz Mcfall, 'Pragmatics and Politics: The Case of Industrial Branch Assurance in the UK,' *Journal of Cultural Economy*, 3, no. 2 (2010).

49 Clark, *Betting on Lives,* describes compellingly the coexistence of competing and contradictory political aspirations for insurance techniques in eighteenth-century England, while the friendly societies that coexisted with British commercial life assurance companies in the nineteenth century used insurance as a technique to further fraternal and communitarian ends. See also Mcfall, 'Pragmatics and Politics,' for more on insurance's political malleability

50 O'Malley, 'Risk and Responsibility.'

51 O'Malley, 'Risk and Responsibility,' 196–7.

52 Graham Burchell, 'Liberal Government and Techniques of the Self,' in Barry et al., *Foucault and Political Reason*.

53 In Donzelot, 'Promotion of the Social,' 404.

# 7 Honesty, Fidelity, and Insurance in Eighteenth- and Nineteenth-Century England

GREGORY ANDERSON

By the late nineteenth century fidelity insurance was firmly established in Britain as the main mechanism for risk transfer in handling potential loss exposures resulting from the violation of trust. Although during the course of its development fidelity insurance was successfully adapted to meet a wide range of new contingencies, this chapter will deal with its original and primary function, which was to provide protection against acts of dishonesty by trusted employees in public and private companies and by officers of state.

The historical process by which fidelity insurance achieved this position of importance was by no means a straightforward one. I will show how it developed out of a much older tradition in which security, for persons holding positions of trust, was provided by the widespread use of private arrangements based upon a high-trust culture and depending upon kinship, fidelity, and social networks linked to family and friends. This historical background provided both an opportunity and an obstacle to the early promoters of fidelity insurance. Indeed the very use of the word 'fidelity,' with its wider connotations of loyalty and faithfulness as well as honesty, is strongly suggestive of the historical ties this form of insurance had with this much older cultural tradition. The first promoters of fidelity insurance sold their product as a superior replacement for personal security, but at first encountered scepticism and even hostility from those who believed that the security provided by personal arrangements was somehow morally superior to that provided by insurance.[1] However, the existence of a large and ready-made market among employees, private employers, and public companies as well as the departments of state, all needing security against the threat of dishonesty, could be readily exploited by insurers once their assessment of the risks associated with such dishonesty became more sophisticated. The emergence of fidelity insurance also occurred during a period of transition when personal arrangements and other customary practices were being gradually replaced by firmer legal principles and more binding contractual arrangements mirroring the growth of a new commercial and financial economy. The legal system was already encroaching on this new economy, providing remedies for various forms of default and fraud long before fidelity insurance appeared on the scene. In particular, there was growing concern about commercial crimes in the workplace. The creation of 'new' indictable white-collar crimes provided an essential platform from which fidelity insurance was eventually launched. Compared to the old system of personal suretyship, fidelity insurance provided a better solution to the need for new and more formal contractual arrangements in the workplace to protect against employee dishonesty. In particular, it proved to be well suited to the needs of large-scale corporate employers, both the old corporations and the new joint-stock companies, where workers were subject to increasing managerial control. A similar situation was faced by the officers and appointees of the state, who had historically required individual security but who in the nineteenth century began operating in new areas where trust and guardianship were statutorily required.

## The Development of Fidelity Insurance

Fidelity insurance originated in England in the first half of the nineteenth century. The London Guarantee Society, established in the capital in 1840, is generally credited with being the first fidelity company in the world. Its first prospectus encapsulates its potential market and describes the background from which it emerged:

> The Guarantee Society has been established to obviate the defects of the suretyship by private bondsmen which is universally acknowledged to be attended with various inconveniences and objections … the Guarantee Society undertakes on the payment of a small premium … to make good in case of default by fraud or dishonesty, any loss which may be sustained to an amount specifically named and agreed upon in their policy and by such means obviate the necessity for private surety.[2]

Although a number of other companies entered the field in the mid-nineteenth century, not all were successful, with some either failing to mature or being eventually 'wound up.' These difficulties, which affected insurance generally in the first phase of joint-stock promotion, led to some loss of confidence in fidelity insurance, especially in official circles. However, its credibility was considerably strengthened by the 1867 Guarantee of Companies Act, which set out general conditions for compliance before departments of state were allowed to accept a company's guarantee. Despite this, progress was initially very slow, and as late as 1872 the premium income of all operating companies was only £70,000. From the 1880s a fresh impetus was provided by employer's liability companies, which began to transact fidelity business, and by 1890 there were no fewer than thirty fidelity companies operating in Britain. In the twentieth century Lloyd's of London also entered the field, providing excess cover against potential catastrophic losses by employees, who were otherwise only covered by ordinary schedule policies. From the early twentieth century many specialist fidelity companies, faced by an increasingly competitive environment, disappeared as their business was absorbed by the larger corporate insurance companies in a wave of mergers and takeovers that saw fidelity insurance increasingly subsumed into the accident departments of these larger companies.[3]

## Security in the Old Economy

Fidelity insurance developed as part of the transition towards a new system for enforcing employee compliance and monitoring their performance in the workplace. New procedures such as fidelity insurance did not abruptly replace older mechanisms, but developed alongside them and gradually subsumed their functions over time. Indeed, the traditional culture for generating trust in British business continued to flourish into the nineteenth century and beyond, as the long success story of family firms bears witness.

In the eighteenth century and before, trust and loyalty in business were heavily dependent upon social networks, religious affiliation, kinship ties, and sentimental and affective attachments. A number of historians have drawn attention to the importance of one's 'friends' in this period, and this was nowhere more apparent than in business, where social obligations and mutual self-interest linked patrons and clients together. This extended to the workplace, where the trust between partners and between masters and their servants rested not merely upon economic imperatives but also upon affective feelings and emotional bonds.

For young men starting out in life the first introduction to this culture was likely as not to be through an apprenticeship, a formal period of training that involved serving a master faithfully and becoming part not only of a master's workforce but also of his household and family. Some two-thirds of young men and women in the eighteenth century left home for 'formative periods of life-cycle service' as servants and apprentices in other people's households.[4]

Apprenticeships were common across the economy but were particularly important in the career development of commercial and professional occupations. Young men who wished to become merchants or lawyers first served a period of formal training before setting up on their own account. During their training, apprentices were expected to study their masters' temper, while masters in turn were expected to lead by example.[5] Apprentices were formally contracted to their masters, but their covenants were as much a moral as a legal bond. The solemnity of the contract was sometimes reinforced by the apprentices' swearing of oaths of loyalty, and the apprenticeship indentures usually proscribed behaviour employers regarded as inappropriate or morally hazardous, such as drinking, swearing, and gambling. There is little doubt that contract enforceability in the case of apprenticeship was effective, since the future employment of apprentices was conditional upon their past conduct. However, the contractual nature of such arrangements did not preclude a moral dimension. Hard-nosed pragmatism and sentimental attachments intermingled effectively, as was reflected in the warmth and friendship that often existed between masters and their young charges, especially in the counting-houses of the old merchant class.[6]

Apart from apprenticeship, there existed additional instruments to sustain the contractual relationship between masters and their servants. Surety bonds were often posted for commercial employees and were designed to protect employers against breach of contract. Historically, surety bonds were utilized in a variety of default situations. They were commonly used to secure loans, as forfeits in "malicious petitions" in bankruptcy, or as security for individuals who failed to appear before the courts, but by the early modern period their most common use was probably as employment bonds. While the ubiquity of private suretyship is well known, with a history dating back to biblical times, the practice had come to flourish in the high-trust culture, based upon patronage and property, of early modern England. It also became notably subject to greater legal control with the Statute of

Frauds in 1677, a milestone in the history of suretyship, which sought to eliminate abuses in the enforceability of verbal contracts arising from acts of fraud and perjury. In order to be enforceable all contracts now had to be written and signed, including any promises that a surety made for another's defaults and debts.[7] The inclusion of surety within the emerging law of contract recognized the importance of this form of protection as part of a wider pattern of debt recovery. Much of the concern was with the potentially disastrous consequences of offering surety too easily. It was an immutable rule of suretyship that no person would ever lightly offer surety to a stranger. "He that hath surety for a stranger',' the Old Testament proverb had warned, 'shall smart for it: and he that hateth surety is sure.'[8] Shakespeare in *The Merchant of Venice* highlighted the dangers awaiting the unwary provider of surety in the famous forfeiture of Antonio's bond to Shylock. Written around the same time, William Burton's sermons on suretyship were a warning that charity and affective feelings should not lead those who might act as sureties into acts of folly, since a default could be financially disastrous for them.[9] The moral dimension of surety bonds was crucial, as in practice the surety would only agree to provide security if there was little or no expectation of losses occurring. The surety was only secondarily liable to pay, and all efforts would normally be made to ensure that the principal, usually a relative or close friend, who was effectively in debt to the surety, paid in the first instance. If this did not occur the financial impact upon the surety might be considerable. Losses under suretyship could turn former friends and relatives into the most bitter of enemies.[10]

By the eighteenth century the use of surety bonds in the workplace was becoming more common. Although the bonds could be used to cover any non-excluded failure to carry out an expressed obligation (performance bonds), the provision of security to cover employee dishonesty was becoming more important. This was in line with the growing number of employees with greater financial responsibilities and more direct access to their employers' funds. These men, for it was at this time an exclusively male preserve, usually filled positions as clerks, an occupation whose range by the late eighteenth and into the nineteenth centuries extended from the most menial posts to the highest administrative, confidential, and financial responsibilities in government, commerce, and finance. Among the latter were the officers of the East India and Hudson's Bay companies, the Royal Exchange Assurance, and the Sun and London Assurance as well as of the Bank of England and the Treasury and other great departments of state. These men formed the nucleus of an expanding class of well-paid, well-educated, middle-class clerks located mainly in London.

Private suretyship for such men was usually regarded by both their sponsors and employers as a social formality and a form of moral security. The East India Company, for example, used two legal instruments, bonds and 'covenants of indenture,' to limit the opportunistic behaviour of its employees. Employees were obliged to provide pre-employment bonds, signed by two sureties on their behalf, which theoretically offered legal redress against malfeasant behaviour through the Courts of Chancery. However, there is no evidence of legal action ever being taken against sureties, and indeed in an internal statement in 1785 the company's solicitor could not explain the historical reasons for such bonding, since 'in this respect it had been ever what it now is and that there had been some good cause for it but they did not intimate even a guess what it might be.'[11] During this period the East India Company preferred enforcement mechanisms from within the firm, such as the dismissal or suspension of rogue employees, rather than involve the courts.

The weaknesses of private suretyship became more apparent as the economy expanded and the number of employers and their clerks increased. Apart from the well-known moral hazards facing those who acted as sureties, employers faced an equal degree of uncertainty, since they were often unable to check on either the continuing solvency or the health of sureties. A parliamentary enquiry into a series of frauds in the Port of London revealed that no surety had ever been rejected there for many years and one surety, it was discovered, had a criminal record.[12] Monitoring problems such as these were more acute for large-scale employers. At the same time, the expansion of the urban white-collar labour market in the nineteenth century, especially in London, exposed the difficulties young men with fewer social connections faced in finding willing sponsors as part of their search for employment.[13] Although suretyship did not disappear, it gradually became much less important as a solution to the problem of employee honesty.

## White-Collar Crime in the New Economy

Concern about the honesty of those men who were employed as clerks increased in direct proportion to the growth of the new financial and commercial economy. In a number of ways during the eighteenth century 'the law was brought into line with the needs of new forms of property and securities.'[14] Many of the statutes passed were designed to protect currency, credit, bills, and other commercial issues, with a large number dating from the period of office of Lord Mansfield at King's Bench between 1760 and1788. What were regarded previously as misdemeanours were now classed as felonies, and some, like 'coining,' became capital offences.[15]

The operation of trust in the workplace must be understood within the context of this new economic and legal experience. During the course of the century the law of theft was extended to the workplace, being first applied to industrial workers with a landmark act passed in 1749 that made it a criminal offence for a worker to purloin materials that were entrusted to him; customary practices that were considered perquisites by many workers were increasingly regarded as theft by their employers. Repeated legislation in the eighteenth century changed the penalty structure for successful prosecutions in such cases from straightforward restitution, a civil breach of contract, to seizure of property and even jail as an option.

Although clerks remained a relatively small occupational group until the nineteenth century, their role in the world of money, credit, and securities was a strategic one and their money-handling activities provided opportunities for dishonesty. Despite the high level of trust that operated between clerks and their masters, the criminal law was eventually introduced into the counting house, firstly with a number of special acts that referred to those employed in the Post Office and banks before the first 'modern' and 'general' statute in 1799 (39 Geo. 3, c. 85) dealing with the embezzlement by clerks and trusted servants in the course of their work. It has been suggested that the test case for this legislation was that of a clerk in Esdaile's Bank, one of the major country banks, who received a note to the value of £100 that he put to his own account rather than to the credit of the customer who had paid it in. The purpose of the enactment was to distinguish between the common law of larceny, which involved unlawful possession following trespass, and one in which the initial possession was in good faith but was subsequently misappropriated.[16]

In practice embezzlement proved to be the most difficult of crimes to define, prove, and prosecute. The prevailing view is that, although it was a purely statutory offence, embezzlement was never adequately defined by statute, and there is general consent among legal historians that in the nineteenth century the law of theft, which covered embezzlement, was one of confusion since juries had to make the correct finding between either larceny or embezzlement, or convictions were quashed. A related problem in embezzlement cases, and one that was tested in the courts on a number of occasions, was the nature of the relationship between the employer and his clerk. For embezzlement to be proven there had to be a master-servant relationship in existence, but if the clerk or other trusted employee could prove that the relationship was that of a principal and his agent then the accused could not be guilty of embezzlement, since the failure to account for monies due to the principal was then a matter of debt and therefore in law constituted a civil action. This legal distinction was especially important for fidelity insurance companies, since it was incumbent upon them to issue policies that protected employers from civil action, as fidelity policies could only safeguard employers if the relationship was one of' 'master and servant.'[17]

An additional and overriding complication was that it was often difficult to distinguish between the errors of ill-trained clerks and managers and their fraudulent activity, a situation that was exacerbated by the inadequacy of early accounting and book-keeping procedures. Against this background it was naturally difficult to assess the extent of embezzlement. Because of the legal complexities involved, crimes might occur that were impossible to indict or might remain deliberately hidden from the public gaze because of the 'reputational' damage their disclosure would inflict upon all the parties involved: the employers, the individuals concerned, and their families.

## Commercial Morality and Security in the New Economy

Whether or not there was a real increase in the rate of embezzlement in this period is impossible to say, but by the nineteenth century the continued expansion of the 'money' economy and the growth of commercial occupations created more uncertainty among employers by increasing the opportunities for white-collar crime in the workplace. Embezzlement may be seen as the flip side of company fraud. Both were middle-class crimes, but while company fraud was difficult to prosecute or was tolerated as part of the business process, attitudes to embezzlement, many of which were small-scale crimes, hardened with the early introduction of criminal sanctions.[18]

Concern about white-collar crime was probably at its greatest in the City of London, since it was there that the new money economy was most visible. By the 1830s and 1840s London was on the cusp of its pre-eminent role as a global financial centre. The City was the hub of a metropolitan world in which money was made, invested, and recycled, and clerks were at the heart of these transactions. The number of men in white-collar occupations in England had by 1851 reached 130,000, with a preponderance living in London, where they were an essential body of workers and a significant economic presence.[19]

However, the level of honesty and gentlemanly conduct in the City was, it was feared, being undermined by the speculative mania that gripped London and the rest of the economy at this time. The waves of limited liability promotions involving banks, insurance and trading companies, and especially the railways were too frequently associated with fraud and mismanagement and raised once more the spectre of the 1720 South Sea Bubble. While brokers, merchants, and investors made and lost fortunes, their clerks, who often carried out their masters' dealings on the stock exchange, sometimes acted independently, lured by their own pursuit of wealth and personal advancement, except that in the frenzied buying and selling of stock they were more likely to face financial disaster and perhaps succumb to dishonesty as a result. The dangerous level of personal speculation by clerks certainly fuelled fears in the City about the threat of embezzlement. Such was the level of concern that it led in the middle of the nineteenth century to a committee of the London Stock Exchange forbidding its members from transacting speculative business with clerks in private and public companies without the knowledge of their employers, although in truth the problem continued throughout the century, and often with disastrous consequences.[20]

The threats of embezzlement, fraud, and uncontrolled speculation helped create a virtual moral panic about the state of the country's commercial morality. In 1843 the editor of the *Illustrated London News* declared that 'commercial dishonesty will become the rule and integrity the exception.'[21] Some historians have even suggested that business and personal ethics at this time were being seriously compromised by the climate of greed and that the social rules, moral concepts, and sensibilities that controlled middle-class behaviour in the outside world were proving to be much less effective inside the workplace.[22] The fear of middle-class occupational crime was given substance by the public exposure of organized fraud in the Port of London among customs officers and of systemic weaknesses in the system of private bonding in operation there, a situation that the early proponents of fidelity insurance were quick to exploit by showing that not only was the new generation of commercial young men sometimes unable to find security from within their own social circle, but that the legal protection of private suretyship for employers was more apparent than real.

Against this background, it is not surprising that the proposal for fidelity insurance should emanate from within the City of London and that it should seek to commend itself to the business community by declaring that one of its objects was 'to promote commercial stability and security.' Neither was it a great surprise that the idea was first developed by representatives of some of the City's oldest corporations, viz. the East India Company and the Bank of England. Henry Roberts, a Bank of England clerk, helped by a member of the stock exchange, is credited with first suggesting the idea of forming a committee to investigate the possibilities of fidelity insurance. The members of this committee formed the London Guarantee Society in 1840. Ironically, given its primary purpose, one of the biggest initial problems the London Guarantee Society faced was concern about its own level of solvency. Actually, such concern was not surprising given the background of fraud and mismanagement associated with the first wave of insurance company promotions. So great was the level of public scepticism that the Guarantee Society offered any business for which a policy was being drawn an invitation to inspect its deed of settlement to ensure it was satisfied that the necessary funds were in place.[23]

More fundamental moral questions were raised, however, about the very nature of fidelity insurance itself. It seemed to some critics that such insurance must of necessity regard defalcation as more of a loss than a crime. The reaction of the first fidelity insurers was to laud as their 'great moral object' the 'diminution of crime,' but in its first prospectus the Guarantee Society was forced to admit that for some individuals 'no moral restraint whatever will influence them.'[24] The exposure and prosecution of embezzlers was regarded in some quarters as the best deterrent, and in the nineteenth century fidelity companies often pursued defaulters through the courts; some companies included this as a 'condition precedent' and were willing to pay the legal costs if a conviction followed. As we have noted, however, the law on embezzlement was so complicated that by the twentieth century fidelity policies became closer in principle to pure accident insurance and usually omitted the need to prosecute, and avoided legally contentious terms like 'embezzlement' altogether. One historian of white-collar crime has argued that in practice fidelity insurance 'could only cushion the blow of clerical fraud and did nothing by way of prevention.'[25] It was certainly true that most fidelity policies could not cover the very largest frauds, but both in their willingness to prosecute embezzlers and, more importantly, through the careful construction of their contracts, the companies helped to ensure that employers operated adequate internal audits and other measures in order to prevent the occurrence of fraud.

More worrying for the first promoters was the view, widely held at the time, that, in contrast to personal security, fidelity insurance might undermine personal morality. Why, critics argued, would some unscrupulous individual have less compunction about defrauding an impersonal insurance company rather than a friend or a relative? This was a concern that went to the heart of this type of insurance, and forced the first fidelity companies to sell themselves as a more effective alternative to private security by arguing that under the old system 'a young man might yield to temptation … secretly encouraged by the hope that his error if detected will be hushed up by his relations for their sake if not for his own,' while in contrast the directors of a fidelity insurance company would be obliged to lay the particulars of individual cases in front of that company's shareholders, with inevitable exposure ensuing. Given the practice in the early fidelity companies of giving cover mainly to named individuals rather than to their employers, there was a distinct possibility of such exposure, and there is no doubt that the early fidelity companies sought to counter such criticism by embodying the characteristics of the old personal system of bonding, since it was not at all unusual for them to re-guarantee private sureties partly to overcome objections to corporate provision. Some of the criticism of fidelity insurance struck closer to the heart of the Victorian value system by suggesting that such cover might somehow undermine a man's 'independence' and 'honest pride;' insurers were forced to retaliate strongly by arguing that, compared to insurance, personal security surely placed a man under an obligation that was distasteful to anyone of independent spirit.[26]

A further 'moral hazard,' though not one that was of much concern at first, involved the impact of fidelity cover upon employers, who it was argued might also behave differently in the face of insurance by seeking to act outside the terms of their policies. Although the same moral hazard was a feature of private suretyship, this threat to behavioural trust was indeed a problem that lay at the heart of this type of insurance, and ultimately could only be resolved by the care with which the fidelity insurers constructed their contracts, something that the surety could never do. However, while the construction of contracts by companies might reduce this moral hazard, it could never entirely eliminate it, as the regular testing of fidelity contracts in the English courts bore witness.[27]

The criticism that fidelity cover might undermine the 'independence' of key employees was potentially damaging to the values of self-help and self-reliance that were in turn expected to shape the careers and attitudes of men, such as confidential clerks, who were historically a potential source of business partners. Such criticism was more relevant in the culture of the old mercantile counting houses, but much less so in an emerging corporate economy. Once employers rather than employees became responsible for paying the insurance premiums, concern about the impact of insurance on the 'independence' of employees became less of an issue, as they were no longer party to the insurance contract. The new contractual arrangements reflected fundamental changes in employer–employee relationships in the nineteenth century, especially in corporate organizations with their large salaried workforces. In contrast to the obligations under suretyship, where the employee was legally bound to protect his employer against loss, fidelity insurance contracts were increasingly granted only to the employer, without either the knowledge or consent of the employee. These corporate fidelity contracts effectively depersonalized employees, who might also face criminal charges if their misdemeanours were indictable, as well as being forced to reimburse the insurance companies for their costs. The development of these 'hard-line' insurance policies partly reflects the demands of the legal system on the fidelity companies, but also the changed and more bureaucratic relationship between employers, insurers, and employees that developed as the nineteenth century progressed. More than sixty years after the introduction of fidelity insurance an industry representative could confidently assert: 'While a certain type of employer – rapidly dying out in these matter-of-fact days – was wont to rely upon the integrity of his staff, to put them upon their honour and trust to their better natures as his sole safeguard against peculation and embezzlement, such blind confidence does not enter much into business relations nowadays.'[28]

Early moral concerns about the use of fidelity insurance gradually disappeared in the face of a changing business culture whose need for an increased supply of white-collar employees after 1850 rapidly outgrew both the capabilities and the underlying principles of private suretyship in favour of new administrative and contractual arrangements.

## Fidelity Insurance and Corporate Business

While the spread of fidelity insurance in the nineteenth century reached out to all areas of the economy, with private companies being as prominent as public ones, it was with the latter that it became mainly associated. Apart from the old corporations such as the East India Company and the City of London, the banks, railways, and other incorporated enterprises that followed in the wake of the joint-stock legislation between the 1830s and 1860s were all targets for the fidelity companies, as were the officers of central and local government and court officials. In particular, the fidelity companies proved very adept at responding directly to the requirements of large-scale employers, replacing, for example, individual with collective policies that better catered for both the higher turnover and larger number of employees and the internal labour markets that were features of such organizations. By the late nineteenth century the fidelity companies had taken the process a stage further with job categories or groups of unidentified workers, rather than individuals, being insured, usually at a lower rate than on individual policies.[29]

In the first half of the nineteenth century corporate enterprises were faced with a high degree of uncertainty with respect to employee honesty and fidelity. While some social scientists believe that low levels of trust are a systemic problem in large business organizations irrespective of either time or place, this problem was also a historical consequence of large firms outgrowing the managerial, accounting, and auditing procedures that were available to them.[30] Old 'monied' corporations like the East India Company had struggled to develop adequate and enforceable employment contracts or systems of personal bonding to control employee dishonesty in the eighteenth century and had been among the first clients of fidelity insurers. Fidelity insurance also matched the need for new arrangements in the Bank of England during its period of 'modernization' in the 1830s and 1840s, which culminated in the Bank Charter Act of 1844. In 1836 the court of directors put a stop to their very lenient treatment of financially embarrassed clerks and ordered that bankruptcy would in future be followed by dismissal while, at the same time it forbade any officer from engaging in business or trade outside the bank. Not only was one of the bank's clerks a prime mover in the creation of the London Guarantee Society in 1840, but in the following year the bank set up the first 'in-house' mutual guarantee scheme for its own clerks, which in turn led to the formulation of a similar scheme for the other banks.[31]

Fidelity insurance also developed at a time when legislation to control companies was weak and largely ineffective and before the professionalization of accountancy had taken place. Under the 1844 Companies Act protection against embezzlement and fraud was very limited, and although the Companies Acts of the 1850s increased the demand for accountants, there was no required standard of skill in place until after the Institute of Chartered Accountants was established in 1880. Accounting procedures did improve for large companies over time, but only with the Companies Act of 1900, reinforced by further legislation in the first half of the twentieth century, did both public and private limited companies require compulsory audits that ultimately provided the main safeguard against fraud.

Given the shortcomings of internal audits in the middle of the nineteenth century, it was not surprising that some of the newly incorporated businesses, having been the victims of large-scale fraud by their senior officers, turned increasingly to fidelity insurance to provide large-scale security cover. From the 1840s the newly amalgamated railway companies, the first giant enterprises anywhere in the world, began to utilize fidelity insurance companies to sift recruits according to their character, and applicants were obliged to purchase cover before they were considered for employment. Existing staff who were refused fidelity cover following investigation into their personal backgrounds were likely to be dismissed. The early railway companies also used fidelity insurance as a powerful disciplinary weapon, since at this time they could rely upon fidelity insurers to prosecute individuals who were guilty of defalcation if there was any likelihood of conviction.[32]

In the long run, however, the use of fidelity insurance by corporate firms like banks and railways proved to be only a transitional solution to the problems of trust and dishonesty. Accounting practices improved more quickly in the larger companies partly in response to major frauds and partly to safeguard shareholder interests. Also, corporate businesses like banks and railways were in the forefront of creating centralized managerial systems during the nineteenth century, although the pace and timing of this 'managerial revolution' varied enormously. Fidelity insurance was, at first, a preferred solution to the problem of managing the honesty of employees in these companies, but it did not always remain so. Large companies came increasingly to rely more upon external audits, which arguably dealt more effectively with the internal organizational causes of dishonesty; at the same time, fidelity companies began to face competition from changes in these organizations' internal provision of security. The 'internalization' of a range of activities otherwise carried out by the market has been a recurrent feature in the history of large corporations, so it is hardly surprising that, when circumstances allowed, the management of employee honesty was also brought 'in-house.' By the 1860s and 1870s the joint-stock banks and railway companies began to form their own guarantee funds with deductions from pay as a normal condition of service, and such arrangements, apart from anticipating modern company pension funds, much reduced the need for large-scale fidelity insurance cover as a prerequisite of employment. This process was a piecemeal and in some ways an experimental one drawn out over many years, with different arrangements for dealing with security cover for employees sometimes coexisting in the same corporate organization, but by the twentieth century the overall effect was that the need for large-scale insurance cover first declined and then eventually disappeared.

## Fidelity Insurance and the State

The state's need for security to cover breaches of trust and honesty by its servants was by its very nature both more complicated and more varied than the demands placed upon private employers. Firstly, whereas it was entirely at the discretion of private employers whether to make use of security provision for their employees, for certain officers of the state there was a statutory requirement for security. Secondly, the sheer scale and variety of the responsibilities and commitments of the various branches of government, particularly by the second half of the nineteenth century, opened up new areas where the provision of security was statutorily required.

It was no surprise that the most pressing and earliest need for security was among those officers of the Crown operating in the area of tax collection. The Customs and Excise Department had records of bonds dating back to the seventeenth and eighteenth centuries either to cover duty payments by merchants, in the nature of a solvency guarantee to protect the revenue, or to provide security for customs officers. As the state entered new areas of 'money-handling' activity, new and more specific moral hazards arose. The formation of the Post Office in the eighteenth century, for example, led to the formulation of some of the earliest workplace-specific legislation regarding the threat of embezzlement as well as to a statutory requirement that its servants acquire security. Before the appearance of fidelity cover, unless individual servants of the state could provide security for themselves, all of these bonds were arranged by private suretyship.[33]

Following the crisis in private suretyship among officers in the Board of Customs in the 1840s, it was no surprise that the state was in the forefront of the search for a viable alternative. At first, Parliament permitted certain revenue officers to deposit a sum equivalent to the amount of security required, but this could benefit only those with sufficient means. Although the attitude of the Lords of the Treasury towards fidelity companies was at best ambivalent and sometimes openly hostile, insurance bonds from the London Guarantee Society were accepted for customs officers in 1842 following an act that regulated legal proceedings against fidelity companies, and in 1849 the British Guarantee Association was also authorized to provide cover. However, the range and nature of the duties of officers of the early Victorian state extended beyond those dealing with taxation to include, among others, military officers and adjutants acting as accountants for the Volunteer Corps. The Admiralty and the War Office were early and enthusiastic candidates for fidelity cover. The credibility of fidelity insurance was much enhanced by the passage of the Guarantee By Companies Act in 1867 and the Government Officers (Security) Act in 1875, which together provided the vital statutory platform from which the fidelity companies could extend their business into the heart of government. Fidelity cover for revenue and taxation officers, while important, turned out to be a transitional solution, and the Treasury permitted the establishment of a Mutual Guarantee society for customs clerks and officers, around the same time as this process was occurring in the banks and railways. And as was the case with corporate employers, the subscriptions that built up in these funds were later transmuted into retirement pensions. Eventually, in legislation enacted just before the First World War, it was decided that, except in very special circumstances, insurance bonds would no longer be generally required for officers of the Crown.[34]

The relationship between the state and the legal system was a key factor in helping to underpin the credibility of fidelity insurance in the nineteenth century. Those officers and appointees of the courts who were involved in the handling of money, property, and securities required protection, and fidelity companies actively sought out this business, since 'persons of standing' were usually appointed to such positions and claims were rare. From the courts' perspective, fidelity companies were more secure than private sureties, as those companies who wished to undertake this class of business were obliged to furnish copies of their articles of association, published accounts, and statements of available funds. Such was the solemnity associated with the provision of probate and chancery bonds that they were executed under seal and an affidavit was sworn by the insurance company stating its funds and liabilities.

The state's search for security on behalf of its legal officers and nominees was also part of its historical role in the process of debt recovery. Indebtedness had become a normal part of England's commercial life by the eighteenth century, and changes in the law of bankruptcy were vital in an economy based increasingly on credit. The state had already moved in the direction of protecting the 'honest bankrupt' as early as 1706 and had utilized security bonds that had to be lodged to 'ensure against a malicious petition.'[35] As the credit-based economy grew, the number and probably the rate of bankruptcies increased, and fidelity insurance proved to be particularly well suited to the issues involved in the 'ownership' of property in such situations.[36] The moral hazard that prompted an employer to find security for his clerk, who might deprive him of his money before it entered his possession, was present in the relationship between the state-appointed trustee and the creditors in bankruptcy proceedings. Under the Bankruptcy Act of 1869 permission was granted that the creditors 'shall when they appoint a trustee, by resolution declare what security is to be given,'[37] and the Bankruptcy Act of 1883, which was reinforced by later legislation, accepted the security bonds of approved insurance companies. In those situations where the debtor's position was not so hopeless that the business could not be continued under supervision of a trustee, the debtor was permitted to enter into a deed of arrangement, and under the Bankruptcy and Deeds of Arrangement Acts of 1913 and 1914 trustees appointed to manage businesses in these circumstances were given security from an approved guarantee society.[38]

The same 'insurable interest' operated in the administration of estates when persons died intestate or left a will without appointing an executor and a grant of administration was required. In these circumstances the state-appointed administrator was required to obtain security either from private sureties or, increasingly by the 1870s, from a fidelity provider. In cases where there was a statutory requirement for security the fidelity companies, with their specialized knowledge, corporate structure and strong links to the legal profession, had an advantage over private sureties. Fidelity insurance also developed a role when the state intervened in situations when considerations of property coincided with wider 'welfare' concerns. This was particularly the case in relation to the treatment of the mentally ill. By the nineteenth century in England the 'legal view of mental illness' was the rule.[39] While under certain circumstances the law was used to deprive individuals of their personal liberty in custodial asylums, it also applied the law of 'protection' to those 'alleged lunatics' whose wealth rendered them especially vulnerable. Masters in Lunacy were appointed to consider whether such individuals were of unsound mind, and if so, 'committees of the person' were duly appointed to administer their estates. From 1889 so-called lunacy bonds, which were more tactfully later renamed as courts of protection, were arranged through fidelity insurance companies.[40] Apart from the mentally ill, the vulnerability of the property of children, if they alone were responsible for its administration, was also recognized, and under the Probate Act of 1857 guardians were appointed on behalf of minors for whom security was increasingly provided by registered fidelity companies.

Beyond the widening reach of central government was the growth of local government, and fidelity insurers in this area increasingly advertised their policies on the basis that they had been 'accepted by the Chancery and King's Bench Division of the High Court of Justice, H. M. Treasury, Crown Agents to the Colonies, Masters in Lunacy, National Debt Commissioners, The Inland Revenue Board and by over 1,000 Local Government Authorities throughout the country.'[41] At the local level fidelity cover was closely connected to the more efficient provision of the Poor Law, and when the Local Government Mutual Guarantee Society was established in 1890 all of its trustees and directors were connected either to local authorities or the boards of guardians of the Poor Law. One of the key characteristics of the nineteenth-century Poor Law, following the 1834 Amendment Act, was its power to make detailed regulations and by-laws in its 'management of the poor.' The special authority vested in the Poor Law reflected an important extension of 'administrative' law into social welfare, and the fidelity cover which was extended to the overseers and guardians of the Poor Law helped to underpin this process. Indeed, when the Poor Law was abolished under the Local Government Act of 1929, a good deal of fidelity business was lost to the insurance companies.

## Conclusion

By the twentieth century the shape and scope of fidelity insurance had altered irrevocably, and as a solution to the management of the 'trust' problem it had been mainly superseded by alternative internal arrangements within large corporate employers and by the growth of professional auditors and accountants. However, its role in the transition to more modern managerial systems should not be underestimated, and in some ways it was the first modern attempt to deal with the problem of honesty in the workplace. Its larger role as a provider of security to the state was part of a corporate process, which was especially important where considerations of property coexisted with those of individual welfare. In situations where the extension of statutory powers became necessary in the nineteenth century, it was often underpinned by the use of fidelity insurance. From a longer historical perspective, fidelity insurance was also part of the transition from an 'economy of obligations' to one in which contractual and more bureaucratic arrangements became dominant. Although in the first phase of its development fidelity insurance sought to embody some of the moral values associated with the social obligations of private suretyship, in the long run it, like other forms of corporate insurance, offered a measure of permanence, predictability, and security that individual arrangements could never easily match.

## NOTES

The author is grateful to the warden and fellows of Nuffield College, University of Oxford, for his election to the Sir Norman Chester Senior Research

Fellowship in Hilary term 1993, during which time some of the research on which this essay is based was carried out.

1 The early debate on the relative strengths of suretyship versus insurance is well covered by W.A. Dinsdale, *History of Accident Insurance* (London: Stone and Cox, 1927), 80. See also G. Anderson, 'The Emergence and Development of Fidelity Insurance in 19th Century Britain,' *The Geneva Papers on Risk and Insurance*, vol. 29, no. 2 (2004), 239.
2 H. Raynes, *A History of British Insurance* (London: Pitman and Son, 1964), 279.
3 For the background on the growth of fidelity insurance, see Dinsdale, *History of Accident Insurance,* chap. 5; Raynes, *A History of British Insurance,* 279–83; and Anderson, 'Emergence and Development of Fidelity Insurance,' 238–9.
4 N. Tadmor, *Family and Friends in Eighteenth-Century England* (Cambridge: Cambridge University Press, 2001), 35.
5 On kinship and other ties between masters and apprentices, see Tadmor, *Family and Friends,* 57–8.
6 Charles Dickens in *A Christmas Carol* (1843) has an affectionate account of the warmth of the young Scrooge's apprenticeship in the counting house of old Fezziwig.
7 For the use of surety in the Bankruptcy Act of 1706, see J. Hoppit , *Risk and Failure in English Business 1700–1800* (Cambridge: Cambridge University Press,1987), 35. For the use of surety in Anglo-Saxon law, see A. Harding, *A Social History of English Law* (London: Penguin, 1966), 19. For the inclusion of suretyship in the Statute of Frauds, see J.B. Fitzgerald et al., *The Principles of Suretyship* (Malvern Pennsylvania: Insurance Institute of America, 1991), 5.
8 The quotation is attributed to Solomon.
9 From William Burton's *A Caveat for Sureties* (1593 ) in C. Muldrew, *The Economy of Obligation* (London: Macmillan, 1998), 160.
10 On the principles of suretyship, see Fitzgerald et al., *Principles of Suretyship*, 1–7.
11 Quoted in P. Casa-Arce and S. Hejeeba, Job Design and the English East India Company, working paper, September 2002 (www.lang,harvard.edu/programs/01), 13.
12 Report of the Commissioners appointed to investigate the Customs Fraud in 1843, quoted in Dinsdale, *History of Accident Insurance,* 82.
13 The Guarantee Society sold itself as the 'poor man's friend.'
14 R. Porter, *English Society in the Eighteenth Century* (London: Penguin, 2001), 135.

15 Porter, *English Society*, 135.

16 Background from Sir James Stephen, *A History of the Criminal Law of England*, vol. 3 (London: McMillan and Co., 1883), 151–4.

17 On the legal technicalities and their relationship with fidelity insurance, see F.D. MacMillan, *Fidelity Guarantee* (London: Stone and Cox, 1936), 4–8.

18 The idea that there was a conflict of standards between the 'immoral' acts of businessmen and corporate bodies when compared to individual clerks is from R. Sindall, 'Middle-Class Crime in Nineteenth-Century England,' *Criminal Justice History* 4 (1983), 5.

19 Mid-nineteenth-century London, its business community, and clerks and their temptations are well described in A. Sanders, *Charles Dickens: Authors in Context* (Oxford: Oxford University Press, 1999), chap. 4.

20 The links between speculative activity, clerks, and embezzlement on the Stock Exchange are from G. Robb, *White-Collar Crime in Modern England, 1845–1929* (Cambridge: Cambridge University Press, 1992), 132–6.

21 Sindall, *Middle-Class Crime*, 3

22 Sindall, *Middle-Class Crime*, 3.

23 From the First Prospectus of the Guarantee Society 1840 and the Deed of Settlement for the same society. LGS records, Ibex House, London.

24 First Prospectus of the Guarantee Society.

25 Robb, *White-Collar Crime*, 136.

26 Details and quotations from First Prospectus and Deed of Settlement of Guarantee Society.

27 Key cases involving fidelity insurers and their clients are covered in MacMillan, *Fidelity Guarantee*, 4–8.

28 Quoted in H.A. Balston, 'Fidelity Guarantee,' *Royal Exchange Assurance Magazine*, 1911, 3.

29 On the development of the fidelity insurance contract, see Anderson, 'Emergence and Development of Fidelity Insurance,' 239–42.

30 The problem may be one of detection, i.e., of which team member is cheating, and then of obtaining convincing evidence for the courts. See M. Casson, 'Culture as an Economic Asset,' in A. Godley and O. Westall, ed., *Business History and Business Culture* (Manchester: Manchester University Press, 1996), 48–77.

31 On the changing internal arrangements in the bank, see W.M. Acres, *The Bank of England from Within*, vol. 2 ( London: Oxford University Press, 1931), 487.

32 Large-scale railway frauds in this period are examined in Robb, *White-Collar Crime,* while P.W. Kingsford, *Victorian Railwaymen: The Emergence and Growth of Railway Labour 1830–1870* (London: Frank Cass, 1970),

covers the early use of fidelity insurance by railway companies and the growth of mutual schemes. Analysis of the applications to the Guarantee Society between 1848 and 1870 shows the heavy dependence on the railways and the banks. Of the 373,472 applications in total, 181,576 were from railway companies and 28,500 were from banks, with public companies and insurance companies the next largest categories: LGS records, Results Book to 1870.

33 On early guarantees for officers of state, especially in customs, which also included customs and excise bonds, see Dinsdale, 92–3.

34 For the details of the legislation, which helped to make fidelity insurance more credible, see Dinsdale, *History of Accident Insurance*, 87.

35 On the changing attitude towards bankruptcy, see M. Daunton, *Progress and Poverty* (Oxford: Oxford University Press 1995), 249.

36 Since the law did not permit any property to remain at any time without an owner, fidelity cover allowed trustees to discharge their duties. See C.A. Sales, *The Law Relating to Bankruptcy* (London: MacDonald and Evans, 1956), 59.

37 Dinsdale, *History of Accident Insurance*, 92.

38 Dinsdale, *History of Accident Insurance*, 92.

39 K. Jones, *A History of the Mental Health Services* (London: Routledge and Kegan Paul, 1972), 153.

40 Dinsdale, *History of Accident Insurance*, 94.

41 Information on local government fidelity cover for such as Poor Law officers is from documents held by the author and privately supplied by the archivist of Guardian Royal Exchange.

# 8 Competing Appeals: The Rise of Mixed Welfare Economies in Europe, 1850–1945

MARTIN LENGWILER

The period between the 1850s and the end of the Second World War was crucial for the expansion of a variety of insurance branches in Europe – for life insurance as well as for accident, sickness, disability, or old age insurance. Moreover, the insurance market, historically dominated by commercial insurance companies and friendly societies, was fundamentally transformed as the state entered the market through the foundation of the first types of social insurance since the latter decades of the nineteenth century. In most branches of the market, as in accident, disability, old age, or sickness insurance, private and public actors now offered competing coverage and had to find ways of accommodating their rival positions. Second, and partly as an effect of the rise of social insurance, the decades after 1880 witnessed a massive expansion of the clientele of insurance. What previously had appealed to the labour aristocracy and to a small, wealthy part of the middle classes became a standard form of provision for the working and the middle classes.[1] This remarkable expansion of the insurance clientele was partly due to the new social insurances, which focused primarily on the working classes, later also including the employees – both groups that did not yet belong to the customers of commercial life insurances. As well, life insurance companies also reacted to the new competitors by developing new products reaching beyond their traditional clientele and addressing the emerging mass market for insurance.

The argument of this chapter is that the growing appeal of insurance after the late nineteenth century was provided by neither commercial insurance companies, friendly societies, nor the statutory insurances alone, but by the *competition and interaction between public and private actors within the insurance market*.[2] This mixed, public-private history of insurance is also mirrored in emerging new institutional constellations. After the end of the nineteenth century, the different fields of insurance were increasingly administered by a heterogeneous combination of private (commercial or mutual) and public or statutory actors. Moreover, the national patterns of interaction between public and private actors played an important role in shaping the nationally specific paths on which the European welfare states developed.

This chapters focuses on two areas of insurance, in which the mixed economy of public and private actors developed in an exemplary form: industrial life insurance and health insurance. Industrial life insurance represents a branch of commercial life insurance in a field that was partly also claimed by statutory insurance plans, notably in the fields of burial and old age insurance for the new clientele of the working classes. In health insurance, the institutional and social development was different. Here, parts of the working class had already been insured since the early nineteenth century by friendly societies, long *before* the wealthier social strata. At the end of the century, however, the state and later also commercial insurers began offering health insurance, either as social insurance, mainly for the working or the lower middle classes, or as private health insurance for the salaried and self-employed population.

## Bridging Business History and Social History: Methodological Challenges of the Analysis of Mixed Welfare Economies

Until recently, the mixed economies of life insurance were neglected in social and economic history: the historiography of insurance concentrated *either* on the development of private, corporate insurance *or* on the history of social insurance and the welfare state. This problematic split was partly due to disciplinary traditions. The history of insurance was traditionally divided between the disciplines of economic history (dealing with the history of commercial insurance) and social history (concentrating on the history of the welfare state and on the mutual insurance of the working class). Under this disciplinary framework, the interdependencies between public and private insurance traditions were often left out. The historiography of the welfare state, for example, tended to focus on the expansion of statutory insurance plans and the genesis of the interventionist welfare regimes and to neglect complementary traditions of private insurance.[3]

This 'etatistic' approach has been challenged over the past decade by a new trend in welfare history that started to combine the perspectives of private and public insurance institutions into one picture and thus bridged the institutional gap between public and private worlds of welfare. The starting points for this methodological shift have been the results of the comparative welfare studies of the 1980s and the consequential need to explain the fundamental variations between the systems of social insurance in modern nation states.[4] Over the past years, a series of studies emerged, often inspired by Peter Baldwin's path-breaking book *The Politics of Social Solidarity*, analysing the role of private insurers in the history of the welfare state. Examples are the studies on the two-tiered system of the British old age provision by Pat Thane or Robin Pearson, the works on the role of commercial insurers in the history of health and old age insurance in the United States by Jacob Hacker or Jennifer Klein, the analyses of significant local and occupational social policies in the history of the French welfare state by Paul Dutton or Timothy Smith, or the study on the history of the Swiss three-pillar system of old age provision by Matthieu Leimgruber.[5] By stressing the heterogeneity and fragmentation of modern welfare systems, these studies confirm that the history of social insurance consists of a complex – part co-evolutive, part conflictive – interaction between statutory and private actors, be they philanthropic societies, associative mutual funds, or commercial life insurance corporations.

The theoretical challenges posed by the plurality of social insurance systems are currently an important issue in the social sciences and the historiography of welfare states. For example, sociological studies on recent transformations of 'classic' welfare systems (such as the German or the Scandinavian cases) in an era of deregulation and privatization have stressed the notion of a 'mixed welfare economy,' transcending the traditional conceptual juxtapositions of institutional distinctions (corporatist versus statutory regimes), political traditions (social democratic versus liberal/paternalist regimes) or – as in the widely used typology of Gøsta Esping-Andersen – on the quality and scope of welfare benefits (in Esping-Andersen's terms, on the degree of 'decommodification' and 'destratification').[6] Moreover, in expansion of Esping-Andersen's typology, studies of southern European welfare systems have outlined a 'southern type' or 'southern syndrome' of welfare states also based on a mixed welfare economy. Welfare systems in southern Europe are often marked by a sociogeographical division, with rather generous welfare provisions for the privileged industrial workers in the north and a system of only basic social assistance provisions for the mainly agrarian and often informal workforce in the south.[7]

Peter Baldwin has recently coined the concept of 'styles of statism' as an analytical tool to understand the emergence of mixed welfare economies.[8] This concept goes beyond the ambition of typologies and aims at delineating general qualitative and historical differences between welfare states, including the differences between public and private welfare institutions or between insurance-based and tax-based welfare benefits. Baldwin argues that the analysis of heterogeneous, public-private constellations of welfare actors calls for a new theoretical understanding of statism. Whereas traditional concepts of statism, for example of a Weberian descent, are based upon a homogenous ideal-type of a rational and bureaucratic state, Baldwin suggests a framework allowing for heterogeneous and hybrid constellations and transcending common categories such as liberal versus interventionist or federal versus centralist. Instead, he proposes the concept of 'styles of statism' as an open and qualitative conceptualization of states, a framework also more appropriate for the historical variations of welfare state developments: 'A two-dimensional axis of social policy endeavour between active and residual welfare states is now, after two decades of empirical comparative work, inadequate ... We need, as a starting point, a typology, or at least a grasp of the possibility, of various kinds of states.'[9]

In the following analysis, I will concentrate as mentioned on the fields of industrial life insurance and health insurance. The chapter includes three case studies. The first deals with the spread of industrial life insurance in different European countries since the 1850s. The second and third case studies investigate two opposed systems of health insurance: on the one hand the rise of a market for private health insurance, parallel to the social sickness insurance, in Germany with its strong tradition of social insurance after the 1880s; and on the other hand, as a comparison to the 'etatist' German case, the emergence of the statutory health insurance system after 1910, administered by private sickness funds, in Switzerland, a country with only a weak central state authority.

## Appealing to the Mass Market: The Success of Industrial Life Insurance after 1850

Industrial insurance, or *Volksversicherung* as it was called in Germany (literally, 'people's insurance'), was offered by commercial insurance companies as a cheap life insurance for working-class clients. It consisted of a more standardized contract than the regular life insurance with reduced benefits (mainly offering a lump sum for the burial expenses or a small annuity) and cheaper premium rates. Many insurance companies also scrapped the medical examinations of policy applicants, and customers often benefited from profit-sharing systems. Also, industrial insurance was marked by a professionalized marketing endeavour based on a large number of underwriters acting in the neighbourhoods of their potential clients. By habits such as the weekly home visit of the uniformed insurance agent, companies made sure that industrial insurance became part of the everyday life of their customers.[10]

As mentioned, industrial insurance usually offered endowment insurance with a one-off payment for loss of wages and as a compensation for funeral costs. In the Anglo-Saxon countries, customers could also get contracts for pension insurance. The clientele of industrial life insurance included comparable numbers of men and women.[11] Benefits were normally limited to a maximum amount, which in Germany corresponded to 1500 marks, about eighteen months' wages of an industrial worker.[12] Policies for children were quite popular – working-class parents thus tried to provide for the potential loss of children's income. In Germany, about half of the policies covered the lives of underage children.[13]

The rise of industrial insurance in the latter part of the nineteenth century is partly an effect of growing competition between the insurance industry and the emerging activities of the state, in particular in offering insurance products for the growing working classes. In Great Britain, the competition between public and private actors was an indirect one, as each developed its own distinct product for insuring the new clientele. Since 1829, the national government had offered voluntary pension insurance to the working and middle classes. This was partly an extension of the traditional pension schemes for the civil service, which most absolutist bureaucracies had already introduced in the eighteenth century to foster the loyalty of their public servants.[14] The extension of state pensions beyond the civil service was directed particularly to low-income earners and was motivated by the criticism of William Gladstone, then chancellor of the Exchequer, levelled against commercial insurers and their profit-oriented business. In 1864 Gladstone extended the scheme by enrolling post offices as marketing agents for government insurance. However, the scheme suffered from high premium rates and bureaucratic hurdles; by 1883 the number of yearly insurance contracts was still below four hundred.[15]

Despite its commercial failure, voluntary government insurances were symbolically important because they triggered the launch by commercial insurers of comparable products for the working classes. With its newly designed industrial insurance, the life insurance industry launched its own product within the emerging mass market for life insurance. The new insurance, which in most cases consisted of provisions to cover the costs of a funeral, was also competing with similar provisions offered by the widely popular friendly societies.[16] First and most successfully of all companies, the Prudential Assurance Company introduced small life insurance policies in 1854 to the British market. Within a few decades it grew to be the undisputed market leader among British life insurers. By 1873 the Prudential already counted over three million customers in the industrial insurance branch, occupying a share of three-quarters of this rapidly expanding market. By the late 1880s it also overtook its competitors in the market for ordinary life insurances.[17] By 1909, one year after the introduction of the first national old age pension (with the Old Age Pension Act), there were no less than twenty-seven million life insurance policies administered by the insurance business (half of them by the Prudential), amounting to about two-thirds of the whole population.[18] The insurance industry, headed by the Prudential, was also highly successful in influencing government policies in insurance matters. In 1911, for example, the British government had to drop the idea of integrating survivor insurance into the National Insurance Act, which first established a national health insurance, because the planned provisions for survivors were in direct competition with industrial insurance. By openly threatening to take the government to court with massive claims of compensation, the insurance industry successfully forced Lloyd George to drop the planned survivors' insurance.[19]

In Germany, the rise of industrial insurance was a direct reaction to the state's intervention in the insurance market, in particular to Bismarck's establishment of the national old age and disability insurance in 1889, which was limited to the working class.[20] Contrary to Britain, where compulsory old age insurance provided by the state arrived after the insurance industry had already occupied the market for industrial life insurance, in highly federalized Germany the life insurance industry was fragmented and lacked the critical mass to build up a strong market position before the state's intervention in the 1880s. To do business in the whole German empire, an insurance company had to obtain around a dozen concessions from the German *Länder*.[21] Thus, the German life insurers had to accommodate themselves to the *de facto* nationalization of a large part of the growing market for life insurance. They tried to profit from the popularization of old age insurances through the social insurance scheme by offering their own insurance products for the working classes. Copying the British model, they offered industrial insurance, under the German term of *Volksversicherung*, which was used as a complementary to the low benefits of the national old age insurance.[22] Comparable to the British market, the business in industrial insurance was dominated by two companies, the Friedrich Wilhelm and the Victoria.[23] Until the First World War, the *Volksversicherung* was a considerable success. Between 1902 and 1910 the share of the population with life insurance rose from 10 to 20 per cent, an expansion primarily based on the spread of industrial insurance policies, held by about 10 percent of the population, mainly among the working classes and employees. Employees were particularly attracted, as they had to wait until 1911 to be included in the statutory old age insurance.[24]

The second factor in Germany behind the rise of commercial life insurance was, as in Britain, the competition between commercial insurers and friendly societies. By offering products for the working classes, commercial insurers entered the traditional market of the friendly societies, first in Britain and later in Germany. The strategy of the commercial insurers profited from three structural problems faced by the friendly societies. Firstly, many friendly societies were based upon an exclusive culture, often barring low-income earners and women from membership, which made such societies increasingly unpopular and resulted in the foundation of a second generation of societies led by the previously excluded groups. Secondly, most societies were organized on a regional, local, or corporate level, which became a growing handicap for workers trying to shift their membership from one to another society. People leaving their society usually lost all their entitlements and were thus discriminated against, for example for reasons of age, by the new society they entered.[25] Thirdly, most small societies had difficulties in developing technically advanced products such as pensions, because they often lacked professional management and the necessary economies of scale.[26] Such structural difficulties contributed to the growing unattractiveness of the traditional sector of friendly societies among an increasingly mobile working class.

Industrial insurance spread in most countries of northern Europe and in the United States. In 1909 Britain was still the biggest market with a share of 66.8 per cent of policies among the population, followed by the United States (23.1 per cent) and Germany (11.8 per cent).[27] Whereas in the Anglo-Saxon countries industrial insurances survived the First World War and the interwar period, the German market collapsed after 1918 as a consequence of inflation and consecutive devaluation of the insurance capitals. In particular, with the inflation crisis in 1922–23 most of the industrial insurance schemes went bankrupt. After this blow, the popularity of life insurance among the working classes never recovered.[28] In the Catholic countries of southern and central Europe – for example in France, Belgium, Spain, and the Austro-Hungarian Empire – industrial insurance was either completely missing or developed only later after the end of the First World War. This was due partly to the underdeveloped insurance industry in largely agrarian countries and partly to legal reasons, for example the ban on insurance for children, prevalent in Catholic regions and motivated by moral and religious fears about the incentives for infanticide.[29]

The success of industrial life insurance is the effect not only, as is often argued in the historical literature, of a marketing revolution in insurance, particularly the introduction of professionalized agency systems.[30] It also reflects a deeper transformation in the culture of prevention of the working and middle classes. The traditional preventive ideals of friendly societies with their fraternizing and often male bonding sociability were gradually replaced in the second half of the nineteenth century by a modernized, individualistic model provided by the commercial insurance companies. Although the commercial model of prevention was to a certain degree discriminatory – by adapting the premiums according to age and sex – it was still more inclusive than the associative model, as it dropped a series of medical, occupational, and geographical entry barriers still common among the mutual societies.[31] From its beginning, industrial life insurance was a venture for a mass market appealing to as wide a clientele as possible.

Prevention now meant a form of translocal, anonymous insurance, opposed to the local sociability of the mutual societies. Thus, an insurance policy changed from a symbol of the associative rituals of mutualism to a mass-produced consumer good for individual and familial protection.[32] This new, individualistic model of prevention appealed not only to the working classes but also to the employees of the rapidly expanding service sector.[33]

### In the Shadow of Social Insurance: The Spread of Private Health Insurance in Germany since the 1880s

The second example, the rise of private health insurance in Germany, differs from the case of industrial insurance (at least in the British context) in that an existing private market of sickness funds was nationalized in the 1880s and a second generation of private insurers had to build up a parallel market, complementary to the social insurance system. This eventually led to a segmented system of health insurance with a social insurance part for workers and the lower-earning employees and a private insurance part for self-employed and higher-earning employees. As mentioned above, the Bismarckian insurance legislation of the 1880s replaced much of the private market of accident, sickness, disability, and old age insurance by compulsory national insurance schemes, first for the industrial working classes and later expanded to salaried employees (by the *Angestelltenversicherung* as part of the *Reichsversicherungsordnung* 1911).[34]

Before the introduction of statutory health insurance in 1883, sickness insurance was mainly provided by mutual societies, corporate sickness funds, or compulsory local sickness funds (the *Ortskrankenkassen*), a specifically Prussia-German type of fund.[35] As in Britain and elsewhere in Europe, the market was traditionally dominated by mutual funds; the commercial life insurance companies were not involved because sickness insurance was a low-profit business compared to the ordinary life insurance market. Whereas in accident insurance and in old age and disability insurance, Bismarck succeeded in setting up new statutory or corporatist organizations for the administration of the insurance, in health insurance the Iron Chancellor had to compromise with the friendly societies and the corporate health funds, which were highly sceptical about the proposed plans for a national scheme. The 1883 legislation thus delegated the management of the new statutory insurance to the already existing funds. Friendly societies and other private sickness funds were allowed, after a registration process, to keep their clientele, now under the new statutory framework.[36] Indeed, most private societies registered for the compulsory scheme and transformed themselves into semi-public actors; they included about two thousand mutual societies and five thousand corporate funds.[37] Thus, with the Bismarckian nationalization of the mutual societies in 1883, there were hardly any genuinely private insurance associations left in the market for health insurance. Only a few sickness funds, mainly small mutual societies, did not register and continued to be genuinely private organizations.[38]

In the first decades after the introduction of compulsory health insurance in 1883, there was therefore hardly any competition between public and private insurers; the registered funds dominated the market. The status of the few private sickness funds remained marginal until the First World War. They were further weakened by the departure of practically all employed members (workers and after 1911 also employees) who fell under the compulsory social insurance and needed to get insurance with a registered fund. Thus, by the turn of the century, most of the old, private funds had perished.[39]

Only after shifting their strategy and focusing more on the self-employed professions, not included in the compulsory health insurance, did private insurance associations recover. Between 1900 and the First World War, a dozen insurance associations were founded, mainly in the legal form of mutual societies, offering insurance for the self-employed or complementary insurance, mainly for death benefits, for the clientele of compulsory health insurance. The new funds included the Kranken- und Sterbekasse für selbständige Handwerker und Gewerbetreibende zu Braunschweig' (founded in 1902), the Deutsche Beamten-Krankenversicherung (founded in 1905, as civil servants – *Beamte* – were also excluded from compulsory insurance), and – by far the biggest association – the Leipziger Fürsorge, Versicherungsanstalt für Beamte und freie Berufe (founded in 1904).[40]

This minor role of private insurers in the health insurance market was reinforced by discriminatory regulations. After 1883 the market was reorganized and divided into three parts: first, the market for compulsory insurance (covering the working classes and, after 1911, salaried employees up to a maximum income level); second, the market for voluntary (i.e., private) health insurance consisting of those members of the middle classes (employees above the maximum income and the self-employed) that were not compulsorily insured; and third, the market for private medical practice, composed of the wealthier bourgeoisie and the nobility – a clientele with a financial status allowing them to pay for medical services without any insurance.[41] The discriminatory part of the law of 1883 was that it did not restrict the registered insurers (public or semi-public organization) to the compulsory market alone, but also opened the market for voluntary health insurance for both private and public insurance funds. Already before the First World War and again in the interwar period, many of the public insurance funds entered the private market, either by offering special contribution rates for private clientele (cross-subsidized by contributions from their compulsory clientele) or by founding subsidiary companies specialized for private customers.[42] Private sickness funds were disadvantaged, as they had to compete with large and financially strong public insurers for a comparably small market of private health insurance.[43]

Only after the First World War did the market for private health insurance expand to a lucrative size. The inflation of the First World War, the inflation crisis of 1922–23, and the economic crisis of the early 1930s convinced the middle classes – particularly the self-employed – of the advantages of health insurance. The economic crises only triggered a trend that had deeper roots and had already begun during the First World War. With the extension of industrial social insurance to salaried employees in 1911, insurance became a publicly respected form of financial precaution, in particular for the self-employed and the wealthier middle classes. Thus in the interwar period, the middle classes not yet covered by social insurance looked for health insurance coverage to a previously unknown degree.[44] After 1918 the market for private health insurance, significantly known as *Mittelstandsversicherung* (middle-class insurance), became the fastest growing part of the insurance market. In 1924 there were already one million insurance contracts, rising to 8.5 million by 1939 and over 10 million by the end of World War II (compared to about 40 million insured persons in the statutory health insurance).[45] It helped a lot that the National Socialist regime basically followed a business-friendly policy in insurance matters. Most importantly, in 1935 the Nazis barred public insurers from interfering in the private market and thus set the private insurers on a par with their public competitors.[46] Thus, private health insurance was *the* success story in the interwar insurance market.

Both public and private insurance organizations profited from this boom, but the private companies were far more successful in attracting new clientele and quickly surpassed the statutory funds in number of private insurance contracts.[47] The Leipziger Fürsorge, for example, the association poised to become market leader in the 1930s, quickly grew from 21,962 insurance contracts in 1923 to 361,996 in 1926.[48] Similarly, the number of private health insurers mushroomed in the 1920s and 1930s. Before the First World War, the market counted a dozen societies; in 1930 there were already 175.[49] Most of them were organized as mutual insurances, following the tradition of some older friendly societies they replaced, but a growing amount – by 1930 about one-fifth – chose the legal form of a joint stock company.[50] This entry of the commercial insurance industry is a clear sign of the increasing profitability of the market. Four of the five commercial health insurers of the interwar period were founded during years of post-war inflation, between 1921 and 1926.[51] Another indicator of the significance of the private health insurance market is that in the 1920s private health insurers started to organize their collective interests by founding the Verband privater Krankenversicherungs-Unternehmungen Deutschlands (Leipziger Verband) (1926), the Verband der Versicherungsanstalten für selbständige Handwerker und Gewerbetreibende Deutschlands (Dresdner Verband) (1924), and the Verband deutscher Beamtenkrankenkassen (Koblenz) (1927).[52]

The success of private insurance companies compared to public funds is astonishing, and all the more so as the public funds still invested in marketing campaigns tailored to the clientele of the private insurance market.[53] This is partly due to the clever resumption by private associations of the old traditions of craft and trade associations – most insurance associations were organized along professional lines and had thus the backing of the main professional associations. Similarly effective was private insurers' strategy of imitating popular technical aspects of social insurance, such as a tariff based on group (instead of individual) premiums or the expansion of coverage not only for sick pay (the classic provision of private health insurers in the nineteenth century) but for a variety of medical services.[54] Moreover, private insurers could offer some exclusive benefits and thus provide their customers with an advantage over the clientele of public insurers. These privileges included treatment as a private patient (with higher compensation for the medical treatment) or the free choice of a medical practitioner.[55]

As mentioned above, after 1933 the private insurance associations profited from the political support of the National Socialist Party.[56] Even before coming to power, the committee for social insurance of the NSDAP published a memorandum in 1932 that endorsed the structure of the German welfare state with its corporatist social insurances and dismissed any encompassing tax-financed welfare system (*Staatsfürsorge*). This position was reiterated in the 1934 law on the structure of social insurance (*Gesetz über den Aufbau der Sozialversicherung*) with which the National Socialists basically preserved the Bismarckian structure of the welfare system.[57] However, the alternative plans of a generalized tax-financed welfare system were never totally buried. Adherents of an interventionist social policy approach such as the Reichsarbeitsministerium (the Ministry of Employment) under Robert Ley repeatedly suggested a fundamental overhaul of the social insurance system. When Austria and the Sudetenland (the German-populated regions of Bohemia and Moravia) were annexed – both regions with a universal national health insurance in place – the National Socialists had to adapt the German system in 1941 by doubling the income limit qualifying individuals for compulsory insurance for both areas (from 3,600 to 7,200 Reichsmarks), a measure that guaranteed that most of the population was covered by the statutory insurance scheme. The Reichsarbeitsministerium argued that this radical expansion of the statutory system should be generalized for all regions of the Reich, or at least that additional professions should be included within the compulsory scheme.[58] However, these plans never materialized. Reforms of the health insurance system were implemented only to the extent that they allowed the independence of a market for private health insurance. Demands to completely nationalize private health insurance and abolish the basis of the private insurance associations had no significant support among the Nazi hierarchies because they threatened to undermine the loyalty of the self-employeds and employees – both crucial supporters of the Nazi regime.[59]

The case of German health insurance shows how the rise of a private insurance industry, supported by the interests of its middle-class clientele, was able to transform a system originally dominated by public insurance funds into a segmented insurance market, deeply split between a public and a private sector. Proposals for reform of the system, for example by extending the range of compulsory health insurance, stood no chance against the combined interests of privately insured patients, general practitioners, and private sickness insurances. In the postwar period, at least in the Federal Republic of Germany, the basic organization of German health insurance remained untouched. To this day, German health insurance is still organized in a two-tiered system with several structural features that discriminate against clients of statutory health insurance.

## Spread of Social Insurance through Private Actors: The Delegation of Public Insurance Plans to Private Insurance Associations in Switzerland after 1910

The Swiss system of health insurance emerged in a fundamentally different way than Germany's but was also dominated by private sickness funds. However, the origins of the Swiss welfare state in the late nineteenth century were closely related to those of the German example. Before the introduction of social insurance legislation, sickness insurance in Switzerland as in Germany was mainly provided by an expanding sector of friendly societies. These funds emerged in an atmosphere of liberalized freedom of trade after the foundation of the modern Swiss federal state with its liberal constitution of 1848. Predominantly located in industrialized regions, they included a variety of organizational forms such as local and corporate funds, occupational societies (mainly craft and trade associations), or religious and trade unionist societies. Most funds were small mutual societies operating at a local or regional level; only one, the Helvetia, operated on a national base.[60] In the industrialized areas, as in the cities of Basle and Zurich or the canton of Glarus, up to 30 per cent of the population was affiliated with a sickness fund. On the national level the proportion was 4 per cent (1868), comparable to the level in Germany.[61] In contrast with later development in Germany, private health insurers in Switzerland consisted only of mutual societies, with no commercial insurers.

In the 1880s, parallel to the passage of social insurance legislation in Germany, a similar project was initiated in Switzerland but eventually failed after the turn of the century. The dominant political movement in Switzerland, a coalition of the liberal and radical bourgeoisie, supported the adoption of the Bismarckian system. However, a first proposal for German-like compulsory accident and health insurance failed in 1900 to win the necessary popular vote – a defeat at the ballot box that surprised most of the political establishment, which widely supported the draft. The reasons for the unexpectedly strong opposition were political and economic. Before the First World War, the fiscal basis of the federal government was tightly restricted, with no direct but only indirect taxes and duties.[62] These fiscal limitations, combined with the direct democratic constitution allowing for a poll on each national law, made it very hard to enact proposals such as social insurance legislation that demanded a considerable extension of state activities. Opponents of the national accident and health legislation warned of imminent tax increases (although the law did not touch the tax issue) and appealed to voters' anticentralistic attitudes, a strategy particularly successful among the French-speaking minority of Switzerland.[63]

After the 1900 defeat, the radical-liberal government had to change gears and decided to sacrifice the controversial national health insurance plan. The proposal was reduced to the hardly disputed introduction of compulsory accident insurance. In this truncated version, it was approved by a ballot in 1912. In the final version, the law included a back-door measure for the promotion of compulsory health insurance plans: it stipulated a federal obligation to support municipal and cantonal authorities willing to introduce compulsory health plans on a local or regional level. The law arranged for an incentive, a national subsidy to reduce the prospective costs for the municipal or cantonal authorities. The amount of the subsidy was related to the number of persons insured by the plan. Originally it was set at between 40 and 60 per cent of the expenses of the sickness fund; with the inflation during and after the First World War the subsidy amounted to about 20 per cent.[64] Also, it was left to the subordinate authorities whether to rely on the existing, private insurance funds or to introduce new public funds in order to administer the proposed health plans.[65] Thus, as often in Switzerland, the national government tried to bypass opposition to a national welfare state by taking the federal back door.

Under these circumstances, the spread of compulsory health insurance in the decades after 1912 took a specifically Swiss path, typically delegating the administration of the compulsory insurance plans to private sickness funds instead of founding public funds. Social insurance plans were not declared mandatory from above as in Germany but were diffused from below, on the local and cantonal level. Federalism was thus not a structural barrier to the development of the welfare state, as has been suggested in recent studies.[66] It offered, on the contrary, a framework in which some cantons and cities competed for the most advanced social insurances. In the years following the legislation of 1912, most cantons discussed the introduction of health insurance plans, and about half decided in favour of it. Among the early cantons to introduce compulsory health plans were Basle in 1914, Lucerne in 1915, Zug in 1916, Zurich (cantonal level) in 1916, and Schwyz in 1917. The postwar era and the 1920s, a period of recovering public finances, witnessed a second wave of local or cantonal social insurance legislation. Social insurance was further popularized by the effects of the Spanish flu epidemic in 1918.[67] Health plans were introduced by Saint Gall and Berne (cantonal level in both cases) in 1919, Appenzell (Innerrhoden) in 1920, Ticino in 1922, Grisons in 1923, Uri in 1924, and by the city of Zurich in 1928.[68]

This spread of compulsory insurance legislation caused a long-term boom among the private sickness funds. The sector grew from 453 funds with a total of 361,621 insured persons in 1914 to 946 funds with 968,748 insured in 1920, 1148 funds with 1,640,482 insured in 1930, and 1160 funds with 1,937,179 insured in 1935. The number of insured people grew by around 100 per cent per decade while at the same time the insurance funds, due to a process of concentration, considerably expanded their size. In 1935 the segment of the population secured by health insurance (in a public or private scheme) was already 48 per cent. More than three-quarters of the sector was administered by private sickness funds; the share of public funds was thus less than a quarter.[69] Health insurance had become popular not only among the working classes, the typical clientele of public health plans, but also increasingly among the middle classes seeking coverage with private health insurers.

The diffusion of public health plans did not threaten the institutional status of private sickness funds. As in Germany, private health insurers took the opportunity of the boom to strengthen their professional association. In the years after the First World War, the professional association of Swiss sickness funds, the Konkordat der schweizerischen Krankenkassen, doubled its membership. The Konkordat transformed itself from an association offering its individual clients freedom of movement between the affiliated funds into a powerful political lobby organization. Since then, it has by and large been successful in influencing cantonal and municipal legislation and securing its members' privileged market position even under the new public health plans.[70] The Koncordat secured the privileged status of private funds in the lucrative markets of industrialized or metropolitan regions by successfully fighting the establishment of public funds.[71] In the highly industrialized and comparatively wealthy canton of Zurich, for example, the cantonal law for health insurance stipulated that municipalities in favour of a public health plan had first to contact the private sickness funds for the administration of their plan; the establishment of public funds was allowed only in cases where no agreement with private funds could be reached (accordingly, only one town in the canton, Winterthur, set up a public fund).[72]

The coverage and benefits offered by the public health insurance plans were originally quite generous but grew increasingly restricted over the 1920s and 1930s. All plans were based on per capita premiums and subsidized by government contributions in order to keep the level of premiums, for social reasons, cheaper than in the private insurance schemes. Some of the subsidies came from the federal state, but most plans involved financial support by local or cantonal means. Whereas some of the first plans of the prewar era stipulated generous universal health insurance for the whole population (up to a certain maximum income), the plans of the interwar period tended to emulate the German system of class insurance (*Klassenversicherung*), limiting compulsory insurance primarily to industrial workers and salaried employees and reflecting the difficult budgetary situation of public households in the wartime and postwar years.[73] In public as in private health insurance, benefits usually included sickness pay and compensation for medical provisions. The coverage for provisions was sometimes quite generous, as in social democratic Zurich where not only regular health care but also dental treatment, midwife services, and stays at health spas were covered. During the economic crisis of the 1930s, many public health plans accumulated deficits, as contributions had to stay low – for social reasons – while expenses grew rapidly. Under these circumstances, many public plans were forced to restrict their provisions; Zurich, for example, cancelled coverage for dental treatment and midwife services.[74]

The privileged position of private health insurers affected the national landscape of compulsory health insurance, which evolved in distinct patterns. In the lucrative industrialized regions of the north and east of the country, the insurance market – for both private and social health insurance – was dominated by private sickness funds. In the peripheral and poorer, agrarian regions of the central and southern parts, private insurers ceded the market for social insurance to public funds (as in the cantons of Ticino and Grisons and the central cantons of Lucerne and Uri). In the remote alpine regions, such as parts of the cantons of Grisons, Ticino, or Valais, where the provision of medical services was extremely costly, the federal state even offered superior subsidies on condition that the health plan be administered by a public insurer, thus barring private sickness funds from these areas.[75] Only the city of Basle departed from this pattern by introducing, in 1914, a public fund (albeit one reimbursing only medical services, with no sickness pay).[76] In the French-speaking cantons of the Romandie, the mutualités successfully resisted all attempts to set up any comprehensive social insurance. The Romand cantons introduced only a limited form of health plan restricted to insurance of children and pupils.[77]

From a long-term perspective, the parallel expansion of compulsory health insurance and private sickness funds had three important implications for the health insurance system in Switzerland. First, it institutionalized a form of delegated public health insurance, in which private organizations were responsible for implementing social insurances and in exchange received a considerable amount of their income from public subsidies. In the interwar period, the ordinary and extraordinary fiscal subsidies for all sickness insurers amounted to about 20 per cent of their total expenses.[78] In contrast to old age insurance in Switzerland, the basic framework of the delegation and funding structure of health insurance remained unchanged even after the Second World War. Reform of health insurance was discussed during and after the war, but the agenda-setting of the federal government prevented implementation of the plans. For political reasons the government's priority was to introduce national old age insurance, a plan that eventually succeeded in 1947.[79] Although the British Beveridge plan was also debated in Switzerland and the Koncordat of sickness funds even supported a moderate project for homogenization of health insurance at the national level (still administered by the private funds), the parliamentary process was delayed until after the implementation of old age insurance. Finally in 1949, as a first step to an encompassing national scheme, a law for a national insurance scheme against the risks of tuberculosis was proposed and submitted to a national vote. A coalition of right-wing and bourgeois parties supported by the national association of physicians (fearing a further nationalization of the health care system) was successful in fending off the proposal – only a quarter of votes cast were in favour of this modest national health plan.[80] After this devastating defeat, the federal government refrained from any radical reform plans and left the system of health insurance basically unchanged until the 1990s.

The second implication of the mixed health insurance system was that, because of the strong position of private insurance funds, important aspects of the organization of social health insurance resembled private insurance contracts rather than the Bismarckian model of social insurance. Premiums were, as mentioned above, calculated per capita – as in private health insurance contracts – but through public subsidies were kept beneath the level of private health insurance premiums. A more redistributive financing system, such as the payroll contributions in Germany, which reflected level of income of the insured person, was then kept off the agenda. Similarly, some cornerstones of the original social insurance legislation in 1912, such as equal level of male and female contributions, had to be revised under the pressure of private sickness funds arguing for a more risk-adequate contributory system. In the early 1930s the national office for social insurance officially revised the rules for gender-equal contributions and allowed public and private health insurers to increase the female tariff by a maximum of 25 per cent.[81]

Third, the spread of social health insurance in the interwar period indirectly contributed to the rise of private insurance in the postwar era. With the rising living standards of the working class after the Second World War, the breakthrough of health insurance was due less to the spread of local and regional compulsory insurance plans than to the rise of health insurance as part of firm-based social policies. The wage increases of the postwar era meant that in the long run the number of people covered by compulsory insurance plans (limited to a maximum income) actually decreased. The new middle classes, however, did not abandon their health insurance contracts but continued them in the form of private insurance. Moreover, with the chronic labour shortages of the 1950s and 1960s, many employers started to offer health insurance plans as part of their employment contracts. Thus, by 1970 around 80 per cent of the population – including most of the lower-income classes – were covered by some sort of health insurance. The insurance rate rose to over 95 per cent by 1990. Therefore, the final introduction of a *national* compulsory health insurance in 1996 – still administered by the same private insurance funds – was only a small step beyond the previous mixed system of public and private health insurance plans.[82]

## Conclusion: Appeals of Insurance in Mixed Welfare Economies

To conclude I will summarize a few of the interdependent effects that public and private insurance actors had on the development of those forms of insurance discussed above. We can distinguish three levels on which private and public insurances interacted: a social, an institutional, and a qualitative-technical level. On the social level, the above examples showed that since the establishment of the first statutory insurances, commercial and mutual insurances entered a race to enlarge their clientele. The appeal of insurance could address different groups of new customers. In the case of industrial life insurance, it was mainly the working class that profited from new offers of insurance policies, as commercial insurers tried to answer the challenge of statutory old age insurance by developing their own affordable life insurance policies for the lower-earning population. In health insurance, it was instead the middle classes that were gradually convinced of the benefits of insurance. Here the main actors were the mutual societies, traditionally strong in the market for sickness insurance, which were confronted by the challenge of statutory insurance plans. Although marked by completely different systems of national health insurance, the cases of Germany and Switzerland both show that in the economically uncertain years during and after the First World War the mutual insurers succeeded in reaching beyond the low-earning working classes, the traditional clientele of statutory insurance plans, to persuade the wealthier middle classes, until then no customers of sickness funds, to obtain private health insurance.

Institutionally, the cases reveal different national-specific mixtures of public-private welfare economies. In the case of industrial life insurance, the commercial insurance industry reacted to the statutory old age insurance plans by designing a complementary product that was not threatened by the spread of statutory plans, but could on the contrary profit from the preventive attitudes propagated by social insurances. Indeed, at least in the Anglo-Saxon countries industrial life insurance was a considerable success, and even in Germany, the homeland of social insurance, industrial insurance prospered parallel to the statutory insurance scheme and only perished in the inflation crisis of the 1920s, which damaged all capital-based forms of insurance, not just industrial life insurance. In the case of health insurance, the two cases show alternative forms of a mixed welfare economy, depending on the institutional weight of the social insurance system. In the German case the market for health insurance was largely dominated by public sickness funds administering the social insurance scheme of 1883. Private insurance funds (commercial companies and mutual societies) played only a minor albeit increasingly significant role as insurers of the middle classes not included in the compulsory health insurance. In the interwar period the private sector eventually succeeded in establishing a private parallel market of significant size (about a quarter of the social insurance market). Since then, the combined interests of clients, physicians, and private insurance funds have been able to block all attempts to expand the social insurance scheme. In the case of Switzerland, a country with a traditionally weak federal state and a strong federalist tradition, the roles of public and private actors were permuted. Here, the project of a national compulsory insurance scheme failed at the turn of the century and was replaced by a decentralized system of local or regional social insurance schemes (more in line with the Swiss federal tradition). Under these circumstances, compulsory health insurance – where the system was introduced – was organized as a delegated system where insurance was provided by the existing private sickness funds and only exceptionally by public insurance organizations. In this delegated system, which exists until today, the number of insured persons grew *from below*, slowly but steadily.

Finally, there are a series of important influences between public and private insurance systems on the qualitative and technical level. On the one hand, private insurances, such as the sickness funds, often adapted their benefits to the standards of social insurance by extending, for example, the range of medical services insured or by assimilating the tariffs to the group tariffs of statutory insurance. However, some crucial differences still remained, for example in the structure of the contributions. In Germany as in Switzerland, for instance, the per capita contributions of the private sickness funds followed an individualistic approach, whereas the payroll contributions of the German statutory health insurance represented a model of financial solidarity of the clients. Thus, through the rise of the parallel system of German health insurance, the private insurance sector ultimately limited the redistributive effects of the modern welfare state.

## NOTES

This chapter is based upon a research project on the history of sickness insurance in four European states (Germany, Switzerland, Britain, and France), focusing on the interactions between private and public actors and on the decades between the First World War and around 1950. The project is funded by the Swiss National Research Foundation. The author would like to thank Geoffrey Clark and Matthieu Leimgruber for their most valuable comments.

1 For the early spread of life insurance in eighteenth-century Britain: Geoffrey Clark, *Betting on Lives: The Culture of Life Insurance in England, 1695–1775* (Manchester: Manchester University Press, 1999); for Germany: Eve Rosenhaft, '"But the Heart Must Speak for the Tidows": The Origins of Life Insurance in Germany and the Gender Implications of Actuarial Science,' in Marion Gray and Ulrike Gleixner, eds., *Formatting Gender: Transitions, Breaks and Continuities in German-Speaking Europe 1750–1850* (Ann Arbor: University of Michigan Press, 2006).

2 The term 'friendly societies,' common in the Anglo-Saxon countries, is also used here for comparable sickness funds in Germany (*Hilfskassen*) or France (*mutualités*). Formally, friendly societies were often organized as mutual societies (hence the French term *mutualités*). I will use the term 'friendly societies' rather than 'mutual societies' because the field of mutual societies is a heterogenous and contradictory area of the insurance industry. The working-class-related friendly societies were not the only actors creating mutual societies. In the latter decades of the nineteenth century, some of the big insurance corporations were also founded as (or converted into) mutual societies. With this step, the insurance industry tried to fight against popular criticisms of its huge commercial profits. As mutual societies were formally non-profit organizations, the 'commercial' mutuals appeared to be more customer friendly than their joint-stock competitors. In fact, profits were still made, also by mutuals, in the form of financial 'reserves.' See Viviana A. Zelizer, *Morals and Markets: The Development of Life Insurance in the United States* (New York: Columbia University Press, 1979) 19.

3 For the economic history of insurance: Ludwig Arps, *Auf sicheren Pfeilern: Deutsche Versicherungswirtschaft vor 1914* (Göttingen: Vandenhoeck & Ruprecht, 1965); Ludwig Arps, *Durch unruhige Zeiten: Deutsche Versicherungswirtschaft seit 1914* (Karlsruhe: Verlag Versicherungswirtschaft, 1970); Timothy Alborn, *Conceiving Companies: Joint-Stock Politics in Victo-*

*rian England* (London: Routledge, 1998); Robin Pearson, 'Towards an Historical Model of Services Innovation: The Case of the Insurance Industry, 1700–1914,' *Economic History Review* 50, no. 2 (1997); Peter Borscheid, *100 Jahre Allianz, 1890–1990* (Munich: Verlag Allianz AG, 1990). For some classic accounts on the history of the welfare state: Peter Flora, ed., *Growth to Limits*, 4 vols. (European University Institute Series C) (Berlin: de Gruyter, 1986/87); Peter Baldwin, *The Politics of Social Solidarity: Class Bases of the European Welfare State 1875–1975* (Cambridge: Cambridge University Press, 1990); Gerhard A. Ritter, *Der Sozialstaat: Entstehung und Entwicklung im internationalen Vergleich, 2nd ed.* (Munich: Oldenbourg, 1991).

4 Stephan Leibfried and Michael Zürn, 'Von der nationalen zur postnationalen Konstellation,' in Stephan Leibfried and Michael Zürn, eds., *Transformationen des Staates?* (Frankfurt am Main: Suhrkamp, 2006), 31; Flora, *Growth to Limits*; Baldwin, *Politics of Social Solidarity*.

5 Pat Thane, *Old Age in English History: Past Experiences, Present Issues* (Oxford: Oxford University Press, 2000); Robin Pearson, 'Who Pays for Pensions? Das Problem der Alterssicherung in Grossbritannien im zwanzigsten Jahrhundert,' *Zeitschrift für Unternehmensgeschichte* 48, no. 1 (2003), 48–57 (see also Peter Borscheid, ed., Special issue on pension systems ['Alterssicherungssysteme im Vergleich'], *Zeitschrift für Unternehmensgeschichte* 48, no. 1 [2003]); Jacob C. Hacker, *The Divided Welfare State: The Battle over Public and Private Social Benefits in the USA* (Cambridge: Cambridge University Press, 2002); Jennifer Klein, *For All These Rights: Business, Labor and the Shaping of America's Public-Private Welfare State* (Princeton: Princeton University Press, 2003); Paul Dutton, *Origins of the French Welfare State: The Struggle for Social Reform in France, 1914–1947* (Cambridge: Cambridge University Press, 2002); Timothy Smith, *Creating the Welfare State in France, 1880–1940* (Montreal: McGill-Queen's University Press, 2003); Matthieu Leimgruber, *Solidarity without the State? Business and the Shaping of the Swiss Welfare State, 1890–2000* (Cambridge: Cambridge University Press, 2008). For an analysis of the mixed welfare economies in the history of poor relief: Michael B. Katz and Christoph Sachsse, eds., *The Mixed Economy of Social Welfare: Public/Private Relations in England, Germany and the United States, the 1870's to the 1930's* (Baden-Baden: Nomos, 1996).

6 *For example: Ugo Ascoli and Costanzo Ranci, eds., Dilemmas of the Welfare Mix: The New Structure of Welfare in an Era of Privatization* (New York: Kluwer, 2002); Herbert Obinger, Stephan Leibfried, Claudia Bogedan, Edith Gindulis, Julia Moser, and Peter Starke, 'Wandel des

Wohlfahrtsstaats in kleinen offenen Volkswirtschaften,' in Stephan Leibfried and Michael Zürn, eds., *Transformationen des Staates?* (Frankfurt/M: Suhrkamp, 2006).

7 Maurizio Ferrera and Elisabetta Gualmini, 'Reforms Guided by Consensus: The Welfare State in the Italian Transition,' in Maurizio Ferrera and Martin Rhodes, eds., *Recasting European Welfare States* (London: Frank Cass, 2000), 194f.; Maurizio Ferrera, 'Welfare States and Social Safety Nets in Southern Europe: An Introduction,' in Maurizio Ferrera, ed., *Welfare State Reform in Southern Europe: Fighting Poverty and Social Exclusion in Italy, Spain, Portugal and Greece* (London: Routledge, 2005).

8 Peter Baldwin, 'Beyond Weak and Strong: Rethinking the State in Comparative Policy History,' *Journal of Policy History* 17, no. 1 (2005), 15.

9 Baldwin, 'Beyond Weak and Strong,' 19.

10 Ernst Lederer, *Entstehung, Entwickelung und heutiger Stand der Volksversicherung in Deutschland* (Erlangen: Jacob, 1914), 40f.

11 Lederer, *Entstehung*, 73.

12 Lederer, *Entstehung*, 1.

13 Lederer, *Entstehung*, 60ff.

14 Thane, *Old Age*, 236–41.

15 Laurie Dennett, *A Sense of Security: 150 Years of Prudential* (Cambridge: Granta Editions, 1998), 57–68; Alfred Hagemann, *Über die Benutzung postalischer Einrichtungen zu Zwecken der Volksversicherung in England und Deutschland* (Giessen: Brühl, 1910), 7–11; Lederer, *Entstehung*, 147ff.; Georg Zacher, *Die Arbeiter-Versicherung in England* (Berlin: Troschel, 1899), 27f.

16 Paul Johnson, *Saving and Spending: The Working-Class Economy in Britain, 1870–1939* (Oxford: Oxford University Press, 1985).

17 Dennett, *A Sense of Security*, 107f.; Lederer, *Entstehung*, 73.

18 Dennett, *A Sense of Security*, 108, 155ff.; Lederer, *Entstehung*, 87. For the introduction of the Old Age Pension Act: Bernard Harris, *The Origins of the British Welfare State: Society, State and Social Welfare in England and Wales, 1800–1945* (Basingstoke: Palgrave Macmillan, 2004), 80f.; Baldwin, *Politics of Social Solidarity*, 99–115. After the introduction of the national old age insurance in 1908, a similar competition between statutory and commercial insurance emerged as the private insurance industry gradually entered the market for occupational pensions; see Pearson, 'Who Pays for Pensions?' 52ff.; Thane, *Old Age*, 243–54.

19 Dennett, *A Sense of Security*, 185–91.

20 Gerhard A. Ritter, 'Bismarck und die Grundlegung des deutschen Sozialstaates,' in *Verfassung, Theorie und Praxis des Sozialstaats*, in Franz Ruland,

Bernd Baron von Maydell, and Hans-Jürgen Papier, eds., (Heidelberg: C.F. Müller, 1998), 790f. See also Christoph Conrad, *Vom Greis zum Rentner: Der Strukturwandel des Alters in Deutschland zwischen 1830 und 1930* (Göttingen: Vandenhoeck & Ruprecht, 1994).

21 Heinrich Braun, *Geschichte der Lebensversicherung und der Lebensversicherungstechnik* (Nürnberg: Koch, 1925), 270f.

22 Arps, *Auf sicheren Pfeilern*, 307ff., 464ff., 583ff.

23 Lederer, *Entstehung*, 87; Braun, *Lebensversicherung*, 347.

24 Alfred Manes, *Versicherungswesen* (Leipzig, Berlin, 2nd rev. ed., 1913), 42ff.; Lederer, *Entstehung*, 87.

25 E.P. Hennock, *British Social Reform and German Precedents: The Case of Social Insurance, 1880–1914* (Oxford: Clarendon, 1987), 96; P.H.J.H. Gosden, *The Friendly Societies in England 1815–1875* (Manchester: Manchester University Press, 1961), 61f.; P.H.J.H. Gosden, *Self-Help: Voluntary Associations in Nineteenth-Century Britain* (London: Batsford, 1973), 60–2. For a case study on Bristol, UK: Martin Gorsky, 'Mutual Aid and Civil Society: Friendly Societies in Nineteenth Century Bristol,' *Urban History* 25, no. 3 (1998). For the European context, see also Martin Lengwiler, 'Insurance and Civil Society: Elements of an Ambivalent Relationship,' *Contemporary European History* 15, no. 3 (2006).

26 Gosden, *Friendly Societies*, 264ff.

27 Lederer, *Entstehung*, 87.

28 Arps, *Auf sicheren Pfeilern*, 307ff., 464ff., 583ff.

29 Lederer, *Entstehung*, 89f.

30 For example, Dennett, *A Sense of Security*, 125–46.

31 For Britain: Gorsky, 'Mutual Aid'; for Germany: Max Teichmann, *Die Grundlagen der deutschen privaten Krankenversicherung* (Leipzig: Meiner, 1937), 11–21.

32 Timothy Alborn, 'Senses of Belonging: The Politics of Working-Class Insurance in Britain, 1880–1914,' *Journal of Modern History* 73, no. 3 (2001), 576f.; Gorsky, 'Mutual Aid.'

33 Pearson, 'Towards an Historical Model.'

34 Ritter, *Der Sozialstaat*.

35 Florian Tennstedt, *Geschichte der Selbstverwaltung in der Krankenversicherung von der Mitte des 19. Jahrhunderts bis zur Gründung der Bundesrepublik Deutschland* (Bonn: Verlag der Ortskrankenkassen, 1977), 13–22.

36 Florian Tennstedt and Heidi Winter, 'Einleitung,' in 'Quellensammlung zur Geschichte der deutschen Sozialpolitik, 1867–1914,' sec. 1, 'Von der Reichsgründungszeit bis zur kaiserlichen Sozialbotschaft (1867–1881),' vol. 5: *Die Krankenversicherung für gewerbliche Arbeitnehmer zwischen Selbst-*

*hilfe und Staatshilfe* (Darmstadt: Wissenschaftliche Buchgesellschaft, 1999); Tennstedt, *Krankenversicherung*, 13–22.

37 Tennstedt, *Krankenversicherung*, 27.

38 Hans Göbbels, *Arzt und private Krankenversicherung: Wesen, Geschichte und Bedeutung der deutschen privaten Krankenversicherung, insbesondere unter dem Gesichtspunkt ihrer Beziehungen zum Arzt* (Berlin: Springer, 1940), 69f.

39 Göbbels, *Arzt*, 69f.

40 Göbbels, *Arzt*, 69f.; Rudolf Hahnemann, *Die deutsche Krankheitskostenversicherung (private Krankenversicherung)* (Leipzig, 1931), 22f.

41 Göbbels, *Arzt*, 56ff.

42 Göbbels, *Arzt*, 70ff.; Walther Heyn, 'Gesetzliche und private Krankenversicherung,' in Walter Rohrbeck, ed., *Zur gesetzlichen und privaten Krankenversicherung* (Berlin: Springer, 1941), 82f.; Johannes Apelbaum, 'Zu den Problemen der privaten Krankenversicherung,' *Zeitschrift für die gesamte Versicherungswissenschaft* 28 (1928), 269.

43 Teichmann, *Grundlagen*, 7.

44 August Schneider, 'Entwicklung, Stand und Aufgabe der privaten Krankenversicherung,' in Walter Rohrbeck, ed., *Zur gesetzlichen und privaten Krankenversicherung* (Berlin: Springer, 1941), 54.

45 Walther Heyn, 'Begriffsbestimmung,' *Zeitschrift für die gesamte Versicherungswissenschaft* 43 (1943), 90; Heyn, 'Gesetzliche und private Krankenversicherung,' 78; Schneider, 'Entwicklung,' 53.

46 Teichmann, *Grundlagen*, 7.

47 Hahnemann, *Krankheitskostenversicherung*, 67.

48 Hahnemann, *Krankheitskostenversicherung*, 21.

49 Hahnemann, *Krankheitskostenversicherung*, 65.

50 Hahnemann, *Krankheitskostenversicherung*, 61–6.

51 Teichmann, *Grundlagen*, 46.

52 Hahnemann, *Krankheitskostenversicherung*, 69–78; Apelbaum, 'Krankenversicherung,' 260ff.; Schneider, 'Entwicklung,' 54.

53 Heyn, 'Gesetzliche und private Krankenversicherung,' 103, 121f.

54 Heyn, 'Gesetzliche und private Krankenversicherung,' 81f., 85f.

55 Heyn, 'Gesetzliche und private Krankenversicherung,' 85f.; Teichmann, *Grundlagen*, 20f. Private insurance policies also had some disadvantages, at least for some customers, such as the increased premiums for women (usually 30 per cent more than the male premium) or the strict exclusion of all previous illnesses at the start of the membership. Teichmann, *Grundlagen*, 11ff., 22; Schneider, 'Entwicklung,' 58ff.

56 For example, Schneider, 'Entwicklung,' 61ff.

57 Heyn, 'Gesetzliche und private Krankenversicherung,' 80.

58 Heyn, 'Gesetzliche und private Krankenversicherung,' 91f.; Schneider, 'Entwicklung,' 62f.

59 Heyn, 'Gesetzliche und private Krankenversicherung,' 78–80, 88–98; Schneider, 'Entwicklung,' 61–3. Robert Ley still supported an integration of all social and private insurances into a general welfare system, called the 'Sozialwerk,' combining old age insurance, the health services (*Gesundheitswerk*), social housing, vocational training, and public wage policy: Schneider, 'Entwicklung,' 62f.

60 Eduard Niederer, *Das Krankenkassenwesen der Schweiz und das Bundesgesetz vom 13. Juni 1911* (Zürich: Rascher, 1914), 67ff.

61 Martin Lengwiler, *Risikopolitik im Sozialstaat: Die schweizerische Unfallversicherung, 1870–1970* (Köln: Böhlau, 2006), 50–8. For a description of the different types of sickness funds: Niederer, *Krankenkassenwesen*, 67–175.

62 Cédric Humair, *Développement économique et Etat central (1815–1914): Un siècle de politique douanière suisse au service des élites* (Bern: Peter Lang, 2004).

63 Lengwiler, *Risikopolitik im Sozialstaat*, 50ff.

64 Jürg H. Sommer, *Das Ringen um soziale Sicherheit in der Schweiz: Eine politisch-ökonomische Analyse der Ursprünge, Entwicklungen und Perspektiven der sozialen Sicherheit im Widerstreit zwischen Gruppeninteressen und volkswirtschaftlicher Tragbarkeit* (Diessenhofen: Rüegger, 1978), 458.

65 Niederer, *Krankenkassenwesen.*

66 Herbert Obinger, Klaus Armingeon, Giuliano Bonoli, and Fabio Bertozzi, 'Switzerland: The Marriage of Direct Democracy and Federalism,' in Herbert Obinger, Stephan Leibfried, and Francis G. Castles, eds., *Federalism and the Welfare State: New World and European Experiences* (Cambridge: Cambridge University Press, 2005), 264, 291f.

67 Alb. Gyger, *50 Jahre Konkordat der schweizerischen Krankenkassen, 1891–1941* (Solothurn: Vogt-Schild, 1941), 43f.

68 Walther Rickenbach, *Das Obligatorium in der Krankenversicherung mit besonderer Berücksichtigung der Schweiz* (Zürich, Wald: Hess, 1930), 148–57.

69 Hans Hünerwadel, *Die Krankenversicherung nach dem Bundesgesetz über die Kranken- und Unfallversicherung, vom 13. Juni 1911, ihre Entstehung und ihre Auswirkung* (Bern: Huber, 1938), 172f.

70 Gyger, *Konkordat*, 31.

71 Gyger, *Konkordat*, 18f., 31.

72 Hünerwadel, *Krankenversicherung*, 59.

73 Hünerwadel, *Krankenversicherung*, 63.

74 Hünerwadel, *Krankenversicherung*, 60–3, 81–93; Martin Lengwiler and Verena Rothenbühler, *Macht und Ohnmacht der Ärzteschaft: Geschichte des*

*Zürcher Ärzteverbands im 20. Jahrhundert* (Zürich: Chronos, 2004), 49, 56–60.

75 Hans Hünerwadel, *Die besondere Stellung der ‚Gebirgsgegenden' in der Krankenversicherung und in der Krankenfürsorge* (Zürich: Verlag der Schweizerischen Krankenkassen-Zeitung, 1923), 3–5.

76 Hünerwadel, *Krankenversicherung*, 47; F. Aemmer, *Die öffentliche Krankenversicherung im Kanton Basel-Stadt* (Zürich: Verlag der Schweizerischen Krankenkassen-Zeitung, 1925); Hünerwadel, *Stellung*. For a detailed synopsis of all cantonal health plans: Hünerwadel, *Krankenversicherung*, 45–64; Rickenbach, *Obligatorium*, 126–46, 147ff.

77 Hünerwadel, *Krankenversicherung*, 63.

78 Hünerwadel, *Krankenversicherung*, 175.

79 Leimgruber, *Solidarity without the State*.

80 *Schweizerische Krankenkassen-Zeitung* 35, 1943, 66f., 160ff.; Sommer, *Soziale Sicherheit*, 459ff.

81 Hünerwadel, *Krankenversicherung*, 69f.

82 Jens Alber and Brigitte Bernardi-Schenkluhn, *Westeuropäische Gesundheitssysteme im Vergleich: Bundesrepublik Deutschland, Schweiz, Frankreich, Italien, Grossbritannien* (Frankfurt/M: Campus, 1992).

# 9 Employers and Industrial Accident Insurance in Spain, 1900–1963

JERÒNIA PONS PONS

One of the most pressing social contingencies in industrial societies was the problem of industrial accidents, which could have important consequences for workers and their families.[1] From the end of the nineteenth century, 'reformist states' promoted insurance, of either a compulsory or a voluntary nature, to cover this eventuality.[2] In the majority of cases, demand for this insurance originated with the workers, but it affected employers both in terms of their responsibility and with respect to costs. The stance employers adopted in the face of the legislating and reforming state, which could be either one of rejection or one of acceptance and collaboration, influenced the creation of different models of industrial accident insurance coverage in these societies. Other key influences were the positions adopted by different governments as well as the labour demands of the workers. The attitude of employers towards insurance in particular countries was especially decisive. This fact is fundamental when it comes to understanding the evolution of both the legal framework and the management of insurance itself, as well as the repercussions on the number of industrial accidents.

Employers, in general, went from initial opposition to industrial accident insurance to one of acceptance and collaboration.[3] However, the different attitudes towards and timing of industrial accident insurance were extremely varied and were driven by the social, economic, political, and cultural determinants of each country. In the case of Spain, the country used for analysis in this chapter, the employers themselves were not a homogeneous group and thus adopted different postures with regard to industrial accident insurance.[4]

The Commission of Social Reforms was set up in Spain in 1883 with the aim of studying questions related to the improvement or welfare of both the agricultural and industrial working classes, and which therefore affected the relations between capital and labour.[5] In the commission's study of industrial accidents in Spain, it became evident that the employer's responsibility for these accidents was virtually never recognized.[6] Judges, lacking the technical preparation to find out the real causes of accidents, almost never held the employer to be responsible.[7] The law of industrial accidents of 1900 changed this situation, and for the first time held employers responsible for the accidents of their workers in industrial, mining, and construction activities as well as in those agricultural activities where machines were used.

This new law is now considered to be the beginning of social security in Spain.[8] The law did not oblige employers to insure their workers, although it did contemplate this possibility. Employers could insure their workers through a commercial insurance company or in an employers' industrial accident mutual.[9] This latter possibility marked the start of a new relationship between employers and insurance that transcended insurance against industrial accidents and was to gradually evolve with the passage of time.

After this law was passed, insurance mutuals were created to cover the risk of accidents in industrial areas, and especially by employers most affected by the risk of accidents. Although it is true that employers took out insurance due to the responsibilities the new law had recently obliged them to accept, they soon found advantages in the practice of insurance and, above all, in the control of the insurance process. Agricultural employers, for their part, resisted or ignored these insurance practices for decades, and their only objective was to prevent a similar law being passed with regard to agricultural activity.[10]

## Employers' Industrial Accident Insurance Mutuals during the Voluntary Stage

Industrial accident insurance mutuals were created by employers from 1900 onwards in the industrialized zones, mainly Catalonia, the Basque Country, and Asturias, and also in Madrid and Zaragoza. These mutuals always received preferential treatment, firstly in the 1900 law and then in the successive legislation relating to industrial accidents.[11] The aim of successive governments was to obtain the collaboration of employers in order to extend voluntary industrial accident insurance. In chapter 7 of the so-called Dato Law of 1900, it was laid down that both insurance mutuals and joint stock insurance companies wishing to insure employers had to meet a series of obligations. These were: the separation of the operations of this branch with respect to other insurance activities undertaken by the company; a special deposit; acceptance of the legislation concerning industrial accidents; and the need to communicate the statutes, balances, policies, fees, reserves, and statistics related to this activity to the Ministry of the Interior. For employers' mutuals to be set up, they had to include the joint and several liability of their members in their statutes, cover a minimum of one thousand workers, and comprise more than twenty employers. The government favoured the mutuals by exempting them from the payment of taxes and by requiring an initial deposit of only 5,000 to 50,000 pesetas. The amount depended on whether they were authorized to operate in just one or in several provinces. This deposit was much smaller than the deposits demanded from the commercial insurance companies, which varied between 150,000 and 200,000 pesetas.

There are records of the existence of more than twenty employers' industrial accident mutuals in the whole of Spain in 1914, many of them in Barcelona (Table 9.1). The majority of them had brought together employers in the sectors most affected by industrial accidents: construction, transport, or dockyard activities. In other cases, these associations were made up of employers from various sectors and the connection was the local or regional geographical location.

In the first years of their development, employers' industrial accident mutuals enjoyed great freedom of action. Their main characteristics were established during this period. First of all, their geographical scope was reduced. Although there were employers' mutuals on a national scale, the majority limited their activity to one locality, province, or region. Second, the boards of directors were comprised of the principal members, that is to say, by the owners of the largest associated companies or, in some cases, by their representatives. They were run, therefore, by the businessmen themselves, although their management did become more professional with the passage of time. Third, the insurance these mutual societies provided covered two aspects: medical treatment of the injured worker and workers' compensation. Compensation was classified according to whether the disability was temporary or permanent, or whether death occurred.The fourth characteristic, one which persisted for a long time, was based on the notion that the insured (i.e., the client of the mutual) was the

Table 9.1
Employers' industrial accident insurance mutuals in 1914

| Name | Location | Foundation or registration (if data available) |
|---|---|---|
| La Iberia | Barcelona | 1900 |
| Mutua Barcelonesa de Descargadores | Barcelona | 1906 |
| Mutua General de Seguros | Barcelona | 1907 |
| Mutua de Accidentes de Zaragoza | Zaragoza | 1905 |
| Mutua Regional de Accidentes de Trabajo | Barcelona | 1907 |
| Mutua Agrícola del Bajo Llobregat | Hospitalet (Barcelona) | 1908 |
| Mutua Asturiana de Accidentes | Gijón | 1906 |
| Seguros Mutuos de Vizcaya | Bilbao | 1900 |
| Mutua de contratistas generales de obras | Barcelona | 1903 |
| Unión de Corporaciones Patronales | Barcelona | – |
| La Previsión, sociedad mutua de seguros | Madrid | 1901 |
| El seguro Tarrasense contra accidentes de trabajo | Tarrasa | – |
| Sociedad de Seguros Mutuos | Santander | 1906 |
| La Primitiva | Madrid | – |
| La Equidad | Madrid | |
| Mutua Valenciana sobre Accidentes del trabajo | Valencia | 1913 |
| La Providencia | Salamanca | – |
| Mutua Industrial | Madrid | – |
| La Alianza de patronos carreteros | Barcelona | 1908 |
| Mutua de Alquiladores de carruajes | Barcelona | – |
| La Alianza | Sevilla | – |
| Mutua de Faquines del comercio | Barcelona | – |
| Mutua del centro de carpinteros | Barcelona | 1912 |
| El Vulcano | Madrid | – |
| Mutua de Patronos Vaqueros | Barcelona | – |

Source: *Spanish Insurance Yearbook* (Barcelona: Cecilio Bascones, 1913)

employer and not the worker. The main objective of the mutuals was, therefore, to keep employers happy and defend their interests. This last consideration explains the mutuals' policy concerning the creation of hospital infrastructures and their sparse investment in prevention, which were always going to be constrained by the members' interest in paying low premiums and their preference for a refund of part of the premiums (rebates). A comparison of the compensation of injured workers in Spain with that in other European countries demonstrates that the cost of the indemnification was much lower for Spanish employers. For this reason, there was very little incentive to invest in prevention.[12] Before the reform of the law in 1922 compensation was in the form of capital and represented only 50 per cent of salary in the case of temporary incapacity. In the case of death, the capital was the equivalent of twice the annual salary, as opposed to Great Britain where the annual salary was tripled or Denmark where it was multiplied by five.[13] This practice would be modified only later, at least in the majority of cases, after the state intervened in the fixing of premiums, reinsurance, and reserve funds.

These four characteristics contain some of the keys to understanding the change in the collective mentality of the associated employers with respect to industrial accident insurance.[14] The practice of providing insurance through mutual institutions enabled these businessmen to obtain lower premiums, largely because of the practice of rebates (a refund of part of the premium if there were profits at the end of the fiscal year). Lower premiums were also achieved because of the control over the injured workers exerted via the mutuals' own medical service. This was combined with the operation of a paternalistic culture by the mutuals. For example, many 'docile' workers, who suffered accidents in cases that were not very clear with regard to compensation, deferred to their employers. Mutuals were also allowed to organize themselves jointly to put a brake on the tendency towards greater social intervention on the part of the state. In 1914, for example, the employers became concerned about the increase of state regulation in the field of industrial accident insurance. In the first Spanish employers' congress, which was held in Madrid in that year, the bill presented by the government to modify the law of industrial accidents of 1900 was closely scrutinized.[15] The twenty-four employers' industrial accident insurance mutuals, half of them Catalan, met a few days earlier in order to draw up a report and make proposals to the parliamentary commission responsible for the new law, with the intention of directly opposing the government's bill.

Thanks to the analysis carried out by Soledad Bengoechea, we can more fully understand the position of the employers associated with the mutuals regarding the industrial accident insurance prevailing at that time and, especially, their opposition to a reform designed to increase coverage for the workers. Drawing upon legal and medical advice in order to support their case, the employers' mutuals prepared a report in which they drew attention to the almost fifteen years' experience that they possessed in the practice of insurance, while at the same time revealing their paternalistic attitude towards industrial accident insurance, which they saw as part of a wider ethos of Christian charity based on the principles of social Catholicism.[16]

> The fact is, it should be pointed out, that the present report, with the amendments which follow it, are not the isolated thoughts of one thinker, nor of one entity, nor even of a particular region. They constitute the aspirations of the entire class of employers, which, respectful of the humanitarian principle, and just as it is that this principle guides the legislation of industrial accidents, wishes to surround itself with all the guarantees necessary to prevent a swindle.[17]

The employers proposed an amendment to the bill that removed articles they considered inappropriate. But at the heart of their opposition was a fear that the state was beginning to interfere in the management of insurance, whereas previously it had limited its role to one of legislation. For example, the new bill planned to create a new levy on the taxpayer, by means of which it was intended to create a 'special fund' that would be administered by the National Insurance Institute (Instituto Nacional de Previsión), created in 1908. The creation of this fund administered by an official institute would initiate direct state intervention in the management of insurance. Employers considered this to be a threat to the freedom of action they had enjoyed until that time. According to Bengoechea, the employers saw this intervention as 'a dangerous advance of the most exaggerated socialism.'[18]

Another development that was seen as undermining the interests of employers was the broadening of the concept of industrial accidents that was included in some of the articles of the reform. For example, employers were concerned about accepting a 'professional illness' as an industrial accident, given the difficulty in determining at what moment such an illness first appeared or began to develop. Their objection to linking some professional illnesses to industrial accidents was based in part on medical evidence, since according to some doctors a hernia, for example, could be an organic illness, a predisposition of an individual, and its inclusion as an industrial accident might, therefore, open the door to interminable lawsuits.

The paternalistic mentality of the employers was also evident in their expectations about the behaviour of their workers. Too many employers assumed that workers were inherently lazy with a tendency to fall into roguery and vice. According to this view it was necessary to prevent even injured workers from unfairly exploiting their situation. The payment of compensation was, therefore, a major concern since it provided the opportunity for those 'duplicitous' workers to deceive their employers about the seriousness of their accidents. For this reason, employers proposed that payment of compensation start eight days after the accident had happened in order to prevent abuses by workers who, for example, once in receipt of sick pay as well as the aid of some friendly society, might seek to prolong their sick leave if they were receiving a higher income than when they were working. Another proposed modification was that, in cases of partial disability, employers should retain the option, established in the law of 1900, to give injured workers a job compatible with their condition with the same pay as they were receiving when they suffered the accident, instead of compensation of a year's wages. The employers' argument was based on the idea that if a person suffering a partial disability was paid a normal salary, after working for one or two years they would have been compensated for their accident. Finally, employers refused to pay compensation to the family of a worker who died in an accident when the subsistence of these would not have depended on the deceased. This concept of insurance was based on a Christian and paternalistic tradition in which insurance was seen not as a social right of citizens but as a palliative of situations of need, as part of Christian charity. And this ethos was embedded in the insurance practices of the mutuals themselves. The Mutua General de Seguros, for example, in its first years in operation, supplemented payments to some injured workers with special donations in accordance with the docility or deference of the worker as well as of the importance of the employer within the association.[19]

The bill of 1914 was not passed. Further bills were also rejected until, finally, the so-called Matos law was passed in January 1922. This new law had important repercussions through an increase in the expenditure of the mutuals, increasing their fees by up to 50 per cent in some cases as compensation to workers increased. Nevertheless, the employers' principal objective with respect to this insurance was maintained. It continued on a voluntary basis and was privately managed. At the same time, attempts by the social reformers to introduce employers' liability into accidents among agricultural workers were unsuccessful. In February 1919 a bill was introduced in the Spanish parliament to extend the law of industrial accident insurance to the agricultural sector by means of the creation of local mutual societies. The agricultural employers, who were much more conservative and less receptive to insurance, exerted so much pressure that the bill was rejected.[20] This project was only approved during the Spanish Second Republic in 1931.

During the 1920s, the government continued to support the diffusion of employers' mutuals as a formula for extending voluntary insurance against industrial accidents. One effective measure taken in 1925 was the modification of article 109 of the law of 1922, through which the minimum number of workers the employers needed to insure in order to set up a mutual was reduced significantly, from one thousand workers down to one hundred. This reduction enabled the authorization of small mutual institutions. By 1930, forty-two employers' mutuals were operating as opposed to twenty-seven commercial insurance companies. The fact was, however, that the former received only about 14 per cent of premiums collected for this type of insurance, and the rest of the business remained in the hands of commercial insurance companies. Nevertheless, the employers' mutuals helped to change the mentality of industrial employers with respect to industrial accident insurance. For lower premiums than the commercial companies, they could guarantee the medical care of their injured workers, control their progress and the length of convalescence, and also receive a refund of part of the premium if the mutual made a profit. In fact, some mutuals offered their members other types of social insurance that were still not required by the state. From 1923 the board of directors of the Mutua General de Seguros studied the possibility of introducing health, maternity, and life insurance. The paternalistic idea of controlling workers' behaviour continued in these new forms of insurance, a fact that is clearly revealed in the first regulations proposed. One of the articles, for example, proposed to suspend the benefits for sickness, maternity, and death for those workers who were dismissed from the factory or workshop due to a strike or a lockout. However, this article was later removed due to the fact that the right to strike was accepted by law, and because the article 'contradicts the spirit of *social cordiality* which the introduction of health, maternity and life insurance assumes, and it is also the case that the exception mentioned could be interpreted by those concerned as coercion.'[21]

Industrial employers, therefore, were to continue looking for a balance between their interests, based on control of their workers, and reformist measures designed to achieve social peace. Until the 1930s industrial employers found in industrial accident insurance, as well as in other types of social insurance, a mechanism for responding to the needs and risks faced by the working class that was inspired by the principle of Christian charity. The aim was to achieve social calm in times of great conflict with the trade unions and to develop a mechanism for controlling the workers. There were other advantages to the employers' mutuals that could not be gained so directly by taking out insurance with the commercial insurance companies. The employers' mutuals were generally less concerned about the accuracy of the declared wages paid to workers, which was the basis of the premiums, or of the numbers of workers contracted or dismissed in moments of economic difficulty by an associated employer or employers.[22] In spite of these advantages for employers, the commercial companies continued to control a large part of this business by offering a wider range of insurance and other kinds of services. This explains why more than 80 per cent of the premiums for this branch of insurance remained in commercial hands until the 1930s. The mutuals were still not a dangerous rival for the commercial insurance companies at this stage. In fact, both groups of insurers belonged to some of the same associations, such as the Accident Insurance Companies' Legal Committee, which had been created in 1917 on the initiative of the directors of the most important insurance companies operating in this area. They shared the same goal: the defence of the general interests of the private insurance institutions in the face of the state's tendency to gradually take over their functions.[23] However, the collaboration and cordial atmosphere between employers' mutuals and insurance companies was interrupted during the Second Republic, when compulsory insurance against industrial accidents was introduced, and throughout Spain hundreds of employers' mutuals were created that challenged the commercial companies for business.

## Employers in the Light of Compulsory Industrial Accident Insurance

In spite of employers' resistance to the idea of compulsory social insurance, successive governments were to introduce compulsory schemes eventually. Compulsory maternity insurance was passed in 1929, and this development put the employers' mutuals on their guard against a similar process for industrial accident insurance. With the coming of the Spanish Second Republic a new phase was initiated, based on compulsory insurance and on an attempt to unify social insurance. Previously, different governments had attempted to ratify various agreements but sociopolitical circumstances and especially the hostility of the agricultural employers had impeded their implementation. With the Second Republic, and in particular with Francisco Largo Caballero, a socialist, in the Ministry of Labour and Social Insurance, greater impetus was given to the advance of this type of insurance. On 12 July 1931 the decree applying the law of industrial accidents to agriculture was passed, and the regulation developing it was approved on 25 August 1931.[24] In this case, the new law obliged agricultural employers to provide medical care and compensation and, in contrast to accident insurance in industry, it was compulsory in agriculture. Employers had to meet the obligation of medical care through local mutual societies that would be set up in each municipality or area. After years of outright rejection of an increase in their responsibilities with respect to their workers' accidents, except in particular cases, agricultural employers suddenly found that this had been made compulsory. The agricultural employers' organizations, already upset with the government of the Republic over the issue of land reform, decided to draw on the long experience of the industrial employers' mutuals and created similar mutual institutions. If they were obliged to insure, better to do so through their own mutual societies. By 1934 there were already four large industrial accident mutuals in the agricultural sector in Spain, all of them linked to agricultural employers' associations. There were also other small-scale local mutuals. The big four were the Mutua de Seguros Agrícolas (later called MAPFRE), founded by the Spanish Association of Country Estate Owners (Agrupación de Propietarios de Fincas Rústicas de España); the Mutualidad General Agropecuaria, dependent on the Spanish General Cattle Breeders' Association (Asociación General de Ganaderos de España); the Caja de Seguros Mutuos contra Accidentes de Trabajo en la Agricultura, created by the Spanish General Farmers' Association (Asociación General de Agricultores de España [MESAI]); and the Mutualidad Española de Seguros de Accidentes de Trabajo, promoted by the National Catholic-Agrarian Confederation (Confederación Nacional Católica-Agraria).[25]

The compulsory nature of insurance in agriculture was soon extended to industrial activity. The revised text of the law of industrial accidents was passed on 8 October 1932 and further developed by the regulation of 31 January 1933. This new law had three important repercussions: the fact that accident insurance became compulsory; the sub-

> because the Management considered that it was no longer convenient to belong to the said organisation, in view of having seen that a certain hostility towards mutual institutions existed at the heart of the association, and to such an extent that all of the institutions similar to ours have already left this organisation.[30]

The increase in the number of mutuals, and the preservation of privileges such as very low deposits and tax exemption, increased the differences between mutuals and insurance companies. An atmosphere of mutual recrimination developed between them and filled the professional journals and the newspapers of the time.

The agricultural employers' organizations created accident insurance mutuals throughout Spain, but in practice there was an overlap of their activities and those of industrial sector mutuals, since both organizations actually operated across both sectors. The state promoted them as a formula for extending industrial accident insurance, and the employers took advantage of the tax benefits to manage the insurance in their own interests. Insurance in the mutuals was cheaper, and the workers were attended to by a medical infrastructure created by the mutuals themselves. Consequently, the management and the boards of directors of the mutuals (who comprised the associated businessmen with the greatest power) and the medical inspectors whom they designated together determined medical policy, workers' medical treatment, length of time off work, and the rehabilitation of workers. An example of the statistics elaborated by the medical personnel of the Mutua General de Seguro can be seen in Table 9.3, where a record is kept of the time off work of injured workers treated in the General Eléctrica Española company. This information was a vital resource that employers could use to influence their labour relations with injured workers. The identity of injured workers who received medical attention and compensation from an institution was revealed and linked to their employers, and this was especially important among the agricultural workers. Their medical care and compensation relied upon paternalistic landowners, and in a large part of the Spanish countryside it helped to prolong the culture of dependence and *caciquismo* (despotism) that had traditionally dominated the large Spanish estates.[31] Agricultural employers, therefore, adapted this new obligation to their own self-interests, and in the first years of its application in the countryside this type of insurance, managed by their own organizations, was

Table 9.3
Record of injured off work in La General Eléctrica Española, attended by Mutua General de Seguros' doctor, 1941

| Years worked | Age | Off work last year? | Total number of times off work since starting |
|---|---|---|---|
| 1 | 32 | No | 1 |
| 3 | 18 | No | 1 |
| 2 | 24 | Yes | 3 |
| 2 | 31 | No | 3 |
| 9 | 31 | Yes | 2 |
| 8 | 29 | No | 3 |
| 9 | 36 | No | 6 |
| 3 | 30 | No | 3 |
| 6 | 36 | Yes | 5 |
| 3 | 22 | No | 2 |
| 9 | 38 | Yes | 9 |
| 9 | 36 | Yes | 12 |
| 2 | 37 | No | 1 |
| 3 | 18 | No | 2 |
| 2 | 18 | Yes | 3 |
| 1 | 24 | No | 1 |
| 7 | 30 | No | 6 |
| 2 | 36 | Yes | 2 |
| 8 | 35 | No | 3 |
| 2 | 26 | No | 4 |
| 1 | 26 | No | 1 |
| 1 | 15 | No | 1 |
| 3 | 37 | No | 1 |
| 2 | 41 | No | 1 |
| 8 | 32 | No | 3 |

Source: List of services provided in the first-aid post of the General Eléctrica Española, 1941, Mutua General de Seguros archive (unclassified)

once again used as another mechanism for maintaining the dependence of the workers.

Within the industrial sector, the employers' accident insurance mutuals, especially those created in the first decades of the century, had also continued to evolve, especially with regard to the professionalization of their management. Insurance professionals were increasingly incorporated into many mutuals and began a process aimed at the diversification of insurance provision, prompted by the state's interventionist and even nationalizing tendency towards industrial accident insurance. Consequently, many of these institutions diversified and became general insurance mutuals, operating in life insurance, fire insurance, and the like as well as in industrial accident insurance. This was the case with the Mutua General de Seguros, and in December 1935 the manager of this mutual, Salvio Masoliver, defended the start of operations in life insurance to the associated businessmen who were members of the board of directors. In Masoliver's own words, this necessity was based on

> the fact that social policy is constantly accentuating the general tendency of all governments towards state control, a tendency from which, unfortunately, we are not exempt. All kinds of social insurance have to be directed towards us within a relatively short period of time, and current proof of this is the insurance for worker retirement, for the railways and, most recently, for maternity, without taking into account the possibility that compulsory health insurance will soon be added to this list.[32]

By following the path of diversification, the mutuals originally created by employers to fulfil the aim of providing insurance cover for their workers in case of accidents gradually became general insurance companies. The professionalization of management of the mutuals was exceedingly influential in this respect. Nevertheless, the boards of directors continued to be composed of the main representatives of the associated companies for decades to come. These representatives were to determine the evolution of the mutuals, and they never forgot that their principal concern was linked to the management of accident insurance with low premiums and medical attention for injured workers at the least cost.

## Industrial Accident Insurance and Employers' Mutuals during the Franco Regime

After the Civil War (1936–39), at the beginning of the Franco regime, mutuals enjoyed the government's support for managing industrial accident insurance. Neither industrial nor agricultural employers attempted in any way to turn the clock back. No new laws were introduced, and the laws that had been passed during the Second Republic in relation to this branch were not modified. Industrial accident insurance was totally established in practice and accepted as an employer's responsibility. At this stage, the aim was to preserve the management of this insurance in the hands of private insurance. The following decades were used by the mutuals to delay and postpone what seemed inevitable: the nationalization of industrial accident insurance. The unification of different types of social insurance was one of the objectives that had not been met during the Second Republic and, although the situation of autarky prevented its being put into practice during the Franco regime, the idea remained alive.[33]

Between 1933 and 1935 there had been a substantial increase in the creation of employers' industrial accident mutuals. By contrast, during the first postwar years there was actually a reduction in their number, due in large part to the disappearance of a number of poorly performing mutuals, but also because of the effects of the law of mutual societies of December 1941. This law was intended to create some order among the mutual institutions that had been excluded from the regulation of the law of private insurance of 1908. Under the new law, those mutual societies that were not subject to the 1908 law had to include the word 'previsión' in their official title, or some similar term or terms that made express mention of their charitable or social nature. The rest of the societies were subject to the general law, and in the case of employers' mutuals they were also subject to a special regulation of the Ministry of Labour.

This attempt by the authorities governing mutual institutions to exercise greater control caused a great stir among the employers' industrial accident mutuals. Since the mutuals had already diversified their activity towards other branches of private insurance, some of them opted to become commercial companies, making it easier for them to operate in other branches of private insurance such as fire or maritime insurance. Many employers' industrial accident insurance mutuals created due to employers' interest in managing this insurance were thus converting into general insurance institutions, and their strategies and decisions were less and less distinguishable from those of the commercial insurance companies. Following the passage of a law of mutual societies in 1942 that started to restrict the activities of these institutions, some notable employers' industrial accident insurance mutuals became commercial companies. A case in point was Mutua Balear, which became the company Mare Nostrum, while the Sevillian mutual Comercio Industria Agricultura and the mutual Hermes both converted into insurance companies under the same names. The drop in the number of mutuals from 160 in 1941 to 101 in 1945 was due to this process. The managers of the employers' mutuals not only opted for diversification towards private insurance but also collaborated with the government in the management of other types of social insurance.

Early in the postwar period, the government of the Franco dictatorship created compulsory sickness insurance (Seguro Obligatorio de Enfermedad, or SOE). The law covered workers who worked for an employer and offered health care in cases of illness or maternity, as well as economic compensation for the loss of earnings and indemnification for funeral costs in case of death. The family of the insured was also covered. However, the National Insurance Institute, which was responsible for implementing the new insurance, had to utilize private organizations because the state did not have the necessary infrastructure available. The employers' mutuals, which possessed the necessary clinical and health care infrastructure and experience after years of putting industrial accident insurance into practice, were again among the first collaborating bodies.[34] The employers who ran these mutuals continued to have an interest in applying the different kinds of social insurance and were once more able to control their management and development.[35]

Among the employers' industrial accident insurance mutuals operating on a national scale that, in 1944, agreed to offer their services for a ten-year period were well-known mutuals such as Hermes, Mutua General de Seguros, Mutua Balear, and MAPFRE. These mutuals were obliged to have their own personnel and premises in all provincial capitals in order to comply with all of the care provisions and bureaucratic requirements demanded by the agreement. The mutuals managed the collection of the premiums which both employers and workers had to pay, and were responsible for the payment of compensation and the provision of health care services. A percentage was deducted from the premiums to pay for the inspection of health care services, and a further percentage was deducted to fund a plan for the creation of health care facilities (known as the Plan Nacional de Instalaciones Sanitarias) and which was responsible for financing large hospital complexes around the country. When the agreement ended in 1955, the majority of employers' mutuals were left with a significant debt with the National Insurance Institute in relation to these contributions, and for this reason some of them decided to end the collaboration. The majority, however, renewed their agreements until the passage of the basic law of social security in 1963. In spite of the financial difficulties that resulted from the management of compulsory sickness insurance, those businessmen who were members of the employers' mutuals were compensated for providing this service, as they had lower premiums and more direct control over their injured and sick workers.

The employers' industrial accident insurance mutuals continued their activities with very little government intervention. The number of employers' industrial accident mutuals actually reached an historical peak of 235 in operation in 1959. They were able to decide about their assets and the investment of their reserves and surpluses, and they continued with the practice of rebates, which reduced the amount of money destined to infrastructures or prevention. Rumours about the creation of a system of social security started circulating in the insurance sector in the second half of the 1950s. The law of social security, which was intended to finally unify the different types of social insurance in Spain, was passed on 28 December 1963 and was put into effect starting in 1966.

Nevertheless, the Spanish employers' relationship with this form of insurance did not end with this new law. The commercial insurance companies were excluded from a branch in which they had been operating for sixty-three years. With the development of the basic law to instigate social security on 27 April 1966, employers' accident insurance mutuals, for their part, could continue operating as collaborating bodies of the social security. The reasons why the employers' mutuals were allowed to continue administrating this insurance are not clear. It was probably due to a combination of political pressure and the state's need to count on their infrastructure and experience.[36] The employers' mutuals had to separate the branch of accidents from the rest of their business, and this was then constituted as a new mutual that continued managing this type of insurance as a collaborating body of the social security. The bodies linked to the social security could not now make a profit. Although they were allowed to continue with the rebates, a limit was now set and 80 per cent of the mutuals' surpluses had to be dedicated to investments and prevention, while the remaining 20 per cent could be refunded to members in the form of rebates. The employers' mutuals invariably continued to be run by the associated businessmen, although now under greater state control. Starting in 1972, the intervention of the National Insurance Institute finally led to prohibition of the rebates and control of the mutuals' historical patrimony, and from the 1980s on a process of concentration was encouraged.

## Conclusion

The way that the relationship between employers and industrial accident insurance evolved in twentieth-century Spain had to do more with practical and operational issues than with any other factors. The advances in this insurance came about largely as a result of workers' demands or legislative developments, although there were some employers who supported the state's social reform policies. However, the majority of industrial employers, and especially agricultural ones, accepted the insurance without conviction, as an obligation, even at the stage when insurance was still voluntary. In spite of this, the businessmen linked to the employers' mutuals ended up being convinced of the usefulness of this insurance and adapted it to their own interests. With lower premiums than those of commercial companies, they obtained rapid medical attention for their injured workers, were able to exert influence over their recuperation and compensation, and furthermore, if the mutuals made a profit they received a refund of part of their premiums. The policy of the mutuals served the interests of their members, but these were the employers and not the workers. For workers there were many deficiencies with respect to prevention or infrastructure. It was upon costs and rebates, issues affecting the employers, that the mutuals mainly concentrated.

The introduction and development of industrial accident insurance was voluntary and partial for decades, until an institutional reform promoted by the Socialists of the government of the Second Republic approved its compulsory nature and its extension to the majority of workers. Nevertheless, its management continued in the hands of commercial insurance companies and employers' industrial accident mutuals. There was no turning back after the Spanish Civil War because, among other reasons, companies and mutuals had both benefited from the compulsory nature of insurance through an increase in the volume of business. With the implementation of compulsory sickness insurance during the first years of the Franco regime, insurance mutuals and companies continued participating in the field of social insurance. The institutionalization of social security in European countries, and changes in the Franco regime itself, led to the passage of a law of social security in 1963 and the nationalization of social insurance. However, at the last moment, the employers' industrial accident mutuals were allowed to continue managing industrial accident insurance. Whether this was due to pressure from the mutuals, the need to use the medical and health care infrastructure they had created, or the political influence of certain groups of businessmen linked to the mutuals has still not been clearly established. Nevertheless, this decision has effectively conditioned this type of insurance up to the present day. At the same time, some of the mutuals created with the aim of insuring workers against industrial accidents were transformed, with the passage of time, into important insurance companies in their own right due to their diversification into other non-social branches of insurance. Among present-day insurers that followed this path are two important examples: Mutua General de Seguros and MAPFRE, the latter of which is now a multinational in the sector.

NOTES

1 Margaret S. Gordon, *Social Security Policies in Industrial Countries: A Comparative Analysis* (Cambridge: Cambridge University Press, 1988); Peter Baldwin, *The Politics of Social Solidarity: Class Bases of the European Welfare State 1875–1975* (Cambridge: Cambridge University Press, 1991); Paul V. Dutton, *Origins of the French Welfare State: The Struggle for Social Reform in France 1914–1947* (Cambridge: Cambridge University Press, 2003); Bernard Harris, *The Origins of the British Welfare State: Society, State and Social Welfare in England and Wales, 1800–1945* (Basingstoke: Palgrave Macmillan, 2004).

2 For the case of England, see Peter W.J. Bartrip, *Workmen's Compensation in Twentieth-Century Britain: Law, History and social Policy* (Aldershot: Gower, 1987); Walter Dinsdale, *History of Accident Insurance in Great Britain* (London: Stone & Cox, 1954). For Europe, see Margaret S. Gordon, 'Industrial Injuries Insurance in Europe and the British Commonwealth before World War II,' in Earl F. Cheit and Margaret S. Gordon, eds., *Occupational Disability and Public Policy* (John Wiley & Son: New York, 1963), 191–220. For the United States, see Price V. Fishback and Shawn E. Kantor, *A Prelude to the Welfare State: The Origins of Workers' Compensation* (Chicago: University of Chicago Press, 2000).

3 For the case of Spain, see Feliciano Montero García, 'La polémica sobre el intervencionismo y la primera legislación obrera en España 1890–1900. 2ª parte: El debate político-parlamentario,' *Revista de Trabajo* 61–62 (1981), 35–89.

4 More on Spanish employers and their organizations can be found in Fer-

nando Del Rey Reguillo, *Propietarios y Patronos: La política de las organizaciones económicas en la España de la Restauración (1914–1923)* (Madrid: Ministerio de Trabajo y Seguridad Social, 1992); Mercedes Cabrera, *La patronal ante la II República: Organizaciones y estrategias (1931–1936)* (Madrid: Siglo Veintiuno de España, 1983); Soledad Bengoechea Echaondo, *Patronal catalana, corporativismo y crisis política, 1898–1923* (Barcelona: Publicacions de la Universitat Autònoma de Barcelona, 1992); Mercedes Cabrera and Fernando del Rey Reguillo, *El poder de los empresarios: Política e intereses económicos en la España contemporánea (1875–2000)* (Madrid: Taurus, 2002). For the agricultural employers, see Antonio Florencio Puntas, *Empresariado agrícola y cambio económico, 1880–1936* (Seville: Diputación Provincial de Sevilla, 1994).

5 For the creation of the institutions of social reform in Spain, see Juan Ignacio Palacio Morena, *La Institucionalización de la reforma social en España (1883–1924)* (Madrid: Ministerio de Trabajo y Seguridad Social, 1988).

6 On industrial accidents, see Álvaro Soto Carmona, 'La Higiene, la seguridad y los accidentes de trabajo: España (1874–1936),' *Civitas: Revista Española de Derecho del trabajo* 23 (1985), 389–423.

7 Guillermo García González, 'Antecedentes de la ley de Accidentes de Trabajo de 1900 en materia de prevención de riesgos laborales (1873–1900),' in Carlos Arenas Posadas, Antonio Florencio, and Jerònia Pons Pons, eds., *Trabajo y relaciones laborales en la España Contemporánea* (Seville: Mergablum, 2001), 395–403.

8 Manuel Alonso Olea *'La ley de accidentes de trabajo como origen de la Seguridad Social,' Cuadernos de Información Económica* 159 (2000), 145–51. For studies of the evolution of social insurance in Spain, see Jordi Nadal and Carles Sudrià, *Historia de la Caja de Pensiones (La 'Caixa') dentro del sistema financiero catalán* (Barcelona: La Caixa, 1981); Josefina Cuesta Bustillo, *Los seguros sociales en la España del siglo XX: Hacia los seguros sociales obligatorios* (Madrid: Ministerio de Trabajo y Seguridad Social, 1988); Feliciano Montero García and María Esther Martínez Quinteiro, *Orígenes y antecedentes de la Previsión Social* (Madrid: Ministerio de Trabajo y Seguridad Social, 1988); and Mercedes Samaniego, *La unificación de los seguros sociales a debate: La Segunda República* (Madrid: Ministerio de Trabajo y Seguridad Social,

9 There is an important relationship between the mutual societies and the creation of the welfare state. See Martín Leingwiler, 'Insurance and Civil Society: Elements of an Ambivalent Relationship,' *Contemporary European History* 15, no. 3 (2006), 397–416. For the case of Spain and the development of mutual aid societies, see Santiago Castillo, ed., *Solidaridad desde*

*abajo* (Madrid: UGT-Centro de Estudios Históricos y Confederación Nacional de Mutualidades de Previsión, 1994).

10 According to Juan Ignacio Palacios, *La institucionalización de la reforma social en España (1883–1924): La commission y el Instituto de reformas sociales* (Madrid: Ministerio de Trabajo y Seguridad Social, 1988), 7, one of the most visible differentiating factors affecting the evolution of the social question in Spain was the fact that the majority of the population remained tied to agricultural activities.

11 For the evolution of the employers' industrial accident mutual societies in Spain, see Andrés Bibiloni Amengual and Jerònia Pons Pons, 'El desarrollo de las mutualidades patronales de accidentes de trabajo en España. El mercado balear: Entre la competencia y la colusión (1920–1940),' *Revista de Historia Industrial* 15 (1999), 83–104. Also see Jerònia Pons Pons, 'From Obligation to Business: The Creation of Insurance Companies in Spain by Business Industrialists (1900–1963),' paper presented at the 8th European Business History Association Conference, Barcelona, 16–18 September 2004.

12 For the comparison of compensation paid with respect to other countries during the voluntary stage, see Javier Silvestre Rodríguez, 'Wage Compensation for Workplace Disamenities during Industrialisation: The Case of Spain, 1909–1920,' *Labor History* 47 (2006), 43–72; and for its influence on prevention, see Javier Silvestre Rodríguez, 'Workplace Accidents and Early Safety Policies in Spain, 1900–1932,' *Social History of Medicine* 21 (2008), 67–86.

13 Javier Silvestre Rodríguez and Jerònia Pons Pons, 'El seguro de accidentes del trabajo en España (1900–1935): Análisis de su impacto compensatorio y preventivo,' paper presented at the 14th Congreso de la Sociedad Española de Historia de la Medicina, Granada, Spain, 11–14 June 2008. For occupational risk prevention in Spain, see Federico Castellanos and Antón Saracibar, eds., *Historia de la Prevención de Riesgos Laborales en España* (Madrid: Fundación Largo Caballero, 2007).

14 These characteristics have gradually been formulated on the basis of published or forthcoming studies of employers' industrial accident mutuals. Worthy of special mention is the study of the Sociedad de Seguros Mutuos de Vizcaya sobre Accidentes de Trabajo, created in 1900, carried out by Eduardo Alonso Olea: *Sociedad de seguros mutuos de Vizcaya, sobre accidentes de trabajo. 1900-1975: Documento de trabajo 9609* (Madrid: Fundación Empresa Pública, 1996). For the case of the Mutualidad de Accidentes de Mallorca (Mutua Balear), created in 1924, see the analysis in Jerònia Pons Pons, *El sector seguros en Baleares: Empresas y empresarios en los siglos XIX* (Palma de Mallorca: Editorial El Tall, 1998).

15 For an analysis of this first congress of Spanish employers, see Soledad Bengoechea Echaondo, *Patronal catalana, corporativismo y crisis política, 1898–1923* (Barcelona: Publicaciones de la Universidad Autónoma de Barcelona, 1992), chap. 6. The reform bill was presented in Parliament on 8 June 1914 by the minister of the interior, José Sánchez Guerra.

16 Social Catholicism was among the currents of thought that fed the social reform movement, and which promoted the first types of social insurance in Spain through institutions such as the Institute of Social Reforms and the National Insurance Institute, created in 1908. One of its promoters was José Maluquer Salvador, and some of his texts, written between 1906 and 1925, can be consulted, compiled in José Maluquer, *Curso inicial de Seguro Obrero (Los orígenes del Estado de Bienestar en España)* (Barcelona: Orbis, 1986). According to Mercader, social Catholicism was a notable influence on the first social insurance legislation in Spain: Jesús Rafael Mercader Uguina, 'Filantropía, beneficencia y caridad en el primer derecho obrero,' *Civitas: Revista Española de Derecho del trabajo* 137 (2008), 67.

17 Translated from the Spanish. Fragment of the report that appears in the general Memorandum of the First National Congress of Employers' Federations, included in Soledad Bengoechea Echaondo, *Patronal catalana, corporativismo y crisis política, 1898–1923* (Barcelona: Publicaciones de la Universidad Autónoma de Barcelona, 1992), 160.

18 Bengoechea, *Patronal catalana*, 160.

19 In this case, in 1911, the Mutua General de Seguros decided to give the family of a deceased worker, Francisco Maristany, a donation of 1,500 pesetas, as well as the half day's pay they were to receive for life, and a donation of 250 pesetas to the parents of Gregorio Pitaque, a worker deceased in the factory of the widow of Quirico Casanova: Minutes of the board of directors' meeting of the Mutua General de Seguros, 29 December 1911.

20 However, this very same year the first compulsory social insurance in Spain was approved. This was the so-called *retiro obrero*, a compulsory insurance for pensions. It was passed by a royal decree published in the *Gaceta de Madrid* on 11 March 1919. Josefina Cuesta Bustillo, *Los seguros sociales en la España del siglo XX: Hacia los seguros sociales obligatorios* (Madrid: Ministerio de Trabajo y Seguridad Social, 1988), 130–1.

21 Translated from the Spanish. Minutes of the board of directors' meeting of the Mutua General de Seguros, 2 June 1924.

22 This was the case, for example, of the flexibility shown by the Mutua General de Seguros during the crisis that followed the end of the First World War: Minutes of the board of directors' meeting, 27 December 1919.

23 In 1927 the following companies and mutuals were members of the committee: Hispania, Le Patrimoine, Mutua General de Seguros, Winterthur, Northern, Anónima de Accidentes, Caja de Previsión y Socorro, Assicuratrice Italiana, La Vasco Navarra, L'Abeille, and Guardian Assurance: *Anuario Español de Seguros* (1927), 269.

24 For a compilation of the legislation, see *La legislación social en la Historia de España: De la Revolución liberal a 1936*, compiled by Antonio Martín Valverde (Madrid: Congreso de los diputados, 1987).

25 For the history of MAPFRE, see Ignacio Hernando de Larramendi, *Así se hizo Mapfre: Mi tiempo* (Madrid: Actas Editorial, 2001). For its composition, and for the role of these agricultural associations in Spain's political and economic life, see Del Rey, *Propietarios y Patronos*, 71–87. For the case of the employers' organizations in Andalusia, see Antonio Florencio Puntas, *Empresariado agrícola y cambio económico, 1880–1936* (Seville: Diputación Provincial de Sevilla, 1994), especially chap. 2.

26 Samaniego, *La unificación de los seguros sociales*, 317.

27 Translated from the Spanish. Minutes of the board of directors' meeting of the Mutua General de Seguros, 12 December 1932.

28 Jerònia Pons Pons, 'El seguro de accidentes de trabajo en España: De la obligación al negocio (1900–1940),' *Investigaciones de Historia Económica* 4 (2005), 86.

29 For a summary of the position of the commercial companies, see Rafael Iparraguirre, *El primer ataque a fondo contra las compañías de Seguros de Accidentes de Trabajo* (Madrid: Vicente Rico, 1934).

30 Translated from the Spanish. Minutes of the board of directors' meeting, 14 March 1933.

31 In the case of MAPFRE, ever since its creation in 1933 it was linked to the Agricultural group or to the CEDA, a right-wing party that governed the Republic from 1933 until the victory of the left-wing Popular Front in 1936, just a few months before the military uprising of 18 July and the start of the Spanish Civil War. MAPFRE created a network of local delegates due to the fact that 'in the insurance against "agricultural industrial accidents," injured workers had to be paid every Saturday in their locality, just as the agricultural employers paid the workers who worked on their land, and so local delegates were necessary': Ignacio Hernando de Larramendi, *Así se hizo Mapfre: Mi tiempo* (Madrid: Actas Editorial, 2001), 222–9.

32 Translated from the Spanish. Minutes of the board of directors' meeting of the Mutua General de Seguros, 23 December 1935.

33 Samaniego, *La unificación de los seguros sociales*, 344–5.

34 Andrés Bibiloni Amengual and Jerònia Pons Pons, 'The Development of Industrial Accident Insurance from Private to National Insurance in Spain in the 20th Century,' paper presented at the 14th International Economic History Congress, Helsinki, Finland, 21–25 August 2006.

35 Jerònia Pons Pons 'El seguro obligatorio de enfermedad y la gestión de las entidades colaboradoras (1942–1963),' paper presented at the 9th Congreso Internacional de la Asociación Española de Historia Económica, Murcia, Spain, September 2008.

36 Some of the reasons are set out in Juan Velarde Fuertes, 'Problemas en torno al mercado del seguro de accidentes de trabajo en España,' *Revista de Trabajo* 3 (1963), 9–23, and Juan Velarde, A. de Guindos, and M. Lázaro, 'Aspectos estadísticos del seguro de accidentes de trabajo en España,' *Revista de Trabajo* 4 (1963), 9–49.

# 10 Five Ironies of Insurance

AARON DOYLE AND RICHARD ERICSON

Insurance is the world's largest industry. Evan Mills recently wrote in the journal *Science* that if insurance was a country, it would have the third biggest economy in the world.[1] Yet the historical and contemporary centrality of insurance is mostly neglected by academics. Comparable institutions like the mass media and the criminal justice system have whole subfields of hundreds of social scientists studying them. Yet insurance, while arguably as important, remains all but invisible to us sociologists and other academics, as well as to the public.

A few key social theorists like Germany's Ulrich Beck[2] have discussed in broad terms the crucial importance of insurance to understanding modern life. Insurance is the central institution in what sociologists call our contemporary 'risk society.'[3] Unfortunately, discussions of the key role of insurance in modern life are not always grounded in any fine-grained knowledge or study of how insurance actually works, leading to important analytical errors.[4] In neoliberal reasoning, private insurance is presented as the key alternative to relying overly on the state for risk management. Similarly, Beck has suggested that insurance has been a central bulwark against uncertainty in modernity. Beck thus argues that when key 'uninsurable' risks such as nuclear catastrophes emerged starting in the late twentieth century, we moved to a more uncertain 'second modernity.' These various claims about insurance as a guarantor of certainty and security ignore what we will call in this chapter the ironies of insurance.

Elsewhere we have argued that private insurance has come to constitute a vast behind-the-scenes system of informal governance over matters large and small.[5]. Yet to say insurance simply manages risk is oversimplifying. Ideally, insurance, both public and private, might serve to socialize risk and produce social solidarity.[6] However, one theme of the following is that, because of various ironies, insurance often serves instead to reproduce and magnify social inequality.

This chapter highlights various ironic aspects of insurance shown in our previous research.[7] We will define irony here simply as reversal of expectations. Actions have unintended consequences and often produce ironic results. Irony can stem from deliberate attempts by insurers to intervene in the risk environment, attempts that backfire. It is a fact of organizational life that new risks are unintentionally created through the very processes by which other risks are managed.[8] For instance, insurers insisted that a guard dog be hired to protect a collection of hundreds of rare teddy bears in Somerset, England. Unfortunately, the Doberman Pinscher recommended by the insurers went on a rampage and shredded dozens of the teddy bears he was supposed to protect.[9]

Any action can have ironic consequences, but with insurance in particular there are a number of sources of irony. Irony can stem from tensions or paradoxes in defining what insurance is: Is it risk transfer or risk pooling? In its ideal form, does public or private insurance share risk without prejudice among a large pool of people, or does it individualize the risk, so that each pays premiums according to his/her riskiness? Irony can stem from the reactive nature of risk: how insurance feeds back or loops back on and alters the risks it is insuring. Irony can also result from the fundamental paradox in private insurance between good risk management for the consumer and the profit motive. The latter is a key tension or strain that may seem obvious, except that it is often ignored by people in the industry. Irony is fostered by the gaps between industry rhetorics and realities more broadly. Finally, irony can stem from the control efforts of insurers, as we know, from numerous examples in the sociology of deviance and the criminal justice system, that control efforts may have the effect of constructing or reinforcing the very phenomena they seek to control. We will now discuss five ironies of insurance that flow from these sources.

## The First Irony: Unpooling of Risks

Firstly, then, irony can stem from fundamental paradoxes or tensions in the insurance institution itself, differences in vision about what insurance is and should be. Here, our chapter builds on the work of the

American ethicist Aditi Gowri, who wrote of 'the irony of insurance' in her doctoral dissertation.[10] As Gowri points out, there are two fundamental ways of conceiving insurance: as a transfer of risk between two people or as a relationship of risk-sharing among members of a pool. She argues there is a constant tension in insurance practice between these two models. The risk-sharing model makes insurance more of a public, communal measure, approaching social insurance.[11] For Gowri, the irony of insurance is that actuarial risk rating undermines the potential of insurance as such a mechanism of social solidarity, so that pools of people tend to be split into smaller and smaller groups with the purpose of either making them pay their own way or excluding them. This 'unpooling' tendency, she argues, undermines much of the positive potential of insurance. One insurer response is that actuarial risk rating and segmentation is essential as a counter to the problem of adverse selection, but it is debatable whether there is a necessary link between those two things.[12]

This kind of tension between two different visions of insurance is played out in the tort versus no-fault auto insurance debate that has occurred in various jurisdictions. It might be argued that this tension in insurance epitomizes contradictory aspects of contemporary governance more broadly: amoral system management versus individual moral responsibilization. In insurance, this tension is played out in competing tendencies described above: on the one hand, to pool risk equally without prejudice between a large number of insured so that insurance creates 'community,' and on the other hand, to individualize the burden of risk more and more by making insurance ever more differentially available and expensive on the basis of ever-refined risk profiles. The second tendency, overall, seems to be increasingly winning out. Our empirical research shows that unpooling has been exacerbated in recent years, with the emergence of more and more sophisticated actuarial tools that allow risk segmentation of insured populations, for example in life and disability insurance. New technologies allow what one expert called the 'slicing and dicing' of risk pools. Interviewees outlined what one called a 'revolution' in ever-refined risk segmentation. To quote one actuarial scientist we interviewed:

> The whole idea of insurance works on the pooling of risk ... Those categories of the collective were very broad even fifteen years ago ... Now it is going with the philosophy of the rest of society that you are responsi-

> ble ... The whole concept of a pure accident is almost disappearing. There is no pure accident anymore. If you have a claim, you are partially at fault. And you need to change risk categories ... [This is a] move to more and more slicing and individualization, and more and more passing the responsibility back to the claimant. If it goes too far people will say that this isn't insurance any more ...

Insurers increasingly target those consumers who are constructed as 'preferred' and 'super-preferred' risks. Insurance market segmentation and risk pooling go hand-in-hand. Knowledge of risk for marketing is entwined with knowledge of risk for the determination of insurance pools. These 'preferred risks' are seen as doubly desirable as clients, being both wealthy consumers and less risky in terms of claims. Respective rates and insurance contract conditions are established for multiple levels within each of superstandard, standard, and substandard pools. The insured are thereby placed in the insurance equivalent of a gated community, sharing risks only with those similarly situated both in the marketplace and in terms of how their moral character, and thus propensity for dubious claims, is evaluated by insurers. In the extreme case, those seen as the worst risks, often members of disadvantaged or marginalized groups, may be 'redlined,' excluding them from the pool altogether.[13] However, insurers also profit by defining people whom they consider to be substandard risks, as they can be charged higher premiums. While the state regulates what is seen to be unfair discrimination in risk pooling, its effectiveness is limited, and state regulation of equitable pricing of insurance policies is routinely sidestepped. One approach is for the insurer to create subsidiary companies, each of which targets a different market/risk pool segment. Automobile insurers in Canada have been blocked in their efforts to use poor credit ratings as a risk factor and to make people with poor credit ratings pay higher premiums. However, auto insurers are allowed to use place of residence in risk rating, and place has become a highly effective proxy for lower socio-economic status and for minority status. A recent study by Ong and Stoll[14] in the United States shows that, controlling for driving records, people in poor and minority neighbourhoods pay much higher prices for auto insurance.

Treatment of claimants also varies by market segment. Superstandard clients are treated more generously. For example, when this company dealt with motor vehicle insurance claimants, it provided new parts to repair vehicles of preferred clients, and used replacement parts to repair vehicles of other clients. A superstandard insurer we studied specialized in the cross-selling of personal lines insurance to corporate executives who were responsible for their firm's purchase of commercial insurance lines. These executives benefited from favourable terms for their personal insurance, including a very lenient approach to claims, an approach that took their statements of loss at face value.

This favouring of superstandard clients who provide sources of profitability is in stark contrast to discrimination experienced by substandard clients, who are regarded as a threat to profitability. Substandard clients routinely experience insurance company efforts to suppress their legitimate claims. The extent of claims suppression was revealed in a 2001 judgment by the Utah Supreme Court in *Campbell v. State Farm Mutual Automobile Insurance Company No. 981564*. State Farm is well known for promoting consumer trust in itself. For decades it has used the same advertising slogan, 'Like a good neighbor, State Farm is there.' As it turns out, for decades State Farm was not a good neighbour and when needed was not there. In affirming a $145 million punitive damages judgment against the company, the court stated that

> [First,] State Farm repeatedly and deliberately deceived and cheated its customers ... For over two decades, State Farm set monthly payment caps and individually rewarded those insurance adjusters who paid less than the market value for claims ... Agents changed the content of files, lied to customers, and committed other dishonest and fraudulent acts in order to meet financial goals ... State Farm's fraudulent practices were consistently directed to persons – poor ethnic or racial minorities, women, and elderly individuals – who State Farm believed would be less likely to object or take legal action. Second, State Farm engaged in deliberate concealment and destruction of documents related to the profit scheme. State Farm's own witnesses testified that documents were routinely destroyed so as to avoid their potential disclosure through discovery requests ... Third, State Farm has systematically harassed and intimidated opposing claimants, witnesses, and attorneys. For example, State Farm published an instruction manual for its attorneys mandating them to 'ask personal questions' as part of the investigation and examination of claimants in order to deter litigation ... There was also evidence that State Farm actually instructs its attorneys to employ 'mad dog defense tactics' – using the company's large resources to 'wear out' opposing attorneys by prolong-

> ing litigation, making meritless objections, claiming false privileges, destroying documents, and abusing the law and motion process. Taken together, these three examples show that State Farm engaged in a pattern of 'trickery and deceit,' 'false statements,' and other 'acts of affirmative misconduct' targeted at 'financially vulnerable' persons.

These tendencies and their social consequences were also epitomized in a private-sector vehicle insurance market we studied, by a local company that found a niche market in substandard driving risks. The niche market is people for whom vehicle insurance is mandatory, but who have difficulty obtaining it because of their poor driving records. The large multinational companies that dominate the general insurance market do not want these poor risks, leaving room for the local company to create a very profitable business.

The company is highly profitable for four reasons. First, as just mentioned, there is no competition. Second, the insurer only covers liability claims against these drivers to a modest level. Third, the insurer provides financing of premium payments at high interest to consumers who frequently cannot afford to pay up front and therefore have no choice but to pay this interest. Fourth, the company charges very high premiums. Unwanted risks are simply priced too high, although this is rare because, in the words of a company official, 'My attitude is a good risk is one that pays high enough premium.' Moreover, the insurance regulators in the jurisdiction allow the company to circumvent the fairness criteria that apply to companies filing rates for standard risks by allowing separate rates to be filed for the nonstandard risks. The regulators thereby effectively constitute the company as an unfairness company. An official of the company explained in interview:

> If you file rates for a standard type of risk, you can't file a rate for a nonstandard risk because you have to set the rate levels that are going to be fair for all types of drivers. So where a company is, say, identifying the better risk and they set a rate for liability insurance at say $800, they don't want to insure the bad risk because they can't get enough money for it because of the fairness criteria. So our base rate might be $1500 and we only insure the bad ones who come to us.

There is a ruthless deselection of the poor once they are insured with the company. As mentioned above, many policyholders cannot afford to pay the full cost of the policy up front, and so must finance their premiums through the insurance company, at profitable interest rates considerably above market level. Moreover, they are required to pay two months premium in advance on a twelve-month contract, and to have their subsequent monthly payments made automatically through an electronic pre-authorization system from their bank account. In fact, approximately 40 per cent of policyholders cannot keep up this payment schedule; thus 40 per cent of the company's auto insurance policies are cancelled at some time during the twelve-month contract period for non-payment of the premium.

Many of these cancelled policyholders thus join the ranks of the estimated 10 to 15 per cent of drivers in the jurisdiction who drive illegally without insurance. This situation poses a problem for the police because the insurance card is issued for twelve months: the driver can still show the police officer what looks like a valid card even after it has been cancelled. In sum, these arrangements enable and encourage motorists with poor driving records to drive without valid insurance, putting themselves and other drivers at risk, although not the insurance company, which is no longer liable once the drivers' policies are cancelled. While some police officers have learned that all insurance cards from this company are 'red flags' indicating high-risk drivers and are therefore likely to do further investigative checks, this approach is by no means uniform. Given its approach and substandard risk clientele, this company does not even bother employing regular insurance adjusters on staff or on contract, adjusters who would be skilled in dealing with claims relatively gently and diplomatically. Instead this company contracts with a firm of private investigators located in the same office building as the insurance company's headquarters, in order to ensure a much tougher approach with this particular clientele. As ex-police officers, these private investigators are especially adept at detecting fraudulent claims and at having clients see the wisdom of withdrawing such claims. They are also skilled at the preparation of evidence and work closely with their former police department colleagues in prosecuting the company's clients. This represents a very strong contrast with the more diplomatic approach to claims that we found is adopted by insurance firms targeting more upscale risk segments.

More broadly, then, insurance features a tension between risk pooling and individualizing risk, which Gowri has called 'the irony of insurance.' The increasing risk segmentation and unpooling we have observed undercut the risk-socializing potential of insurance.

## The Second Irony: Creating Risk

Insurance features a number of other ironies beyond that described by Gowri. A second kind of irony in insurance stems from the reactive nature of risk and the unforeseen and unintended consequences of the existence of insurance itself creating shifts in the risk environment.[15] A key example is how identifying disabilities as covered in disability insurance regimes ironically produces those disabilities. The insurance regime feeds back into the actions of medical professional and lawyers, which in turn feed back to the insured. Medical, legal, and insurance professionals collectively discover and negotiate the meaning of new disability risks and how they should be addressed through insurance.[16] For example, Malleson[17] reported that one-third of motor vehicle accident victims in North America claim that they are subject to 'whiplash associated disorder' risks. They are treated to a rich menu of medical possibilities that are mediated through insurance-managed care criteria of acceptability and underwritten to the tune of tens of billions of dollars annually.

> Ophthalmologists report whiplash damage to the eyes. ENT surgeons report whiplash damage of the inner ear that causes distressing and disabling dizziness, buzzing in the ears, and sometimes deafness. Dentists report mandibular whiplash leading to chronic and incapacitating temporo-mandibular joint disorder. Orthopaedic surgeons report whiplash to be a potent cause of persistent backache and other musculoskeletal pains, and rheumatologists that whiplash victims frequently develop fibromyalgia [also known as fibrositis: severe muscle aches and pains, unrefreshing sleep, constant exhaustion] ... Psychologists and psychiatrists emphasize that the deleterious effects of the frightening experience of the collision cause victims to develop a post-traumatic stress disorder.[18]

Referring to data reported by the Insurance Research Council,[19] Malleson[20]documents that on average there are 86 visits to health care practitioners in connection with each personal injury insurance claim: chiropractors (25), physical therapists (19), psychotherapists (11), unspecified healthcare practitioners (9), MD/osteopath other than the initial emergency room visit (8), dentists (7), unspecified medical practitioners (6), and MD/osteopath emergency room visit (1). A consequence of this looping effect is that the insured sometimes may even internalize the disability themselves and come to understand they have a disability.

At other times, the insured may see claiming a fictionalized disability as more a matter of convenience. Several disability insurers we interviewed pointed to the fact that disability claims increase with recession, layoffs, and rightsizing of companies. For example, a disability insurance broker said that two pending hospital closings in her city had led to a significant increase in insurance claims from employees desperate for sources of income in the face of losing their jobs.

Such ironies due to the reactive nature of insurance are well known. Insurance provides a structured incentive that can paradoxically encourage risky behaviour on the part of the insured, either deliberately (as in the insured burning down a failing restaurant to collect the insurance), the property of insurance known as moral hazard, or because the insured neglected to take proper preventive measures (for example, not sufficiently safeguarding her car because insurance will cover it if it gets stolen, the term for this being morale hazard).[21]

## The Third Irony: Risky Insurers

While these properties of moral hazard and morale hazard have long been well known, what is much less acknowledged is that insurance ironically creates another set of parallel incentives for risky behaviour by its own employees. In our work we have tried to expand the term 'moral hazard' by situating it as part of a broader term we call 'moral risk.'[22] 'Moral risk' encompasses all the different incentives insurance offers to anyone in the insurance relationship to put others at risk. Simply put, insurance structures incentives for its own people also to cheat and lie, not just the consumer. This irony here stems from the tension between managing the consumer's risks and the profit motive.

A key example: the commission system for life insurance sales[23] has long been a structured source of market misconduct, leading to many inappropriate and harmful sales. Ironically, then, the life insurance commission structure produces another, parallel form of moral hazard, or moral risk as we call it. In early nineteenth-century England, commissions were characterized by Charles Babbage, the mathematician and contemporary 'life assurance' expert, as bribery. As such, Babbage said commissions 'ought to be immediately abolished, or else publicly acknowledged.'[24]

Despite periodic cycles of scandal and recrimination, the life insurance industry continues to rely heavily on commission-based selling. This is in part because life insurance is a tough sell: life insurance is expensive, arcane, addresses remote future possibilities that people prefer not to dwell on, and is intangible and does not have the commodity appeal of material goods. Often the poor, as financially unsophisticated, are particularly vulnerable to deceptive sales. We found it is a widespread practice to sell less affluent families expensive life insurance policies, with most of the cost taken up by investment components of questionable value. This occurs even though most financial advisors acknowledge that such families are much better off with a cheaper product providing only basic coverage, known as term insurance. However, the dubious, more expensive products offer a much higher commission to the salesperson.

One of the most ironic condemnations of the commission system was offered inadvertently by one company we studied. This is a case of irony as revealing. This company abandoned the normal commission system in a small number of cases because they did not want to victimize key clients. Why did they do this? The firm had a lucrative business in employee benefit group plans. As a sideline, this company also sold a few individual life insurance policies to selected key clients whom they dealt with for group sales. The company had adopted a slogan indicating they were 'people you can trust.' Asked to explain this slogan, the executive we were interviewing gave the example that the salesperson who sold these individual life insurance policies to key clients was paid a salary with no commission and was therefore trustworthy. The executive told us:

> This guy is not motivated to sell the wrong product … When we hired him and set him up that way, we had him tested by [a major life insurance company's recruiting system, and that company's recruiter] called me and said, 'You don't want to hire that guy because you know he's not going to be motivated.' I said, 'That's perfect, that's exactly what I'm looking for!' He said, 'You're going to lose money.' I couldn't afford to have [this guy] selling [a key client] the wrong product, one that is too expensive ... because the guy makes a great big commission.

The revealing irony is of course that most other salespeople are indeed paid on commission and therefore not 'people you can trust.'

The quote above referred to the testing process that potential life insurance sales people undergo. Another irony is that, while insureds are selected to be good risks, insurance agents may in these testing processes actually sometimes be selected to be bad risks. An agent selection manual from the Life Insurance Marketing Research Association we examined recommends in broad terms that entrepreneurial risk-takers with a gambling spirit and disregard for the rules be recruited. The manual suggests potential life insurance agents should be asked questions like: 'Do you ever exceed authority or break the rules at work or in school? Give me an example.' In fact, the agent-recruiting manual concludes with the statement 'All rules ... are meant to be broken.' Although the industry pays lip service to attempts to regulate deceptive sales, other institutionalized practices undercut fair sales guidelines and make a mockery of them. All of this of course is particularly ironic in the context that the purchase of life insurance by the consumer historically became a highly moralized exercise in self-governance for the consumer.

Managers in life insurance sales also work very largely and sometimes exclusively on commissions. This gives managers an incentive to perpetuate a revolving door system where they hire short-term employees who will sell to their extended families and friends and then are cut loose as soon as these networks are exhausted. To quote one life insurance veteran we interviewed:

> If you can come up with a hundred names, you get hired. And they tell you they are training you up for a career in life insurance, which is a lie ... the system wouldn't work if it actually required training ... They send out a so-called trainer or unit manager with this new career person, and they call on all those people on that list. And the purpose of that is ostensibly to train him on how to sell insurance. The con is, the purpose is to simply sell insurance (to all the family and friends) ... When you get through the list, they say, 'Okay Fred, you are on your own, go to it.' And at that point they stop paying him ... his draw. He flounders, they cut him loose, and then they have to bring somebody else in, so it is a revolving door.

The life insurance commission structure is a striking example, but not the only one, of structured incentives that put the consumer at risk. Another kind of example is directors' and officers' liability insurance, which according to a recent study by Baker and Griffith[25] 'seems likely to increase the amount of shareholder losses due to securities violations' because it shields directors and officers from the financial impact of such violations, while failing to control the moral hazard problem created through practices such as pricing or monitoring corporate governance.

**The Fourth Irony: Insuring the Uninsurable**

Next we consider another kind of irony that gets at a different kind of challenge insurers face. This kind of irony, present both historically and in many contemporary examples, is that insurers will insure the uninsurable. Insurance literature states that two of the things that make risks uninsurable are if the risk are too large or there is insufficient actuarial data. In fact, insurers in practice will go against both of those credos. They very often proceed in the absence of accurate actuarial data.

Insurance industry efforts to organize security through risk expose the limits of science and technology. They reveal that scientific risk assessment is both a known chance and measured uncertainty,[26] and how science is sometimes used less for the certainty it offers than the doubt it insinuates.[27] These efforts exemplify Adams' observations[28] that 'risk is a close relation to uncertainty. Where we cannot be certain about the relation between cause and effect we clutch at the straw of probability ... Estimates of the probability of particular harms are quantified expressions of ignorance ... [Hence] risk management decisions are moral decisions made in the face of uncertainty.'

Insurers must therefore organize security through non-scientific criteria and types of knowledge that are experiential, intuitive, speculative, evaluative, and emotional. In interview, a senior executive of the Institute of Actuaries of Canada stressed that pricing the insurance product before the costs are known is a 'guessing game' that involves 'trying to put a present value on contingent future events. You know you're going to be wrong from the start. You want to be least wrong.' In another interview, a former chief actuary of a major property and casualty insurer looked skyward and said, 'God knows what insurance policies will eventually cost, a very difficult science. It is judgment, it is experience, it is feel, touch,' always subject to changes in law, company operations, political environments, and market conditions.

These observations hold across all lines of insurance. Life insurance is widely regarded as the exemplification of actuarialism, with neat life expectancy tables, adjusted for longevity factors such as whether the policyholder smokes.[29] However, life insurance underwriting can also be highly speculative and contingent. Indeed, life insurance appeared long before actuarial tables were invented, and in many respects it remains a form of 'betting on lives.'[30] Aggregate actuarial data do not translate directly into local underwriting contexts because population characteristics vary within each local risk pool. There is a great deal of new, specialized underwriting of medical conditions without actuarial history. Insurers copy each others' products in competitive market conditions without much understanding of the risks they may be taking on. There is also a proliferation of financial product features tied to life insurance policies, again without actuarial history and much understanding of the risks involved. These features are driven by competitive market conditions, and subject to financial market vagaries that can variously spell windfall profits and catastrophic losses for life insurers and their clients. Life insurance profitability and viability is also subject to a complicated loss ratio formula that involves guesstimates about such matters as future administrative expenses, policy lapse rates, reinsurance arrangements, and investment return projections.[31]

Contemporary earthquake insurance serves as another example. Scientific understanding of earthquakes is very shaky, making prediction of losses extremely difficult. As the CEO of one company that sells earthquake insurance put it, 'I mean you might as well blind yourself and get dizzy before you throw a dart in terms of picking a number.' The industry's financing arrangements have also been shaky. If a catastrophic earthquake had occurred in Vancouver, Canada, in the late 1990s, numerous companies that had significant earthquake exposure would not have been able to pay their policyholders and would simply have folded. There were, of course, financing arrangements in place, there was reinsurance, and there was a compensation scheme whereby solvent companies would band together to pay off policyholders of bankrupt companies. Even so, it was estimated that a catastrophic earthquake in Vancouver could cost $10 billion, and the industry only had financing in place at that time to cover $3 billion to $4 billion. As one insurance executive in Vancouver, whose company sold a lot of commercial earthquake coverage, told us bluntly, 'Well, if I really thought we were going to have [an earthquake], I wouldn't live here.' This insurance executive was speaking to us in a high-rise office building in downtown Vancouver; he said, 'We looked at this building and we decided it's probably going to sway and snap off at the fifteenth floor. But we haven't moved.' He went on to note, 'If a major quake happens in Vancouver, it probably is going to fry the industry.' People in the insurance industry have been working with the government in Canada to remedy that problem, but it demonstrates the more general point that some insurers insure the uninsurable.

This undercuts a key claim of Beck,[32] of a new modernity that is characterized by a new type of uninsurable risks. Insurers have long insured risks like this that are of a huge scale and not very calculable.[33] Again, insuring the uninsurable stems from the tension between good risk management for the consumer and the profit motive.

## The Fifth Irony: Creating Fraud

The final irony concerns how the crackdown on insurance fraud creates more and more insurance fraud.[34] As much literature from criminology and the sociology of deviance attests, efforts to control crime and deviance often end up producing the very phenomena they seek to control.

More than thirty years ago, H. Laurence Ross conducted a classic sociological study of adjusters at three U.S. auto insurance companies, reported in his book *Settled Out of Court*[35] Ross found that:

> The adjuster typically believes that few people cut false claims from whole cloth, but that nearly everyone exaggerates his loss. This exaggeration is expected, and the adjuster sees his job as being to reduce the valid claim to an appropriate size. The claimant discovered in an exaggeration is the rule, rather than the exception, and nothing is gained by embarrassing him. Even more is this the case when exaggeration is expected but dishonesty cannot be proven, as in the case of subjective pain and whiplash injury.[36]

In the thirty years since Ross's study was published, some things have not changed in the insurance industry but others have shifted dramatically. Just as Ross found then, today many in the industry still assume that a large proportion of claimants exaggerate. However, Ross barely discussed fraud in his book,[37] noting simply that a 'small minority' of claims warranted further investigation due to the possibility of fraud. However, since Ross wrote, there has been an explosion of insurance industry anti-fraud efforts, targeting not only wholly fabricated claims but, perhaps more importantly, cracking down on the mere 'exaggeration' described by Ross as a somewhat routine part of the claims process. In recent years, North American home and auto insurers have presented fraud as a very serious social problem. Insurance people regularly proclaim things like 'insurance fraud is the second leading source of criminal profits next to drugs.' To quote an industry source:

> The crime of insurance fraud is growing in Canada; its economic impact is exceeded only by that of tax evasion. Insurers in Canada believe that at least 10 to 15 percent of … claims are fraudulent. That's about 1.3 billion dollars a year.

There has been a massive crackdown by the North American insurance industry on fraud in the last two decades, especially in the property and casualty (home, auto) and disability sectors. The first Special Investigation Units (SIUs) of private police within American insurance companies were established in the 1970s[38] and have multiplied dramatically since the mid-1980s. In 1992 approximately 240 companies had SIUs. However, by 1997 approximately 1,200 companies had such units. This expansion in SIUs has been accompanied by the hiring of more investigators within each company's SIU. During the same five-year period one major company's SIU grew from approximately 300 to 1,200 investigators. In 1992 the National Insurance Crime Bureau (NICB) was created in the United States, headed by a former army general who had been one of the higher-ups in the 'war on drugs.'[39] The general now declared war on insurance fraud. Insurance companies have pushed the American justice system to get tough with fraud. Almost every American state now defines insurance fraud as a felony rather than a misdemeanour.

These dramatic figures – that 10 to 15 per cent of claims are fraudulent – raise the question: how do we know how much fraud is out there? Other industry insiders admit that such figures have little statistical foundation. An editorial entitled 'The Mismeasure of Fraud,' written by the editor of *Canadian Insurance* magazine, makes the following assessment:

> Although we have seen in countless media the estimate of fraud in Canadian property and casualty insurance – 10–15 percent of claims or roughly $1.3 billion – few actually know where this measurement came

> from or, for that matter, how accurate it is. My exhaustive research has turned up only one reference to this number. A judgment in a 1992 New Jersey Supreme Court case stated that 'insurance fraud is a problem of massive proportions that currently results in substantial and unnecessary costs to the general public in the form of increased rates. In fact, *approximately ten to fifteen percent of all insurance claims involve fraud*' (italics in original). No one really knows how much these particular judges knew about fraud, but the estimate lives on. Since the Canadian Coalition Against Insurance Fraud clearly borrowed the name from its U.S. counterpart (Coalition Against Insurance Fraud), it is quite likely that this number was also extrapolated to fit the Canadian environment.[40]

In fact, as many in the industry admit, the extent of insurance fraud is impossible to know, for several reasons. Most crime in general goes unrecorded. This is particularly true of most insurance fraud, because it is secret and seldom dealt with formally. It is a so-called victimless crime. One top of all this, there is another problem: it is actually very difficult for the insurance industry to define precisely what is meant by fraud. In our project, we asked many people who work in insurance to define fraud. Firstly, none of them referred to criminal codes or legal definitions. In public contexts, stressing the need to crack down, insurance people offer a broad definition. Fraud is 'any intentional deception for financial gain … from fabricated claims, to inflation or padding of legitimate claims.' But in everyday working contexts, the definition narrows. A manual for adjusters says that 'slight exaggeration in the amount of the claim itself will not constitute fraud … however, falsifying documents would.'

So how do you draw the line between slight exaggeration and fraud? I asked that question of someone who organized a five-hour training program on fraud. He told me, 'If *you* could give us the answer to this, you'd be a hero.'

Others in the industry make distinctions between 'soft-core' abuse of the system and 'hard-core' criminal fraud. We interviewed a consultant who developed data analysis systems to detect insurance fraud. He said an example of 'soft core' in auto insurance claims is the claimant who has a minor neck injury that becomes a major injury, usually on the urgings of a lawyer. 'Hard core' is an 'injury ring' that stages a fake auto accident followed by multiple claims from several 'injured' parties. Similarly, an investigator for a workers compensation insurer distinguished between '20 percent abuse' and '5 percent criminal fraud' among all claims. He said 'abuse' is largely accounted for by 'malingering individuals … off for a couple of extra weeks longer than necessary simply because they've gone back to the doctor and said, "I need a couple of extra weeks" … we're in an injury system, not an adversarial system. On balance of probabilities, we give the nod to the claimant.'

If soft-core abuse or exaggeration is described by some insurance personnel as not distinctly criminal, and, indeed, something that many or most claimants do, it is also seen within the industry as the more expensive part of the fraud problem overall, as compared to hard-core fraud. A survey of 353 American property and casualty insurers[41] revealed that the soft-core problem was seen as more costly. Thus, while industry anti-fraud publicity campaigns dramatize individual examples of wholesale hard-core fraud such as staged auto accidents, they are also targeted at reducing what is perceived as a more expensive soft-core problem by deterring 'average' claimants from exaggerating their losses.

Ross suggested that both claimants and adjusters routinely stretch the truth as part of the process. Historically, knowing that is it built into the process, the industry has not been concerned to define soft-core abuse or exaggeration as fraud.

Why did the crackdown on fraud come when it did? A U.S. industry executive indicated to us that the massive boom since the 1980s in fraud policing has been driven in part by increased pressure on insurance companies to keep premiums down. In the past, increased claims costs could more easily be passed on to the consumer in higher premiums, and companies may have been reluctant to antagonize consumers with fraud policing. The executive indicated, however, that regulations in various states that restrict premium increases – for example, those as a result of Proposition 103 introduced in California in 1988 – forced the companies to take stronger anti-fraud measures instead to reduce claims costs and to bolster their competitive position and profits. The executive's comments have been supported by some recent analyses by legal and business scholars. As Jaffee and Russell[42] write: 'Prior to Proposition 103, ... the costs of fraud … were simply passed on to consumers … when Proposition 103 placed a ceiling on premium levels, the firms had to control fraud and their expenses in order to maintain profits levels.' Insurers would have been reluctant to police fraud as heavily prior to Proposition 103 because of possible consumer backlash. As Jaffee and Russell go on to suggest:

> It is essential for this argument, of course, to understand why insurance firms did not find it in their best interest to control fraud … even before the passage of Proposition 103. A possible mechanism for this effect is based on the consumer ill-will that an insurance firm may create when it falsely accuses a customer of fraud. In this case, there may be a 'bad equilibrium' in which all firms in the industry ignore insurance fraud, in order not to create a reputation as a firm that falsely accuses its customers. In this situation, it is possible that a major regulatory change such as Proposition 103 may push the system toward an alternative 'good' equilibrium, in which all firms in the industry fight fraud.[43]

A recent statement on insurance fraud in the United States from the Insurance Information Institute[44] similarly acknowledges that insurance companies faced a cost crisis in the mid-1980s that was partly responsible for the industry's introducing a crackdown on fraud at that time:

> In the mid-1980s, the rising price of insurance, particularly auto and health insurance, together with the growth in organized insurance fraud, prompted many insurers to reexamine the issue. They began to see the benefit of strengthening antifraud laws and more stringent enforcement as a means of controlling escalating costs.

As one of our interviewees said, 'they were squeezed for money. And it looked like … a cost-free way. You don't have to raise premiums, you don't have to lower your service, you just get cash. And no one is going to stand up and say, "I'm the fraud lobby," and lobby for keeping the money. So it looked good.'

When you crackdown on fraud, the irony is you find more and more fraud. Insurers say the numbers are up dramatically, but, of course, if you go looking for insurance fraud you will find it, as the social reaction perspective indicates with crime in general.[45] This is something that the criminologist Jason Ditton[46] calls a 'control wave.'

One official told us:

> The scary part is, as we continue to increase the fight, we continually uncover more and more fraud. So people say, 'You are putting all these dollars in there, but the problem is increasing.' You can't say something is fraudulent until you find it … It has probably always been there; it is just that more has been uncovered than ever before.

Ironically, then, a crackdown on fraud leads to more fraud. This irony is also linked to inequality, as poor and marginalized people are most often suspected. Baker and McElrath[47] studied the claims process and found that adjusters use socio-economic criteria to flag suspicious cases. One adjuster said, '"I look at the car they drive, the other things in the house." Also mentioned were the character of the home or neighborhood, employment status, business or professional background, immigrant status ... perceived wealth, and what another adjuster called "a life-style that indicates a basic honesty."'

Our interviews also found ethnicity was used as a red flag for potential fraud. Particular ethnic groups were instantly suspected. One manager said his staff starts with the name on the file as an indicator of ethnicity: '[We have] adjusters who will look at an insured and say "that kind of person with that kind of name is likely to do this."' One adjuster told us, 'East Indian clientele are always looking to scam you.' Another said,

> In the 1970s it was the Polish, in the 1980s it was the Chinese, and now it's Russians ... Another company has an adjuster who is East Indian ... He would tell all of the adjusters, 'Never believe a word that these East Indians say because it's our culture'... Is that stereotyping? Well, no, it's probably just smart.

## Conclusion

Insurance has been part of the fine print as modernity has unfolded in all its complexities, fine print that we may seldom force ourselves to read but that we ignore at our peril. Some have argued that insurance can be understood as a key guardian against uncertainty. We have suggested here that the role of insurance as a manager of risk is complicated by various fundamental tensions in the institution, and we have outlined five ironies of insurance that stem from these tensions. These complicate the role of insurance as protector and guarantor of security, especially, we have argued, for the poor and marginalized.

## NOTES

As this chapter was in preparation, Richard Ericson died suddenly in October 2007. This was a huge loss to many of us who knew and loved him, to academia in general, and to the study of insurance in particular. As I wrote in the acknowledgments to my first book, 'It is practically impossible to imagine a better mentor than Richard Ericson … I have been profoundly fortunate to be his student.'

1 Evan Mills, 'Insurance in a Climate of Change,' *Science* 309, no. 5737 (12 August 2005), 1040–4.
2 Ulrich Beck, *Risk Society: Towards a New Modernity* (London: Sage, 1992); idem, *World Risk Society* (Cambridge: Polity Press, 1999); idem, 'Living in World Risk Society,' Hobhouse Memorial Lecture, London School of Economics and Political Science, 15 February 2006.
3 Beck, *Risk Society*.
4 Richard Ericson and Aaron Doyle, 'Catastrophe Risk, Insurance, and Terrorism,' *Economy and Society* 33, no. 2 (2004), 135–173.
5 Richard Ericson, Aaron Doyle, and Dean Barry, *Insurance as Governance* (Toronto: University of Toronto Press, 2003).
6 Deborah Stone, 'Beyond Moral Hazard: Insurance as Moral Opportunity,' in Tom Baker and Jonathan Simon, ed., *Embracing Risk: The Changing Culture of Insurance and Responsibility* (Chicago: University of Chicago Press, 2002), 52.
7 This work selects from, updates, and builds on material from a bigger project on public and private insurance for which we completed 224 interviews, mostly in Canada but some in the United States and Britain (for a fuller report, see generally Ericson, Doyle, and Barry, *Insurance as Governance*, and Richard V. Ericson and Aaron Doyle, *Uncertain Business: Risk, Insurance, and the Limits of Knowledge* (Toronto: University of Toronto Press, 2004) Interviewees included people with a wide range of responsibilities in the insurance industry or public insurance, professionals in expert systems that serve insurers, representatives of consumer associations, members of the general public who were consumers, industry regulators, senior civil servants, and members of Parliament. Unless otherwise specified, quotes in the article are taken from these interviews. Observational research included attending industry conferences and observing sales operations, loss prevention operations, and claims-related examination practices.
8 Bridget Hutter and Michael Power, eds., *Organizational Encounters with Risk* (Cambridge: Cambridge University Press, 2005).
9 Maev Kennedy, 'Guard Dog Mauls Elvis's Teddy in Rampage,' *The Guardian*, 3 August 2006.
10 Aditi Gowri, 'The Irony of Insurance: Community and Commodity' (PhD diss., University of Southern California, 1997).

11 See also Stone, 'Beyond Moral Hazard.'
12 For an argument against this claim by insurers, see Tom Baker, 'Containing the Promise of Insurance: Adverse Selection and Risk Classification,' in Richard Ericson and Aaron Doyle, eds., *Risk and Morality* (Toronto: University of Toronto Press, 2003).
13 See the various articles in Gregory D. Squires, ed., *Insurance Redlining* (Washington, DC: Urban Institute Press, 1997).
14 Paul M. Ong and Michael A. Stoll, 'Redlining or Risk? A Spatial Analysis of Auto Insurance Rates in Los Angeles' (Working Paper, School of Public Affairs, UCLA, 2006).
15 Carol Heimer, *Reactive Risk and Rational Action: Managing Moral Risk in Insurance Contracts* (Berkeley: University of California Press, 1985).
16 See chapter 3 in Ericson and Doyle, *Uncertain Business*.
17 Andrew Malleson, *Whiplash and Other Useful Illnesses*. (Montreal: McGill-Queen's University Press, 2002).
18 Malleson, *Whiplash and Other Useful Illnesses*, 12–13.
19 Insurance Research Council, *Auto Injuries: Claiming Behavior andIits Impact on Insurance Claims* (Oak Brook, IL: Insurance Research Council, 1994).
20 Malleson, *Whiplash and Other Useful Illnesses*, 258–9.
21 Heimer, *Reactive Risk and Rational Action*.
22 Richard Ericson, Dean Barry, and Aaron Doyle, 'The Moral Hazards of Neo-liberalism: Lessons from the Private Insurance Industry,' *Economy and Society* 29 (2000); Ericson, Doyle, and Barry, *Insurance as Governance*.
23 For a fuller account of the various moral risks built into life insurance sales, see Richard Ericson and Aaron Doyle, 'The Institutionalization of Deceptive Sales in Life Insurance: Five Sources of Moral Risk,' *British Journal of Criminology* 46 (2006), 993–1010, from which the material in this section is drawn.
24 Charles Babbage, *Comparative View of the Various Institutions for the Assurance of Lives* (London: J. Mawman, 1826).
25 Tom Baker and Sean J. Griffith, 'The Missing Monitor in Corporate Governance: The Directors' & Officers' Liability Insurer,' *Georgetown Law Journal* 95 (2007), 1796-1842.
26 Frank Knight, *Risk, Uncertainty and Profit* (New York: A.M. Kelley, 1964 [1921]).
27 Francois Ewald. 'The Return of Descartes' Malicious Demon: An Outline of a Philosophy of Precaution,' in Tom Baker and Jonathan Simon, eds., *Embracing Risk: The Changing Culture of Insurance and Responsibility* (Chicago: University of Chicago Press, 2002), 273–301.
28 John Adams, 'Risk and Morality: Three Framing Devices,' In Richard Ericson and Aaron Doyle, *Risk and Morality*, 87–90.

29 Ericson and Doyle, *Uncertain Business*, chap. 2.

30 Geoffrey Clark, *Betting on Lives: The Culture of Life Insurance in England 1695 1775* (Manchester: University of Manchester Press, 1999).

31 Ericson and Doyle, *Uncertain Business*, chap. 2.

32 Beck, *Risk Society*.

33 Ericson and Doyle, *Uncertain Business*.

34 For a fuller account of the crackdown on insurance fraud, see generally Richard Ericson and Aaron Doyle, 'Criminalization in Private: The Case of Insurance Fraud,' in Law Commission of Canada, ed., *What Is a Crime? Defining Criminal Conduct in Contemporary Society* (Vancouver: University of British Columbia Press, 2004), 99–124, from which the material in this section is drawn.

35 H. Laurence Ross *Settled Out of Court* (Chicago: Aldine, 1970).

36 Ross, *Settled Out of Court*, 45.

37 Ross, *Settled Out of Court*, 95–6.

38 Susan Ghezzi, 'A Private Network of Social Control: Insurance Investigation Units,' *Social Problems* 30 (1983), 521–31.

39 Kenneth Dornstein, *Accidentally on Purpose: The Making of A Personal Injury Underworld in America* (NewYork: St. Martin's Press, 1998).

40 Craig Harris, 'The Mismeasure of Fraud,' *Canadian Insurance*, May 1998,5.

41 Insurance Research Council/Insurance Services Organization, *Fighting Insurance Fraud: Survey of Insurer Anti Fraud Efforts* (Toronto: IRC/ISO, 2001).

42 Dwight Jaffee and Thomas Russell,. 'The Regulation of Automobile Insurance in California,' in J.D. Cummins, ed., *Deregulating Property-Liability Insurance: Restoring Competition and Increasing Efficiency* (Washington, DC: American Enterprise Institute-Brookings Institution Joint Center for Regulatory Studies, 2002), 31; Harvey Rosenfield, 'Auto Insurance: Crisis and Reform,' *University of Memphis Law Review* 2, no, 1 (Fall 1998).

43 Jaffee and Russell, 'Regulation of Automobile Insurance in California,' 32.

44 Insurance Information Institute, *Hot Topics and Insurance Issues: Insurance Fraud*, www.iii.org/media/hottopics/insurance/fraud/ (accessed May 2002).

45 Richard Ericson, *Criminal Reactions: The Labelling Perspective* (Westmead: Saxon House, 1975); idem, *Making Crime: A Study of Detective Work* (2nd ed.) (Toronto: University of Toronto Press, 1993).

46 Jason Ditton, *Contrology: Beyond the New Criminology* (London: Macmillan, 1979).

47 Tom Baker and Karen McElrath, 'Insurance Claims Discrimination,' in Squires, *Insurance Redlining*.